THE
LAST
REAL
SEASON

Other Books by Mike Shropshire

SEASONS IN HELL: With Billy Martin,
Whitey Herzog and "The Worst Baseball Team in History"
—The 1973–1975 Texas Rangers

THE ICE BOWL

THE PRO: A Novel

WHEN THE TUNA WENT DOWN TO TEXAS:
How Bill Parcells Led the Cowboys Back to the Promised Land

RUNNIN' WITH THE BIG DOGS: The True,
Unvarnished Story of the Texas-Oklahoma Football Wars

THE LAST REAL SEASON

A Hilarious Look Back at 1975—
When Major Leaguers Made Peanuts,
the Umpires Wore Red, and Billy Martin
Terrorized Everyone

Mike Shropshire

GRAND CENTRAL
PUBLISHING

NEW YORK   BOSTON

Grand Central Publishing
Hachette Book Group USA
237 Park Avenue
New York, NY 10017

Visit our Web site at www.HachetteBookGroupUSA.com.

Printed in the United States of America
First Edition: May 2008
10 9 8 7 6 5 4 3 2 1

Grand Central Publishing is a division of Hachette Book Group USA, Inc.
The Grand Central Publishing name and logo is a trademark of
Hachette Book Group USA, Inc.

Library of Congress Cataloging-in-Publication Data
Shropshire, Mike.
    The last real season : a hilarious look back at 1975 : when major leaguers made
peanuts, the umpires wore red, and Billy Martin terrorized everyone. —1st ed.
        p. cm.
    Includes index.
    Summary: "A rollicking and ribald first-person account of the 1975 Major
League Baseball season—the last year before free agency took over and changed
the National Pastime forever — for better or for worse!"
    ISBN-13: 978-0-446-40154-8
    ISBN-10: 0-446-40154-4
  1. Baseball—United States—History. I. Title.
    GV863.A1S633 2008
    796.3570973—dc22
    2007047217

The Clan from County Cork—
Jim, Suzie, Sean, Charlie, and Rory

Foreword

That was a hell of a year in baseball, 1975.

It was August, and the race for the American League East championship was coming to a boil. The Orioles were in Chicago, and we were nursing a two-run lead. The White Sox had runners on first and second base, and the batter hit a line drive into the gap in left center. Paul Blair fielded the ball off the wall on one hop, turned and fired it to Mark Belanger, who knew how to position himself as the cutoff man as well as anybody who played the game. Mark took the throw and in one smooth motion, threw a perfect strike to the catcher, Elrod Hendricks, the runner was out at the plate, and we were out of the inning. The play was sheer artistry and a masterpiece of timing. It turned out to be one of those little game-winning events that never appears in the box score. The White Sox announcers' broadcast booth was up there directly behind the visitors' dugout. I could actually hear old Harry Caray up there, bellowing at the top of his lungs, "That's why the Baltimore Orioles keep on winning pennants!"

I laughed, and thought to myself, "Harry's right. And it feels good, too." Pitching and defense. That had been our formula. It worked to the extent that coming into the 1975 season, the Orioles had won our division five out of the last six tries and made it to the World Series three times. We were used to winning and there we were again, entering the home stretch of another pennant battle. And once again, Baltimore had another very, very good ball club. Our team had a Hall of Fame arm, Jim Palmer, and a Hall of Fame glove, Brooks Robinson. I could feel the excitement that builds with being involved in a pennant race. More and more, I was on the field, jawing with umpires. If I thought a guy missed a call, it made me mad and I had to tell him so. I got tossed a couple of times—I'd go home and watch a replay of my performance on the news and feel embarrassed.

Yes, the pressure was great, but not as great as the sheer fun that comes from being around a bunch of players who are so wrapped up in it that they literally cannot wait to get to the ballpark every day. And every day was a challenge that year. In 1975, the managers I would face in the opposing dugouts—Billy Martin in Texas and New York, Jack McKeon and Whitey Herzog in Kansas City, Ralph Houk in Detroit, Dick Williams in California, Alvin Dark in Oakland, Chuck Tanner in Chicago— each one of those guys would manage a World Series champion at some point in his career. And two others, Frank Robinson in Cleveland and Del Crandall, had been centerpiece players on World Series winners as well. They all knew how the game was played, and they knew how to manage, too.

After digging ourselves into a ten-games-under-.500 hole in late May, the Orioles played .650 ball the remainder of the season. Coming into the final week, we trailed Boston by a couple of games. Maybe on a team that is twenty-two games back, you'll find a player or two whose only motivation is polishing his batting average. But when you're in the race, the pennant is the players' passion. That passion might have been fanned by the financial realities of 1975, when a World Series check might match a player's entire salary.

We never caught the Red Sox. They went on to play Cincinnati in the memorable World Series of 1975, while we went home. It hurt. It hurts when you lose after you had played as hard as my guys had. But it was over. What I didn't realize, and what nobody associated with the game fully realized, was that much more than another season was over. The structure of the way the sports business was run was over, too.

That was 1975, the last year of normalcy in baseball.

Free agent times had arrived. Owners, front office executives, players—nobody knew what was going to happen...until it happened. Then it exploded. In about a year, our general manager, Hank Peters, who was the architect of that defensive dynasty the Orioles had put on the field, found himself going to Arizona to meet with Reggie Jackson's agent. Hank had to travel because Jackson's agent was afraid to fly. When Hank got back, he didn't have much to say, other than, "The numbers those people are talking about are mind-boggling."

I realized that from then on, as a manager I would have to accept the fact that assembling a lineup that kept key players in place for years at a time, like we'd done so successfully in Baltimore—well, those times were in the past.

By the time I finished managing in 1982, the New Age of Baseball was in full swing. And I'm happy to say that while the salary aspect of the game has been altered so dramatically, the only thing about the players that's changed is the size of their paychecks. They still play the game with the same heart and intensity as the guys who played their guts out trying to win the pennant in 1975. Apparently, it's also managed with the same intensity, since Bobby Cox, in Atlanta, broke my major league record for ejections.

I still love to watch baseball. I take in every pitch of the playoffs, and the World Series. If I look at the schedule in the middle of the season and see that, say, San Diego is on TV that night playing Philadelphia, I'll probably watch that, too. But if it's still in the second inning, and one of the starters has already thrown sixty-two pitches, then I might turn it off. That kind of stuff makes me want to go light a cigarette.

Earl Weaver
January 2008

Author's Note

This is a baseball biography. Not of a player, but of a season.

It describes a time and a place that no longer exists. It was a season that said farewell and adiós to what can be termed baseball's *pre-agent* era. The men who played the game in those days performed their on-the-field activities with the same make-it-look-easy grace of the modern athletes. But in more essential ways, they were vastly different. Steroids, they thought, were some tribe of evil aliens that appeared on *Star Trek*. Their narcotic of choice was served in a glass. I learned a lot about their social rituals and drinking cliques when I followed the Texas Rangers baseball team around, working as a reporter for a Fort Worth newspaper.

The managers and coaches drank scotch. The position players drank vodka or CC and 7. The pitchers favored a concoction of Everclear, 151 rum, and coffin polish. One hurler was probably ordering doubles the night in Florida spring training when he went berserk and kicked in half the doors in the hotel. He spent the remainder of spring training living beneath a pier, hiding from the law. Management was impressed. He would eventually throw a perfect game.

Nearly every person associated with the game smoked in the dugout tunnels between innings, or stuffed their jaws with various vile forms of "smokeless tobacco," and the only time they didn't spit was standing at attention during "The Star-Spangled Banner." They don't make players like that anymore. They don't have seasons like '75 anymore, either.

That season came at the pre-dawning of baseball's free agent era. Baseball stories on the front of the sports section concerned runs, hits, and errors and not matters of high finance. In 1975, the average salary for a major league baseball player was $27,600. That did come with benefits. They received $19 a day for meal money on the road. If you wanted to find an agent's name in the paper, you had to turn to the real estate section in the classified ads.

In an authentic barroom-noir scene from another hotel and another generation, a traveling reporter (me) sat alone, jabbing at ice cubes with a swizzle stick and watching the little wakes they made in the brown scotch. Anaheim was a lonely place.

A major league baseball player in the exit years of a decent career approached the table, surprising the reporter. This player, surly by nature, his brow now heavy beads of disco sweat, was convinced that his cooperation with the media had cost him his sanity.

The player was direct. "You room by yourself, right?"

"Yeah."

"Then how about me borrowing the room for an hour or so?" His eyes bore the intently earnest and hopeful expression of the family dog after it realizes the backyard chef has charred the brisket.

Impossible to imagine now. A big league baseball player and he's practically *begging*. But there once existed a time when even the All-Star talent lived two to a room.

Much is made of the monied lifestyles of contemporary base-ball Brahmin culture and this era in which the combined sala-ries of major leaguers from the Dominican Republic exceed that country's annual defense budget. Until a federal court mandated that players were free to sell their skills on an open market, the off-the-field landscape was a more modest place.

Simon & Garfunkel sang of America's yearning for the where-abouts of Joe DiMaggio. All they had to do was turn on any TV channel, where Joltin' Joe was selling coffeepots in order to pay the mortgage. Another idol of that era, Bob Feller, who came to the majors with a fabled 100-mile-an-hour fastball, was the topic of a profile in *Sports Illustrated*. After baseball, Feller traveled deep into the nation's off-Broadway precincts, flying his own small plane, working a lounge act, and selling life insurance to minor leaguers. He sounded half-broke and full-bitter.

Look at two other arcangels from baseball's treasured past. On his deathbed, Mickey Mantle talked of trying to sell his used liver on eBay. Meanwhile, Ted Williams's severed and frozen head might endure years beyond his legacy as perhaps the game's greatest hitter. Ted should have at least had enough dough set aside for a decent burial.

The world is still waiting for ex-player Jim Fregosi, who would later manage the Philadelphia Phillies into the 1993 World Series, to complete his baseball autobiography. He has promised to title it *The Bases Were Loaded and so Was I*. As the shadows grew long on his playing career, Fregosi was asked about his post-career inten-tions: "I suppose," Fregosi said after pondering the issue for quite a few seconds, "that I will wind up doing what 90 percent of these guys do. Disappear into the forest."

Yet Fregosi, in his time, ranked among the top-paid players in the game. Consider, then, the financial realities of the players

whose names appeared in the box score but never in the headlines. Such a player was Ken Suarez, a backup catcher prototypi-
cal utility man with the A's in a distant era when the team was
playing in Kansas City. He later would play four positions with
the Cleveland Indians, and ended his career in the morbid early
days of the Texas Rangers.

As a bit player whose real value to his team was a talent for
stealing signs from the opposition dugout, Suarez eagerly con-
cedes that he stayed in the big leagues by fooling scouts and general managers for seven years. He was fully qualified to address
the economics from the perspective of someone who survived the
deep recesses of the labor pool.

"Just to illustrate how things have changed, most ballplayers relied on their income tax *refund* to finance their way through
spring training. Even if you made the big league roster, your first
paycheck wasn't until April 15," said Suarez. "Spring training
was when we all got one of the big perks of those days, back before
players relied on agents for everything that they do. We'd re-sign
our contract with the Topps bubblegum people who put out the
baseball cards. In return, Topps would let us select a gift from a
catalogue. Nice enough stuff. One year, I took a color TV. Another time, a wrought-iron sofa and two end tables wrapped in
clear plastic.

"Then, during the regular season, the profit margin actually
came from the meal money we received on the road. That was
$19 a day. But," Suarez interjected, "at the end of every road se-
ries, we had to tip the visiting clubhouse guy $20, for putting out a
postgame spread of lunch meat and hot dogs and hiring some kids
who were paid nothing to shine our baseball shoes every day."

Suarez cited the reality of life that major league baseball players faced circa 1975. "In those days, you launch a career with some

company like IBM. You might be there the rest of your life. But as a baseball player, I knew for sure that when I reached thirty-two or so, I was through. In baseball, there was no security, but no uncertainty, either." With that in mind, the end of Suarez's career came shortly after he had registered enough days in the majors to qualify for his pension.

The world he describes evokes images of grainy, black-and-white newsreels from the Great Depression, men standing in line for free apples. So Suarez marvels at the image of the contemporary game, seemingly ruled by a new axiom dictating that success in the game is 10 percent perspiration, 10 percent preparation, and 80 percent medication. "The JUICE!" Suarez is howling, but must privately wonder if certain cutting-edge, state-of-the-art hormones could have elevated his career nineteen home runs to a number that would have made fans forget Johnny Bench. "No point in thinking about that," he said, getting philosophical. "Couldn't have afforded them [the hormonal home run launchers]. No. Our drug of choice was affordable. We drank. We celebrated after every win, and drowned our sorrows after every loss."

Over the course of a season, players could rely on a heavy discount on saloon expenses, since adoring fans and certain sycophants known to the players as green flies would recognize the ballplayer and frequently pick up the tab. Additionally, prior to the present scenarios in which a Roger Clemens could sit in his dugout and bid for items at Jackie Onassis's estate auction on his cell phone, players would settle at nothing to stretch their booze supply. Generous flight attendants aboard the team charter flights would allow the big leaguers to loot the beverage carts and fill the barf bags airlines used to supply with the small whiskey bottles.

In the early 1970s, when few baseball players were earning

more than $30,000, a labor lawyer, Marvin Miller, not only freed the slaves but also got them a private 737 and a second home in Palm Beach. But every person in uniform, from the manager to the batboy, was granted a free and unlimited supply of smokeless tobacco.

"Yeah, it was my job to make sure there was plenty around; the manufacturers provided it to the teams for free. All the brands. Beech-Nut. Bull Durham. Red Man. Day's Work. By providing it to the players, the manufacturers hoped that might encourage its use among younger players, younger fans. For some reason, fewer and fewer players used the stuff as time went on. Started making the young ones throw up."

The speaker was Joe Macko, the equipment manager for the Texas Rangers who himself played in the majors very briefly. He would supply, at wholesale cost, another commodity no longer seen in major league clubhouses: cigarettes. "Sometimes, I got free samples . . . those got snapped up right away," says Macko. "The only players who didn't use smokeless tobacco were the ones who smoked. Charlie Hough used to light up between innings even on the nights that he pitched."

Toby Harrah was a shortstop and third baseman whose career spanned baseball's two eras—the Working Man Epoch and the Patrician Age. Unfortunately for Harrah, his All-Star prime was positioned too closely to the former. Consequently, from a salary standpoint, Harrah was never able to partake of the big cheese. "When I was breaking in with the big leagues, players were no different than the neighbors next door," Harrah said, with a tone of chagrin. "I was a starting shortstop in the majors, married, and lived in the Soto Grande apartments in Euless, Texas. Quite happily, I would add."

Harrah was typical of the up-and-coming stars in the long-ago years before anyone had heard of Watergate. He spent his off-season playing baseball in Latin America. "That helped me get needed experience and really refined my game. Really enhanced my playing career. But the reason I went to Venezuela and played was because I needed the cash. It wasn't much. About two grand a month." Players in the winter leagues encountered hardships. Fans would routinely toss small explosives and venomous snakes into the visiting team dugouts. One player arrived home after a short road trip and found a dead horse in his yard.

"Yeah, but it was a wonderful experience," Harrah recalled. So is it possible, at a time when big leaguers lived the middle-class life, that baseball players HAD MORE FUN than the present day Richie Rich generation?

Harrah ponders that issue for a nanosecond and says, "Are you nuts? Man, I love to think what I could have done with five mil a year. Cars. Boats. Clothes. Probably an airplane. I would have put every cent right back into the economy." Harrah reveled in the fantasy, then added, "If I had counted on my baseball salary for survival in later life, I'd be downtown right now, sitting on a curb, holding a sign and a paper cup."

The Toby Harrahs, Jim Fregosis, and Ken Suarezes—relics of baseball's medieval past—played the game when America was a happier place.

America was a happier place. The U.S. really didn't have a president that year. Gerald Ford was more like an interim manager. The nice guy who holds the post for a while, telling jokes and filling out the lineup card until the owner can bring in the next asshole.

But, for all of its nostalgia-laced trimmings, the season of 1975 was a captivating six-month drama that featured great teams, great players, and great managers. The American League season got off to one hell of a bang in 1975. At Shea Stadium (where the Yankees played home games for two seasons while Yankee Stadium was closed for renovation) they conducted opening day ceremonies that also honored the 200th anniversary of the U.S. Army. Two 75mm artillery battalions from Fort Hamilton fired a pregame twenty-one-gun salute. When the smoke cleared, there was a large hole in the centerfield fence, and many of the windows around the private stadium suites were shattered. The season ended on a resounding pyrotechnic blast as well, perhaps the most captivating World Series ever played—between the Red Sox and the Reds.

The Cincinnati team was not an assembly of the rent-a-mercenary type of rosters that dominate the modern game. No, the likes of Pete Rose, Joe Morgan, Johnny Bench, Tony Perez, Dave Concepcion, Cesar Geronimo, Ken Griffey Sr. et al. had been Reds from the outset. They were managed by a man who spoke fluent gibberish (Sparky Anderson at the World Series told me that his bullpen reminded him of birds flapping around, trapped in a chimney). I didn't have the slightest idea what Sparky was talking about. But his 1975 club won 108 regular season games, so having a firm command of the gibberish language must certainly rate as one of the underrated keys to leadership success. Like many of the great major league managers in the history of the sport, Sparky Anderson maintained playing career credentials that would be termed generously as modest. His major league career began April 10, 1959. It ended September 27, 1959. In that one season, Anderson finished among the top ten players in the National League in two categories: grounded into double plays and caught stealing.

Sparky's so-called Big Red Machine must be ranked one of the best baseball teams ever assembled. Certain critics have characterized those Reds as a "Turf" team, but Cincinnati would have dominated on any playing surface, from natural grass, to quicksand or hot lava. Yet its entire twenty-five-player payroll probably amounted to half of what, as this is written, the New York Yankees are paying their third baseman.

In terms of baseball dynasties, the Reds stand out as the sport's last *real* team, and the year of their greatest ascendancy must be remembered as the last real season.

The Arlington Stadium where I watched and wrote about the home team Rangers, like so many of the great ballparks of the time, lies buried beneath a parking lot now, and with it lies a baseball mind-set I describe in this book. It is with a feeling more of disbelief than regret that I concede that those days have vanished forever.

Mike Shropshire
Fall 2007

Prologue

My grandfather, Clyde Moore Shropshire, was born in 1866. How the hell is that possible? Two ways. Clyde was pretty old when my father was born, and I am an old man now. Clyde died in 1948, at a time when I was in the earliest phases of a bonding process with the concept of baseball. Within two years, I accepted baseball into my heart, the same way some people do with Jesus. Sat for an hour, staring at box scores in the newspaper. Some level of autism at work there perhaps, but hopefully that might have been more the product of a genetic linkage. In Nashville, back in the early 1920s, my grandfather owned the baseball team.

The team was the Nashville Vols. They played in the Southern Association, one of the historically embraced franchises from the gilded age of minor league baseball. It was not the teams that people in Nashville remembered or the games of those hazy yesterdays, but rather the park where they played. The story of the Nashville ball field was the story of American baseball itself. At the close of the Civil War, soldiers in the occupying Union forces would gather down in the flats near the Cumberland River and play baseball.

In the city that prided itself as "the Athens of the South," the site was already a popular picnic destination with people who were attracted by the sulphur water that came up through natural springs. Sulphur water is good for arteriosclerosis. People drank it out of fruit jars and watched the Yankee troops play their games. They would soon discover that if the bilious issue of the sulphur springs was heart-healthy, then the leisurely act of watching baseball, with its gentle rhythms, was soothing to the bowels. So baseball became an almost nurturing facet in the matters of humanity that enabled the nation to reunite after the war.

The troops would leave, but baseball stayed, and the park was built right there where the Yankees had laid out their infield. Grantland Rice, rightfully remembered as the best sportswriter in the annals of the concept, came up with "Sulpher Dell." It was a masterpiece of unique configuration, the right field line 262 feet to the flagpole. Right fielders stood on a steep terrace, the base of the wall was twenty-two and a half feet higher than the plate. The wall jutted sharply to a location in dead center 420 feet from the plate. The Nashville Elite Giants of the Negro Leagues played there as well.

I was taken to the Sulpher Dell once, by an uncle, while the Vols were on the road, just to see the place, inhale the enchantment for a few minutes, envy the Camelot days when Clyde owned the team. Of course, when you're a kid, you think that the person who owns the team owns the ballpark, too. So I was immediately consumed with doubt that my grandfather—any member of my family or anybody else's family, for that matter—could lay claim to ever owning something of the magnitude of the Sulpher Dell.

Minor league baseball died hard in Dixie. The Nashville Vols gasped into the 1960s, and then Faron Young bought the property and converted the ballpark into a midget race car track. The ignominious final descent was underway. After the racetrack didn't work, the Sulpher Dell was converted into the city car pound. Then they came with a wrecking ball, demolished the Sulpher Dell, and perhaps the brightest gem in the wall safe of baseball's nostalgic treasures was scooped into trucks and transported to a landfill.

My real indoctrination occurred in another place, more breathtaking even than the Sulpher Dell. LaGrave Field was the home of another of those resonant franchises from the American railroad era—the Fort Worth Cats, an upper tier team in the Texas League. After World War II, the Cats became one of the Dodgers' AA farm teams. The ballpark was on the north side of town, and the Trinity River levee ran immediately behind the left field fence. Then came the great flood of '49, a joyous occasion that drowned ten people and closed the schools for two weeks. LaGrave Field was flooded, and during the drying out process, it burned. The Cats won the Texas League pennant, playing before home crowds that sat in bleacher grandstands built amid the rubble.

The new LaGrave Field that awaited the fans in 1950 was met with unmitigated acclaim. The fans adored the Cats, too, a keystone station in Branch Rickey's farm system for prospects the Dodgers wanted to fast-track. I was among the final generation of an American childhood that had to follow the exploits of the team on the radio. More than the sometimes arcane lyrics of the play-by-play voice, what lingers through the ages are the commercials. The beer commercials, with their songs and uplifting jingles. Southern Select. Hamm's. Jax. Even as a grade schooler, those radio spots really made me want to drink the stuff.

On weekends, it was Dizzy Dean and the CBS *Game of the Week*, brought to a grateful America by the Falstaff Brewing

Company of St. Louis, Missouri. As a youth, I memorized the anthem, and remember it still:

> *Falstaff beer is the right beer, yessiree*
> *Falstaff beer is premium quality*
> *Smooth and bold and mellow brew*
> *Premium quality through and through*
> *Taste it once, and once you do,*
> *You'll sing out for Falstaff, sing out for Falstaff*
> *Sing out for Falstaff beer*

Dizzy Dean was the greatest beer salesman of all time, and through his self-styled broadcast booth poetry—"…I'll tell ya' why Eddie Lopat gets 'em out. It ain't his natural stuff, he couldn't break a wind-er pane, but he's got testicle fortitude…"—he elevated Falstaff from a regional product to the third-biggest-selling brand in the U.S. Diz liked to get suds-ed up on the air, and thank the good people who founded the Falstaff brewery, the Griesedieck family, and he took immense pleasure in his pronunciation of the name: Greasy Dick. CBS executives used to sit chewing their fingernails during the telecasts, hoping that Diz wouldn't say something too outrageous, while everybody in America tuned in hoped that he would.

When people used to refer to Fort Worth as Cowtown, they weren't kidding. Just north of the baseball field, not even a half-mile, you could climb a fence and see cattle and hog pens extending to the horizon. The mammoth Armour and Swift packinghouses loomed in the background. Usually the prevailing winds carried the aromas of the stockyard away from town, and when that didn't occur, the city was cloaked beneath an unseen canopy of cow shit. At least it was organic. Since the ballpark was just down the street, the presence of the pork and beef industry was even more profound. Not only did you get a close-range blast of the morning-after breath that comes from fermenting manure, but LaGrave Field spectators could smell actual blood and guts from the docks behind the gigantic slaughterhouses. They'd take the intestines and genitals and elbow joints and various other parts, let 'em rot in the sun for three or four days, and then grind that up to produce the OK Corral All-Meat Hot Dogs that everybody was eating at the baseball game.

While Branch Rickey stands memorialized as the Abraham Lincoln of major league baseball, his best AA team maintained an all-white roster for eight years beyond the season Jackie Robinson debuted in Brooklyn. So the Cats finally "broke the color line" in 1955. First Negro Cat ever: shortstop Maurice "Maury" Wills. My father took me to the game, but not because of *that*. It was my birthday. Seating was segregated at LaGrave, and the black section, the worst seats in the house, way down the right field line, practically in the parking lot, was jammed. Fans watched the players playing catch in front of the Cats' dugout, wondering which one was the black guy. They figured it out when the game finally started. "They might claim that guy's black, but Jesus...he could pass for Ernest Tubb!" As a major league baseball player, Wills's home-run-to-at-bat ratio was 1 in over 3,200. But Wills knocked one over the left field fence—cleared it by a foot—in the bottom of the ninth to win that one for the Cats.

The nice thing about old baseball stories is that there is always a coincidental subplot. In this case, the Cats' second baseman, on the night when Wills hit the game-winning homer, was named George Anderson. He would become thereafter and forever more known as Sparky Anderson after his season in Fort Worth. Anderson picked a fight with an umpire, and the Cats' radio play guy said, "The sparks are gonna fly tonight!" The Cats always had the right voice for the AM airwaves. Zack Hurt, not realizing he was still on the air after the starter had gotten lifted, said to his listeners, "That son of a bitch couldn't pitch hay to my cow." So the pitcher sued, but the case was thrown out because of ERA evidence.

That '55 Cats team also included an additional trio of regulars who would eventually manage in the major leagues—Danny Ozark, Norm Sherry, and Dick Williams. The Fort Worth Cats bred great baseball minds like Houston breeds mosquitoes. But the spreading epidemic of the deadly minor league attendance virus that began to afflict the sport in those years would kill the Cats about the same time the Nashville Vols shut down, and La-Grave Field, just like the Sulpher Dell, stood abandoned, ignored, neglected, and unloved.

I was working for a newspaper when I visited the vacated La-Grave Field, out of curiosity, and discovered waist-deep weeds poking up from the field-level box seats, and cattle were grazing in the outfield. We assigned a photographer to capture the scene. His name was Russ, and he was one of those photojournalists who used a camera to attract women. So we ran a photo of a bank secretary, wearing shorts, her full red lips beaming on the pitcher's mound, standing next to a bovine creature that chewed grass with the nonchalance of one of those old Cats players grinding down on his tobacco chaw. The indignity ended in 1966. Someone dismantled the metal grandstands, almost overnight, and the ballpark simply vanished. Our paper ran a four-paragraph obit in the sports section, and I wrote the headline: "LaGrave Field Dies in Its Sleep."

Baseball was no longer in my heart. It had abandoned me, slipped off into the darkness like an unfaithful love partner, gone to the 'burbs and moved in with a land developer, leaving behind only a "don't ever try to contact me" note where the TV used to sit. In those years, I was not alone. Baseball abandoned a lot of people.

The slut.

All I could do was dab my eyes and attempt to find solace in a new relationship—minor league ice hockey.

THE
LAST
REAL
SEASON

Chapter 1

October 1974

A burly, all-male, all-white assembly stood in cliquish knots of four or five guys in the pressroom at the Biltmore Hotel in downtown L.A. National media were here on the eve of Game 1 of the World Series, this one unique because it was the first ever all-California spectacle, the Dodgers against the Oakland A's. Baseball media people were a hard lot, ample of girth and opinion, suspicious of outsiders, as surly and unapproachable as the regulars at any rural pub in Ireland. Mostly, the baseball-writing hierarchy consisted of people with faces the color and texture of wet biscuit dough, flesh that was seldom exposed to sunlight.

These men were inclined toward snappishness, due in part to the torment of prostate glands swollen to the size of croquet balls. Their darting, bitter eyes echoed a lifetime resentment over being too short to work for the fire department. They chain-smoked— even though the room had a twenty-five-foot-high ceiling, a thick, choking haze corrupted the oxygen—and they told stories that weren't true. One of them talked out of this puckered, Dick Tracy comic strip mouth that a county medical examiner might identify as an exit wound and told his group, "...and then he said,

1

'Well, this is the first time I ever ate one that came with pepperoni and mushrooms!' Haw. Haw. Haw." The boys bent forward at the waist, they were laughing so hard.

I watched, and listened, wishing to join the group and share in the mirth. Tell 'em my great joke about the epileptic oyster shucker. These were my kind of people, but I was not *their* kind of people, and therefore was excluded. That was because they regarded me as a hippie, probably some chickenshit draft dodger who'd snuck off to Canada. Hippies were unwelcome in press boxes throughout the land, because, as Ronald Reagan had so aptly put it, they (we) dressed like Tarzan, had hair like Jane, and smelled like Cheetah.

Even so, being subjected to occupational quarantine and behind-the-back insults was hardly a consequential drawback to the overall proposition of experiencing an all-expense paid trip to the World Series—courtesy of the newspaper that employed me, the *Fort Worth Star-Telegram.* As an act of extreme generosity, the management people at the paper offered the World Series adventure as compensation for having labored for long months watching the Texas Rangers perform. Who cared if the Rangers were the most low-rent franchise and were regarded as an inferior league in what *Forbes* magazine, among others, insisted was a slowly dying sport? And who cared if nearly all the newspaper readers back in Texas cared absolutely nothing about a World Series staged entirely in California, province of the godless, land of the gay caballero, where the natives all ordered grapefruit on their tacos, where everyone drove foreign-made automobiles, where Okies went to get pissed on, and where the recently exiled president of the U.S. was currently experiencing the heartbreak of phlebitis?

What a gig! After an estrangement that had lasted nearly a decade, baseball was back in my heart. And my liver, too. Why, just that very morning, fresh out of the cab from an interview session at Dodger Stadium, I'd won thirty Wiki-Wiki Dollars in a scratch-off game, and then drank it all up in the icy darkness of Mandy's Caribbean Grotto. Fortified by several hefty beakers of tequila and coconut milk, it was now time to go to work.

The task was to compose a pregame, or pre-series story, known in the newspaper trade as an "advance." In this case, the task was a snap, easier than taking your kid's lunch money at gunpoint. I caressed the keyboard of the manual Smith-Corona that was placed before me in the Biltmore pressroom amid the chattering-typewriter chorale now long extinct from the American workplace. In a presentation designed to pander to the California-loathing readership back home, I composed a story alluding to the per-plexing reality that only out here on the Left Coast, the world's largest can of mixed nuts, could a person fluent in the language of physics become a bullpen hero and the dominant figure on a pennant-winning baseball team. This was Mike Marshall. *Doctor* Mike Marshall. The doctorate had been awarded at Michigan State, in something known as kinesiology, which, as the doctor him-self had told a blank-eyed sportswriter, related to the "interaction of body parts." Marshall had earned the Ph.D. with a thesis he might as well have entitled: "Why Major League Baseball Pitching Coaches Don't Know Their Ass from the Washington Monument."

Marshall, who would soon become the first relief pitcher to win the National League Cy Young Award, had exploited the media mob assembled at a Dodgers workout to press his polemic. "Most pitching coaches are incompetent," he explained evenly, "and they merely perpetuate the old, ignorant ways of pitching. They do so because of their fundamental lack of knowledge of physiology and muscle structure. And, as a result, they destroy pitchers' arms." While Marshall delivered that diatribe, his own

3

pitching coach, Red Adams, stood not far away, smoking a New-
port menthol and rolling his eyes.

The pitcher continued his oral dissertation, explaining how
his Three Laws of Force were actually based on Isaac Newton's
Three Laws of Motion. Okay, I knew all about Newton, having
purchased many screw-top bottles of 59-cent wine from the Isaac
Newton vineyard with its catchy slogan, "What Goes Down Must
Come Up."

But what did Isaac Newton know about baseball, and who was
this pitcher talking all this heresy? Marshall's appearance was as
unconventional as his ideas. Most major league baseball pitchers
were lanky characters who came equipped with the torso of a
buggy whip, and they sure as hell never used words like "perpetuate." Dr. Marshall might measure five-foot-nine if he was wearing
shoes borrowed from Zsa Zsa Gabor, and was as big around as
he was tall. He sported rather spectacular muttonchop sideburns,
and whenever he entered a game, the person in the stands might
have expected the public address man to announce: *Now pitching for
Los Angeles . . . Ulysses S. Grant.*

So, even though Mike Marshall rather reminded me of the
cartoon walrus that sang and danced in Prestone Antifreeze commercials back in the 1950s, the pitcher could say anything he
damn well pleased. For that season, at least, Marshall produced
the stats to back it up. With a body that consisted of half-blubber,
half-rubber, Marshall had taken on the heavy lifting agenda of a
Russian coal miner, appearing in 106 games, and pitched over 200
innings out of the bullpen.

As for his diatribe regarding pitching coaches and their alleged penchant for wrecking arms and careers, Marshall's timing was superb. Two weeks before the start of the World Series,
another kind of doctor, Frank Jobe, had performed a radical and

experimental surgery in an attempt to bring the career of Dodgers starter Tommy John back from the dead. Jobe had taken a tendon from John's right wrist and reattached it to the pitcher's left elbow. Fortunately for both Dr. Jobe and the pitcher, the Dodgers' press guide had confirmed that Tommy John was, indeed, a left-hander.

So I concluded my feature story about the Dodgers' mad scientist, Mike Marshall, with a couple of sentences about the strange goings-on in Jobe's operating room, describing the procedure as "ghoulish" and noting that some Hollywood hotshot could get rich merely by taking the master print of *Frankenstein* and distributing it under the title *The Tommy John Story.*

Then I quickly evacuated the pressroom at the Biltmore, feeling nauseated from the cigarette smoke, my head pounding from the racket of all those typewriters. Near the exit, Joe Falls, the revered columnist from the *Detroit Free Press* (why did they call it free when it actually cost a quarter?) was holding court. Falls delivered prose in the two-fisted patois of the crescent wrench set, a style that was perfectly textured for his readership back in Detroit, the most no-nonsense, no-bullshit city in the whole world.

Joe was a confirmed, born-again traditionalist, and he bemoaned the reality that six long years had rolled by since the Tigers, behind the pitching of Denny McLain and Mickey Lolich, had stunned the baseball community with their breathtaking seven-game World Series triumph over Bob Gibson and the seemingly invincible Cardinals, and Falls was now sadly convinced that nothing of such magnitude would ever occur again. "This isn't right," Falls was saying. "Fall classic, my ass. You can't have a World Series surrounded by all these goddamned palm trees. The atmosphere is...well, hell. There is no atmosphere."

Compelled to interrupt, I said, "What you need to do, Joe, is take a couple of hits of windowpane acid before you go to the game tomorrow. That'll make it all better. Betcha I can score some for you from one of the bellhops."

Falls's face contorted into a knot of utter disdain, and he said, to nobody's surprise, "You're really full of crap, you know that?"

"No. I'm serious. You oughta give it a try," I came back. "It sure worked for me last year in Oakland. God awmighty, man, in the sixth inning, when Yogi replaced Tom Seaver with that fuckin' unicorn, it was the greatest World Series moment since Babe Ruth called his shot at Wrigley Field."

Joe Falls laughed, then said, "Go to hell."

That was when I almost told him that I didn't have time because of an impending appointment to have my ears pierced, but tactfully refrained, having done enough damage as it was.

That was on Friday, and soon I was out on the town. In a city populated almost entirely by an all-you-can-eat buffet of undiscovered ingenues with high cheekbones and low self-esteem, I declined to partake. Actually, I'd long ago learned that ladies with theatrical ambitions don't mix well with men of less-than-pristine elocution skills. Naturally, that excluded all Texans. Once the Texan opened his mouth, the California girl gazed back with an expression that said, "Cram it, buckaroo. Go home and oil your windmill."

Why even bother? So Friday night was largely devoted to the more convivial companionship of the esteemed Johnnie Walker.

Then Saturday came and so did Game 1, and in honor of the occasion, the smog that filled the Southern California sky appeared in more festive shades of brown and gray. In the lobby of the Biltmore, one familiar face from home appeared. Danny O'Brien, general manager of the Texas Rangers, a man of dignity and know-how, who maintained a commendable rise-above-it approach to the tantrums of his field manager, Billy Martin, waved me over.

"Here. Do you know anybody who might want to use these?" said O'Brien. He handed me two tickets to Game 1.

"Sure, Danny. Thanks. I saw a man in here with a little crippled boy, hoping to take the kid to the game."

Three minutes later, I got on the hotel elevator, which was crammed, held the tickets aloft and stood there while some guy took them out of my hand and replaced them with two $50 bills. It was a quick and wordless transaction. Between that and my Wiki-Wiki Dollar windfall, my trip to the Series was already a five-star success.

Then I rode the press bus to the stadium, eager to watch what was going to unfold. This Dodgers–A's match-up might even be fun to write about, since this was a confrontation featuring beyond-the-obvious contrasts.

The Dodgers organization provided the template for the immaculately constructed sports franchise, a paradigm of smarts, class, and cool efficiency. Yes, Walter O'Malley had broken a million hearts in Flatbush when he moved the franchise to the shores of the Pacific, but the evacuation did for baseball what the completion of the transcontinental railroad did for the passenger train people whose industry might not have collapsed had it been run with the top-to-bottom operational foresight that the Dodgers employed. The eternal influx of talent from the team's minor league network was on display once again as the 1974 World Series began. L.A.'s infield—Steve Garvey, Davey Lopes, Bill Russell, and Ron Cey—was the natural successor to the storied around-the-horn quartet of Gil Hodges, Jackie Robinson, Pee Wee Reese, and Billy Cox that hung up National League pennants like laundry drying on the balconies of a Hong Kong high rise.

So 2.4 million fans had come to Dodger Stadium that summer to cheer the team that had won 102 regular season games, and sawed off the Pittsburgh Pirates in five quick games in the National League playoff. L.A. was back in the World Series for the first time in eight years and a clear favorite in the minds of most to beat the A's with the same ease with which the Blue Boys had dismantled the Pirates.

Yes, the A's, whose ownership motif was the mirror opposite of the Dodgers. If the Los Angeles Dodgers functioned like a Swiss bank, then Charles O. Finley and his Oakland Athletics presented all the decorum of a bail bond company. Charlie O. was the renegade on the reservation, a man who felt it a moral obligation to spit in the face of the tradition and long-upheld rituals of the game itself. When Finley emerged upon the scene, major league baseball found itself confronted with a sheer anarchist unconvincingly disguised as an "innovator."

The A's played in Kansas City when Finley, an Indiana native wealthy from the insurance racket, bought the team in 1960. People in K.C. liked Charlie at first. Right off, he decreed that the A's would cease any and all player transactions with the New York Yankees, who'd been exploiting the Midwest rubes on a yearly basis. Then—as the second-division summers in Kansas City dragged by like starving cattle—the fans began to sense that they might have an element of tinhorn despot in their baseball owner.

Charlie began suspending players because of what he deemed "rowdyism" on the team's charter flights. Rowdyism? What had Charlie expected from these guys? An episode of *Masterpiece Theatre*? After Finley had identified Ken "the Hawk" Harrelson as the rowdiest of his rowdies, Harrelson described Charlie as "a menace to baseball."

And after Charlie loaded up his A's and packed the franchise off to Oakland, Missouri senator Stuart Symington did the Hawk one better and, speaking in the U.S. Senate, referred to Finley as "the most disreputable character ever to enter the American sports scene." The mother of an acquaintance of mine, the woman being an ardent follower of the Kansas City A's, lacked access to the congressional floor as a platform to express her feelings toward Finley, but did so more emphatically than Senator Symington. She purchased a doll, labeled it Charlie F., soaked it in kerosene, and torched the thing in her front yard.

After Finley arrived in Oakland, the quality of the A's on-the-field talent improved dramatically. But the burr in Charlie's britches and the pebble in his shoe was that Charlie had decided that the sport itself had become about as exciting as lentil soup. He initiated some radical departures from the norm. When Charlie complained that baseball lacked color, he meant that literally. In Charlie's world, the home team would no longer wear white; the visitor gray. Charlie's A's took the field in their trademark kelly green and gold ensemble...or sometimes, gold and green, and always accented with small-town-Saturday-night white shoes...a fashion statement that resembled, at best, the Baylor University marching band and, at worst, a last-place softball team in South Side Chicago's Marvin Rottblatt tavern league.

Finley advocated the introduction of orange baseballs, and red, white, and blue bases. Finley lobbied for changing "four balls, take your base" to three. That proposal was actually auditioned in an A's exhibition game, and, after 19 walks in a nine-inning game, hastily abandoned.

Charlie mandated that his players wear handlebar mustaches, which was ultimately a measure designed to demean the hired hands, like the car dealer in Texas, who allegedly made his black employees dance the chicken dance during his sales motivation pep rallies. Finley made sure the team's mascot, a mule named Charlie O., became a fixture at both games and away-from-the-ballpark promotional functions. Finley's creative genius provided A's games with ball girls, tarted up in hot pants. It was Charlie's mandate that star A's pitcher Jim Hunter, having grown up in the sticks, would henceforth be known as Catfish. Charlie's public relations notions were geared to a kind of Corn Belt sophistication that was as passé as Buster Keaton movies. In short, Charlie was kind of a hick. His penchant for the abnormal occasionally backfired. Before being famous as a big league manager, Whitey Herzog combed the backwoods and back roads of America, working as a baseball scout. For a while, he was employed by Finley.

Herzog described Charlie O. as "nuttier than a June bug in July." Herzog elaborated. "I found this kid in Florida, a pitcher, who had everything, all the makings for a big leaguer. I asked him what he wanted to sign with the A's. His demands weren't much—a new car and $18,000. The kid's name was Don Sutton. I called Charlie directly, and he didn't care about Sutton's ability. He wanted to know if Sutton had a nickname. I covered the phone with my hand, Sutton was sitting right there, and I asked him about a nickname. He shrugged and couldn't think of one. So I told Charlie the news, and he said, 'No deal,' and hung up. Now if Sutton had told me that people called him 'Peckerneck' or some such, he would have made his Hall of Fame acceptance in an A's hat, instead of the Dodgers'."

Finley's ardent lobbying for the designated hitter rule (Finley also wanted to include a designated runner) came to pass when the American League installed the drastic format in 1973. It was the DH innovation that purists of the sport insisted was as good for baseball as pantyhose had been for finger fucking. Charlie Finley maintained nothing but contempt for anything in baseball that represented the status quo. If Finley had owned the New York Metropolitan Opera, he would have put the divas on Weight Watchers and forced Richard Tucker to stand on stage and sing, "Ninety-nine Bottles of Beer on the Wall."

Oakland fans responded to the Great Innovator's revolutionary themes by ignoring them. Even though the '74 A's had been the only baseball franchise outside of the Bronx to claim three straight World Series championships, their regular season attendance was a pitiful 845,000. In a season in which American League fans throughout the country had been avoiding the ballpark like poison ivy, even the bottom-of-the-keg Cleveland Indians managed to outdraw the A's.

With numbers like those, Finley confided in some people that moving his franchise to Oakland had been a sorry idea in the first place. So Finley calculated that over the course of 81 games, his team had played before slightly more than 3 million empty seats and used that calculation to justify the team's paying security guard wages to a lineup choked with American League All-Stars.

Earlier that season, I'd sat in the A's dugout during batting practice before a Rangers game and talked to a couple of players on the topic of alleged feuding in the clubhouse. Pitcher John (Blue Moon) Odom had exchanged punches with Rollie Fingers in the bullpen, and had come close to blows with Vida Blue amid a throng of reporters after a playoff game. So one could only imagine what took place behind closed doors. Shortstop Bert Campaneris, a six-time All-Star and the greatest Cuban to land on the American mainland since Desi Arnaz, downplayed the rumors of unrest.

"Ees not so unhappy family," Campaneris insisted.

I needed a stronger quote than that. "Okay," I asked the shortstop, "how do you like working for Mr. Finley. He is nice man, yes? No?"

11

"Meester Finley," said Campaneris, his eyes narrowing, "ees the kind of man who likes to put hees hand in other man's pock-eet."

At first, I thought Campaneris might be implying that his owner was the sort of fellow who gets rolled in bus stations throughout the land. What the player meant to say was that when it came to matters of the pocketbook, Finley was tighter than Joe Namath's pantyhose. So the deacons of the high church of baseball frowned on Charles Finley. Yet they could not deny that the A's, with all of the corporate cohesion of a band of Turkish Gypsies, had returned once again to the World Series. But hardly anybody thought the A's could bring down the Dodgers. Oakland had won only 90 games, and with barely a week remaining in the regular season, that silly little team from Texas had drawn so close to Oakland in the AL West standings that the A's could smell the booze on the Rangers' breath.

In the second inning of Game 1, the A's made it known that they would not die easily—might not even die at all. I was stationed in an auxiliary press area along the first base line, way the hell up, with the California sun right in my face. Reggie Jackson took a cut off the Dodgers' starter, Andy Messersmith, and because of the glare and ever-present L.A. haze, I had no idea where the ball had gone. What a ridiculous situation. My job detailed describing a baseball game to an audience of readers who saw a close-up of Reggie Jackson's tonsils just as he swung his bat, courtesy of the camera artistry of the National Broadcasting Company, and eloquently described by Curt Gowdy and Vin Scully, when I couldn't see a damn thing. Then I saw Jackson performing his patented strut around the bases, his chest stuck out like Foghorn Leghorn, the posture that told the world that nobody screws with Mr. October. That top-of-the-second opposite field shot produced a collective moan from the 50,000-plus Dodgers fans—each one blasé and wearing designer sunglasses. Jackson sucked all of the pizzazz from the crowd, and the Dodgers never recovered.

While Mike Marshall delivered his relief artistry for the Dodgers and Rollie Fingers slammed doors on the opposition out of the A's bullpen, this confrontation took on more of the aspects of a World Cup than a World Series. First team that scored won the game. One–nil. Or that was the way it shaped up. That being the case, this Series promised to unfold into a production void of thrills and dramatic tension. The only stat in baseball that indicated an exciting game was the one they called the blown save. If some reliever blew a save, that meant that a team came from behind in the late innings to win or tie a game. As a lover of the game, nothing, to me, could have been more rewarding then witnessing a passionate and sensuously blown save. But with the two bullpens involved here, there would be no blow jobs in the California Fall Classic of '74. Ahead by a run in the bottom of the ninth, Oakland manager Alvin Dark pulled a gambit. After two batters were out, Dark yanked his ace closer, Fingers, and replaced him with the ace, Catfish Hunter, who was not scheduled to start until Game 3. Hunter got the last out.

In the A's clubhouse, about a hundred reporters surrounded Reggie Jackson's locker, another hundred besieged Catfish Hunter, another twenty or so encircled Alvin Dark, and the remainder of the Oakland roster was left free to shower and dress in peace. Finally, the mob began to disperse, and I shoved my way into the notebook-bearing reporters still pumping questions to Catfish. Hunter withstood the inquisition patiently, although his eyes pleaded for a little privacy.

Reporter: If this had been a regular season game, do you think Alvin would have brought you into the game in the ninth like that?

Hunter: You can ask him. But since we played 162 games and that never happened, my guess would be that the answer was no.

Reporter (asking another dumbass question because he thought that was what reporters are supposed to do): So, do you see yourself as a part-time starter, part-time closer now?

Hunter: No.

What a quote! At that point, I should have felt compelled to rush to the nearest pay phone, call the newspaper back home, and scream, STOP THE FUCKIN' PRESSES! But I didn't because I lacked the instincts of a good reporter. Or so I had been told on numerous occasions by various colleagues, a sophisticated collection of fellows who all went to Texarkana on their honeymoons.

Game 2 saw the Dodgers bounce back. Game 2 was much like Game 1, another 3–2 yawn fest. This was L.A.'s Don Sutton working against Oakland's Vida Blue. The teams registered 12 base hits—combined—nine of them singles. Catcher Joe Ferguson won the game with a two-runner for the Dodgers. Sutton weakened in the ninth, then the Ph.D. Marshall trotted to the mound, applied his Three Laws of Force, and while Isaac Newton watched and smiled on some distant cloud, the game ended.

I gazed at the blank sheet of paper in my typewriter. The paper gazed back. Finally, I wrote, "Sorry, honey. No blown saves tonight. I've got a headache." Of course, none of the readers in my paper's circulation realm would have known what their man in L.A. was talking about. It didn't matter. The top of the sports section story for the Monday morning edition would not have involved this World Series game. While the Dodgers were beating the A's, the St. Louis football Cardinals were beating the Dallas Cowboys, 31–28. That marked Dallas's fourth straight loss, so by the time any of the readers might have gotten around to reading about the World Series, they would have already committed suicide.

So the Series moved up to Oakland. Bad ballpark. Uninspired setting. The stands were a long way from the field. At twilight, the fog usually came boiling in from the Bay, and offered a setting more proper for a Dracula movie than a spectacle befitting baseball's most dramatic hour.

Game 3. A night game. Just like Games 4 and 5 would be as well, courtesy of Charlie Finley. Finley had been the leading advocate of playing the World Series under the lights, to hell with tradition, and baseball Commissioner Bowie "the Fox" Kuhn had endorsed the concept. Neither Finley nor Kuhn had to write for a Central Time Zone deadline from the West Coast at night, meaning for my story to make the paper, I would have about six minutes to interview the players, then compose the article.

Also—my assigned location at the Oakland Coliseum turned out to be even crappier than the press box crow's nest at Dodger Stadium where they'd stuck the reporters who did not work for California or New York publications. Now I was stuck in a little cage, underneath the stands actually, behind home plate. My chin was at field level, so, for the next three games, the only view of the pageantry taking place on the field was obscured by the plate umpire's big, fat ass. And each of the umpires assigned to this World Series—Ron Luciano, Bill Kunkel, Doug Harvey, Tom Gorman—had an ass as wide as Nebraska.

I was jammed in there with about a dozen other poor turkeys. Prison cells were more comfortable than this setup. Not that Charlie Finley gave a flip about the human rights of sportswriters. But what else could we have expected from Señor Cheap-O, who presented the crappiest pressroom food service in both major leagues. Lunch meat, white bread, and a fly-infested jar of Miracle Whip.

Oakland won the game, behind Catfish Hunter, the last one he would pitch in an Oakland uniform. Another 3–2 sleep-a-thon.

Again, the teams combined for 12 lousy hits. Rollie Fingers was shaky but still closed the sale. Yawn. Snore.

Game 4 produced more fireworks. Instead of another 3–2 game, this one wound up 5–2. Oakland actually came from behind with a four-run surge in the mid-innings. The Dodgers wilted once again against the Oakland bullpen.

The attempt to describe the action was an insurmountable task. There was more suspense and drama at school board meetings than what this Series produced. In Game 5, the reporters in the field-cage behind the plate could stand it no longer. In the third inning, it was agreed that two writers, selected in a random drawing, would be sent into the stands to attempt a suicide-mission beer run. I was one of the unlucky two. It went smoother than I could have hoped. In less than an inning and a half, I was back in the cage, carrying a box that held six beers, the really good news being that the beer they sold in the Oakland Coliseum came in half-gallon boxes, like orange juice containers. I sipped my half-gallon out of a little Styrofoam coffee cup. That was for two reasons. One, the act of guzzling from the carton appeared gauche, and two, drinking out of the little cup made you drunker. When the game (3–2 again) ended, the World Series with it, everybody in the cage was too messed up to care. After the last out, the writers practically trampled one another as they fought toward the press cage exit. They weren't rushing out to secure beat-the-deadline quotes. Everybody had to take a leak.

So it was over. Nobody seemed sorry. I stood next to Dodgers manager Walter Alston on the press elevator. He was still in uniform. Tall, stoic, and serene; if losing the World Series was a source of anguish to Walter Alston, he sure didn't show it.

The A's held a victory party, of sorts, afterward in the press lounge. They actually popped for champagne, the $6 kind they sold at the Circle K. Charles O. Finley was not present. But the ubiquitous mule, Charlie O., naturally was on the scene. I talked to the mule's handler, some old character that Finley dressed up in a costume that looked like something from an episode of *Death Valley Days*. The guy admitted that his gig was not all that bad—except for the part where he administered the mule's pregame enema, to prevent any on-the-field mascot "incidents."

Evidently, the guy had done his job well enough, so I gave him my vote as the MVP of the 1974 World Series. The mule's valet lost out to Rollie Fingers in the voting. When a relief pitcher was anointed hero of a five-game World Series, it confirmed that the sport's cornerstone spectacle presented all the thrills and spills of a string quartet recital, one that featured the works of Shubert. The instant-gratification generation had taken root in America, and baseball seemed archaic and out of touch. If the sport were going to stage an all-California World Series, the last feature it needed was Rollie Fingers slamming the door. What the games desperately lacked was a scenario where a crippled Kirk Gibson might stagger off the bench and sock the home run that knocked the people in the stands, and the ones who watched on TV, flat on their butts, and leave them saying, "Did I just see what I thought I saw?"

Fortunately, a different kind of season waited in the on-deck circle, a season that would delineate the conclusion of an era, and do it in a manner that restored America's faith in a game that was not dying after all.

Chapter 2

February 2, 1975

A harsh north gale gusted in hard jabs through the thoroughfares of downtown Fort Worth as noon approached. So the large room filled with metal desks, the room that housed the sports department at the *Star-Telegram*, would be largely deserted. On days like this one, the sportswriters all congregated at a coffee shop across the street from the newspaper to watch the wind blow the dresses up over the heads of the secretaries out on their lunch hour.

That situation offered the best time for me to visit the paper—when hardly anybody was there. I didn't have to be there at all. Part of my baseball-writing agreement with the paper involved comp time during the off-season. In three weeks, spring training would begin in Florida, followed by the eternity of the long season, so the free time was running out fast. So I drifted in to check the mail...and the female, a woman who worked in the newspaper library who answered to the name of Big 'Uns. As expected, no sign of life existed in the sports department. So I snatched the latest issue of the *Sporting News* off the copy desk and was prepared to leave when a wiry man wearing a leather jacket that cost two grand, easy, drifted into the room. Anybody could tell from the shape of his face that he was from Southern California. He'd gotten past the security guard, probably, because the security guard himself was over in the coffee shop with the rest of the perverts.

The visitor looked at me, grinned, and said, "You a sportswriter?"

"Uh-huh."

"Well, I've got a hell of a story for you."

"Go ahead, but please make it quick. This place makes me nervous."

"Here's the deal. I'm going to challenge Muhammad Ali to a kick boxing match."

"Good for you. But you've got the wrong guy. I only write ball and bat sports."

The man in the leather jacket refused to be denied. "You've got to hear me out. This is hot stuff. I'm staying at the Texas Hotel. Let's go over there, and I'll buy you a drink or two, and I'll tell you about it."

"Okay."

In truth, somebody else had already agreed to buy me a drink or two around 2:30 that afternoon, so the time was available. The man in the jacket extended his hand and introduced himself. "I'm Chuck Norris," he said.

In the bar at the hotel, the man who would someday become *Walker, Texas Ranger,* the greatest TV drama in the history of the English language, ordered two JB and sodas and pitched his mission. "Kick boxing," he explained, was the ultimate form of sporting combat. "Ali would fall in four rounds, max."

"Does Ali get to kick, too?"

"Sure, but he doesn't know how. Wouldn't stand a chance."

If Chuck Norris had actually been a pro boxer, he would have been classified as a poultry weight. "Maybe you ought to challenge Willie Shoemaker to a kick boxing match, and if you beat him, kind of work your way up," I suggested.

Norris shook his head and said, "I'm serious, but let me tell you about what I am really up to." He ordered two more JB and sodas. "The idea of the kick boxing thing is to gather publicity that will help me raise money to make a martial arts movie."

"What the hell is a martial arts movie?"

Norris cheerfully described the film genre of the future and made a compelling presentation. But, after the third glass of scotch, I wished Chuck Norris all the luck in the world, and reminded him that my job was baseball and nothing else, that he'd been buying drinks for the wrong guy.

"Then how about I line you up with a piece of ass?"

Norris, unfortunately, made it immediately obvious he was kidding, but I said, "You know what, Chuck? You're coming pretty damn close to getting your story in the paper."

It never did, though, because my personal and rigidly enforced canon of journalistic ethics never permitted such a thing.

February 3

According to Lone Star apocrypha, Marvin Leonard, a Fort Worth department store mogul, approached Ben Hogan and asked what it would take to impel Hogan to give golf lessons to Leonard's wife. Hogan mentioned, among other demands, his own private golf course. So that was how Shady Oaks Country Club on Roaring Springs Road in Fort Worth had been founded and constructed, at least according to local legend.

The country club had the reputation for being one of the most exclusive in the whole state, so the closest I'd ever come to the place had been working there as a valet car parker in my teenage years. On one memorable night, a pillar of the community who was prominent enough to have a hospital wing named after him, but not a junior high school, was leaving the club after a wedding reception and walked straight through the big glass front door of the clubhouse. *Crash! Boom!* The gentleman, with admirable aplomb, kept on walking as if nothing had occurred, tipped me a ten-dollar bill, and got inside his white Cadillac. He had bloody scratches all over his face, and he was lucky, really, that he hadn't been killed. He then turned on his windshield wipers, even though it had not rained in over a month, as he drove away, while his wife shouted, "You goddamn country hick!"

Now, about fifteen years later, I was actually inside that same clubhouse. The Texas Rangers baseball team conducted a pre–spring training news conference, a luncheon affair with an open bar. My partner on the *Star-Telegram* baseball beat, Harold McKinney, showed up, the first time I'd seen him in three months. While I'd been assigned to cover the World Series, McKinney had attended baseball's annual winter meeting, the most recent session in New Orleans. McKinney preferred it that way. "Trouble with the World Series is you gotta go to all those games," he'd reasoned. "At the winter meetings, all you have to do is get shit-faced."

Sportswriters from Texas were not the only winter meeting attendees to utilize the occasion for a full-scale assault on the brain cells. Detroit general manager Jim Campbell sat down with his Philadelphia Phillies counterpart for in-depth negotiations involving a multiplayer trade. Campbell felt it necessary to drain two or three quarts of Tennessee tiger sweat to sharpen his bargaining skills. At the end of the session, the deal was made with multiple players involved, a borderline blockbuster transaction. With the dawn's early light, Campbell came up foggy on the details of the deal. In fact, he couldn't remember anything that had taken place, and felt fortunate that nothing had been formalized or finalized on paper. He contacted the Phillies and, as gracefully as possible, backed down from the deal from the night before. That had not been easy. "How do you un-shake a handshake?" Campbell wondered.

McKinney told me that his personal highlight of the New Orleans visit came when he'd been physically threatened by Pee Wee Reese. "Yeah, Pee Wee was glad-handing at this Louisville Slugger hospitality suite, invited guests only, and he flipped out when I sneaked in there and snatched a couple of beers out of the cooler," McKinney related. "Shoulda seen old Pee Wee. He started yelling at me. 'Who in the hell are you?' and 'Put the beers back and get the hell out of here.' Crap like that. Listen man, those Louisville Slugger people are m-e-e-e-n sons-uh-bitches."

This state-of-the-Rangers media event drew a nice crowd. Billy Martin, the manager, himself a member of Shady Oaks, courtesy of Rangers owner Brad Corbett, stood at a little podium and answered some questions from the media. His 1974 Rangers had escaped from the AL dungeon and had made their remarkable and unlikely run at the Oakland A's. Billy Martin had been receiving most of the credit for their amazing turnaround and was all too willing to accept it.

When Billy wanted to be congenial, he maintained an almost theatrical capacity to charm people, this being one of those occasions. He seemed glad to be there, responded enthusiastically to all the questions, and cracked jokes the whole time.

Martin expressed pleasure over his team's one key acquisition from those winter meetings in New Orleans. The Rangers obtained Willie Davis from Montreal to patrol center field in exchange for a couple of minor league prospects. That plugged a hole. The previous season, Texas had proven that a team could win without a center fielder. Cesar Tovar had the job, but center field was not his gig. He wore a whistle around his neck, and he'd blow it when charging fly balls that hit shallow, to warn the infielders that he was on his way. Davis, who had been best known for his seasons with the Dodgers, was beyond his prime, but could still fly. Billy Martin's assessment: "You can't go wrong with a center fielder named Willie." Problem was that, when Martin made that remark, his center fielder named Willie was parked inside the Los Angeles county jail, locked up for failure to make alimony payments.

Somebody asked the manager about rookies who might make the team.

"I haven't seen him pitch yet, but the scouts are really high on this tall left-handed starter," Billy said. "His name is, uh, lemmee think. Jim Umbright."

"No, Billy," broke in Danny O'Brien, the Rangers' general manager. "Jim Umbright is someone else. Our player's name is Jim Umbarger."

"Jim what?"

"Jim Umbarger."

"I'll never remember that in a thousand years. The son of a bitch is going to have to change his name."

Everyone laughed, and finally left, but Billy wanted to stick around and drink some more. Surprisingly, Harold McKinney, my main man at the paper, declined to join us. He said he didn't feel well.

We walked downstairs to the Shady Oaks dining room. Ben Hogan, conspicuous by his presence, sat in there with two other men, playing cards. Hogan and Martin exchanged brief pleasantries. Billy knocked down about a half-dozen doubles in perhaps a half-hour. Experience told me to watch what I said to Martin now that he was embarking into his danger zone, in which the storied manager often, for no cause whatsoever and within a matter of seconds, could transform himself from Dr. Jekyll to Mr. Manson. That surely would not take place here in this dining room with the fine thick carpet, silken white tablecloths, a setting made all the more distinguished with Ben Hogan sitting over there.

The story of the previous day's encounter with Chuck Norris came up.

Billy's mouth twisted into a half-sneer, half-grin. "I could whip Ali's ass in about twelve seconds, and I wouldn't have to fight Jap-style to do it," he announced.

"You're kidding, right?"

"Shit no, I'm not kidding. Ali's nothing but a goddamn pussy."

"I don't know about that, Billy. I was at ringside when Ali fought Cleveland Williams. I thought he was afraid of Williams, since a highway patrolman had put two .357 slugs in the Big Cat's chest, and it barely fazed him. So Ali didn't mess around and beat Williams's head into a bloody sponge."

"You're telling ME that I can't whip Ali?" Billy raised his voice.

"I am saying that might be a tall order."

"THEN HOW ABOUT I BEAT YOUR STUPID FUCKIN' HEAD INTO A BLOODY SPONGE!"

With that, a man in a perfectly tailored charcoal double-breasted suit appeared at the table, identified himself as the manager of the facility, and politely recommended that we get the hell out of his country club. No braver man have I ever seen.

"PISS ON YOUR GODDAMN COUNTRY CLUB!" Billy said, but he did get up and leave, and walking out with him, I turned and looked at Ben Hogan. It was the only time I ever saw him laughing.

On the way out, Martin said, "You stupid piece of shit. You got us kicked out."

"Sorry, Billy. And watch out for the glass door in front of the club. It can be a real doozie."

February 15

This business of becoming a regular in the country club set had gotten stressful.

Two weeks after sitting in too close proximity to one of those patented Billy Martin explosions that rattled windowpanes as far away as downtown Denver, I was back at Shady Oaks. Already leery of a reencounter with the cold face of the club manager who had all but pitched me out onto the street, and certainly not relishing the prospect of Ben Hogan's mocking gaze, I had the burdensome task to stand up in front of an audience of several hundred people and make a speech. Naturally, I was nervous as a crack whore at confession.

The occasion was the winter banquet sponsored by the Dallas–Fort Worth chapter of the Baseball Writers' Association of America. For the second straight year, I had been elected by my peers as chairman of the chapter. An honor? No. A hoax, and a fairly cruel one at that. Yes. A man who wrote sports for a Dallas newspaper coveted the chapter chairmanship to the extent that he'd all but campaigned for it. His popularity index among the rank and file of the membership scored low. That was because the man maintained the day-to-day proclivities of a mean-spirited, backstabbing snitch. So, in a conspiracy designed to bedevil the already tormented soul of the man who wanted the job, a wicked coalition among the group arranged that I, not he, would capture the vote. The reason I'd been handpicked for the chairmanship was because I was least qualified. Administrative skills did not conform to my MO, and also basically I did not know that the writers group (that also included people in the radio and TV media who were known to the typewriter corps as "talking dogs") even existed. I'd been better equipped, probably, to teach Sunday school at the First Baptist Church.

The most haunting aspect of that chairmanship presented itself at this banquet. My job was to appear at a long head table in a big-ass banquet hall, talk into a microphone, thank the attendees for attending, identify and introduce the persons of note, utter platitudes, present insights, look sharp, sound articulate, and make an overall presentation of poise and polish. A tough and demanding duty for somebody who, because of his abnormally elevated sperm count, had a tendency to slur.

In honor of the occasion, I had gotten a haircut, bought a gray suit at Neiman Marcus, eschewed the goofy bush and gone an entire day and a half without even a single can of Lone Star beer. My script contained an opening sentence that went, "I am reminded of the two skeletons hanging in a closet, and one of 'em looked at the other one and said, 'If we had any guts, we'd get the hell out of here.'" Clearheaded, that got scratched.

Baseball fans from all over North Texas jammed the banquet hall. The Rangers had experienced a gratifying off-season. This chronically woe-begone franchise, so sick that it had bedsores, singled out by Satan herself to eat shit throughout eternity, succeeded in escaping the shackles and manacles of humiliation, and finished second. Harry Houdini never did it better.

Consequently, the Baseball Writers of America—representing the whole damn country and not just the Dallas–Fort Worth group—had voted to award almost all of the Association's honors and prestigious hardware to the Rangers. It would have been a lesser upset if *Deep Throat* had won the Palme d'Or at the Cannes Film Festival.

Billy Martin, AL Manager of the Year.

Jeff Burroughs, AL Most Valuable Player.

Mike Hargrove, AL Rookie of the Year.

Ferguson Jenkins, AL Comeback Player of the Year.

Jenkins had been screwed out of the AL Cy Young Award—Catfish Hunter got that one—only because the writers were reluctant to ordain the Texas Rangers as the most decorated team in the history of the league.

The banquet commenced. I advanced to the podium, drew three deep breaths, and reviewed my notes before beginning to speak. The notes consisted of such admonitions as: Don't say "uh." Don't say "fuck." Don't say "cocksucker." Don't tell any ethnic jokes. Don't insult any bankers. Avoid eye contact with the audience. Don't throw up.

I had always thought that in my twelve years of attendance in the Fort Worth public schools, the only thing they'd taught me was that Naomi is I Moan spelled backward. On this wonderful night, however, that high school speech class really came in handy. When the welcoming remarks ended, there was no standing ovation, but in the distance, if one tried, one could detect a smattering of applause. Nobody booed. Nobody heckled. Nobody threw a handful of asparagus at the head table. A resounding success. With hands shaking more from a surge of relief rather than the need for a drink, I turned the remainder of the program over to the pros.

Hall of Famer Lefty Gomez had been retained as the guest speaker. Gomez told the audience he had gotten rich in the years that followed his pitching, after patenting a revolving bowl for tired goldfish. He said that six years earlier, when Neil Armstrong landed on the moon, he told NASA about spotting a mysterious, white object. "I knew right away what it was," Gomez said. "It was a home run ball that Jimmie Foxx hit off me in 1933." He talked about how the American League's somewhat new and still controversial designated hitter manifest "might not have prolonged my career, but certainly would have saved me a lot of embarrassment. I never broke a bat until I was seventy-three years old, and that happened when I ran over one, backing my car out of the garage."

As good and entertaining as Lefty Gomez had been that night, the most intriguing remarks came at the end of the show when Lee MacPhail, president of the American League, made some concluding remarks to the people at the banquet. He said, "The most influential individual in the history of baseball was not Abner Doubleday. It was not Babe Ruth, and no, it was not Jackie Robinson, either. That person is alive and with us today, and he's a New York lawyer named Peter Seitz."

Who? Peter Seitz had been hired by the commissioner as an arbitrator in salary disputes, and Seitz had issued the ruling that had made Catfish Hunter a free agent. MacPhail said that, because of Seitz's finding, most of the balance of influence and power in the game had swung finally "to a skinny, one-armed refugee from the United Steelworkers Union whose name is Marvin Miller."

MacPhail said that through the relentless work of the man who led the Major League Baseball Players Association, the era of Kenesaw Mountain Landis was over, and a "new era was about to begin, and the changes of the era would be radical."

Everybody in baseball knew about Kenesaw Mountain Landis. He had been named for the place where his father had his leg shot off in the Civil War. Nutty thing to do. Anybody who had seen photographs of the man could determine there was something spooky about him. Among the Four Horsemen of the Apocalypse—Fire, Famine, Pestilence, and Death—Landis most resembled the one named Death. In 1915, Landis, a federal judge, had determined that baseball owners were exempt from antitrust laws, and their reserve clause entitled those owners to indenture their player-employees for the duration of their baseball careers. Later, the judge would hand down a prison sentence to a man named Victor Berger, whose crime had been getting elected to the U.S. Congress while running on the Socialist ticket. Landis remarked that it was his "profound regret that I could only give [Berger] twenty years in Leavenworth, as I wish that I could have had him lined up against a wall and shot." The barons of baseball loved the Landis style and appointed him major league commissioner in 1920. Landis promptly banned the eight players already acquitted of throwing the 1919 World Series from the game for life.

But in the crusade that Marvin Miller was in the process of conducting for his tobacco juice–spitting unionists, the Landis Doctrine would gradually become kaput. Because an arbitrator—after the '74 World Series—determined that Charlie Finley had breached Catfish Hunter's contract, Hunter had been declared a free agent. His new contract with the Yankees amounted to an eye-popping $3.5 million over five years. Hunter's deal had been merely the start, according to Lee MacPhail, concluding his remarks to the baseball banquet-goers in Texas. Marvin Miller had pried open the vault.

For lo those many decades, baseball owners shared a plantation mentality. In their minds, the players were little more than the little plastic cowboys and Indians that kindergarten kids liked to line up and fuck over. And the owners swapped the players back and forth like the same kids swapped baseball cards, except the owners were dealing with real people, and not smiling cardboard likenesses. That particular privilege of ownership would become a relic of another time.

Scholars of baseball...and if the legal profession can claim scholars, then baseball damn sure can as well...will long debate the merits of Marvin Miller and his impact on the game. But Lee MacPhail, on a winter night in 1975, proved himself to be the greatest prophet since Nostradamus.

Chapter 3

March 1

Winter, with all its tyranny, headed toward the exit sign. So legions of grateful people migrated to the peninsula of sunshine, salt water, and sand to celebrate nature, celebrate life. The birds were flying north while the chicks were migrating south. Two types of young women strolled the Florida beaches. The ones who had worked since New Year's to lose midriff inches in order to look great in their bikinis, and the other kind—the ones with active metabolisms who did not need to lose any weight in the first place. Because they were there, the National Association of Dirty Old Men conducted its annual convention in the hotels that lined the perimeter of the state. Their eyeballs nearly evacuated the sockets as they ogled the talent, fantasizing as to how this sand candy might look with clothes on.

Major league baseball spring training—the most benign and genteel ritual that America could offer—provided a happy adjunct to the various scenic attractions. Oh, the tranquilizing sounds. The pop of the Spaulding mitt, the energizing c-r-a-c-k of the bats, lovingly crafted from seasoned ash in the factory back in Kentucky. Compare the vivid and soul-enhancing sounds of baseball to the preseason melodies of other mainstream sports. Football: Constant whistles. Thud. Ugghhh! "Get up off your ass and do it again, you fat bastard!" Basketball. More whistles. Thump, thump, thump. The basketball coach at TCU, Johnny Swaim, resigned a week before his team's season opener because he said he could no longer tolerate "the smell of jockstraps and sound of bouncing balls." Oh, and hockey: More whistles, offset by the harsh tinkling sound of dislodged teeth as they hit the ice. Another thing. The game officials in hockey, hoops, and football wore costumes inspired by the same fashion coordinator who designed the "look" for workers on Mississippi chain gangs. Baseball's umpires came to the games in dignified dark suits, just like undertakers and security guards in casinos.

For those reasons alone, baseball in my estimation stood apart as the best of all games. The only game. Particularly in March and especially on the tropical Atlantic coastline. When close to the ocean, I never woke up with a hangover. No headaches. No nausea. Not even a mild case of the shakes. Darwin's theory explained that. We were each and all evolved from some single-cell creatures that slithered up from the sea, if one believed that, thus the enduring healing qualities derived from the surf and salty breeze.

After the first workout of the spring, I presented my notion regarding Darwin's theory to Steve Hargan, a veteran pitcher. "Bobby Darwin [Minnesota Twins outfielder] came up with that? Good for him," remarked Hargan. "And I'll tell you something else. That motherfucker can really lean on a fastball, too."

Those ten-or-so days of spring training that preceded the exhibition games served as the baseball writer's honeymoon. The topic of every story offered the essential aspect of the feel-good story. If no genuine reason existed for out-and-out optimism concerning the upcoming regular season campaigns, at least there was the life-fulfilling concept of hope. With hope came promise, the reason most of the newspaper stories emanating from the green pastures of baseball springtime concentrated on the rookie prospects, challenging for a job on the major league roster and grasping for the fulfillment of almost every little boy's lifetime dream.

The topic of my day one story from Florida was Mike Cubbage, a second baseman. Cubbage had hit .350-something in AAA the previous season. He would someday manage the New York Mets, another nice aspect to major league spring training. Damn near all of those guys would someday do *something*. Before I talked to Cubbage, I'd interviewed the Texas farm director, Joe Klein. If I ever taught a course in Covering Spring Training 101, I'd emphasize that the writer should always talk to the farm director, not the manager, because the farm director always oversells the minor league talent, therefore providing more meaningful quotes. Joe Klein, angular and tanned, with "baseball man" written all over him, never let me down. "Mike Cubbage has the best swing in the entire Rangers organization," Klein said emphatically. Klein had actually managed Cubbage in AA.

Cubbage presented some articulation abilities of his own, which might or might not have been the result of his days at the University of Virginia. The young ballplayer expressed thoughtful confidence in his on-the-field abilities. He felt good about his prospects of landing on the Rangers' roster—if not by the end of spring training, then at least at some point in the regular season. He had a good point. Cubbage had proven himself at every level in the minors. Unlike franchises such as the Cardinals and Dodgers, the Rangers were not three deep at every position. They were one deep, if that. "The only thing that bothers me right now," Cubbage confided, "is my nickname. Cubby. I can't stand that. People call me that, not because my name is Cubbage, but because they tell me I look like some asshole named Cubby who was one of the Mouseketeers."

Jim Spencer, a veteran first baseman, overheard that and interrupted. "I used to watch that show, and I never saw anybody named Cubby," Spencer said. "Of course, the only thing I looked at was Annette's titties."

"Thanks, Jim. Great quote."

"You're going to put that in the newspaper?"

"I'm going to send it in. Only the copy desk will change titties to breasts."

"Annette's *breasts*? That makes me sound like a goddamn deviate."

Jim Spencer always bitched about something. What did Jim Spencer have in common with Dizzy Dean, Hank Greenberg, Rudy York, Al Rosen, and Joe Morgan? They had all once been voted the Player of the Year of the Texas League. Spencer had accomplished that in 1971, playing for El Paso. He said that whenever he hit a home run in El Paso, "after I circled the bases, I circled the stands, and all these Mexicans would hand me a buck." With the Angels, and now the Rangers, that never happened. Spencer bitched about that, too. In 1973, I'd accidentally broken the news to Spencer that he had just been traded from the Angels to the Rangers. When the reality dawned on Spencer that he had gotten shipped to the shittiest team in the big leagues, he'd thrown back his head and laughed out loud. After he'd joined the Rangers, Spencer bitched about the prevailing south wind at Arlington Stadium that turned his home runs into long outs. When Billy Martin let Mike Hargrove play first base and made Spencer the DH, Jim bitched like hell. When Spencer learned that he'd been named as a reserve to the American League All-Star team in 1974, he bitched about that. "There go those three off-days. I was going to have a bunch of people over to watch the game on TV. Crap."

Spencer made great copy. Almost every person in the big

leagues made good copy. I had the best and easiest job in the whole USA. Writing was fun sometimes, and it was even more fun in spring training because of a game I'd invented called Race the Six-Pack. After I'd gathered the necessary quotes at the ballfield, I would buy a six-pack of Budweiser (the eighteen-ounce cans), return to my hotel room, which was about fifty yards from the ocean, pop open a cold one, and begin to type.

Since the *Star-Telegram* uniquely published both a morning and a P.M. edition, the requirement was two stories, plus two "Rangers Notes" one-page sidebars. The stories got transmitted back to the paper on a primitive fax machine, a Xerox telecopier, that worked at the rate of four minutes a page. If the six-pack wasn't completely finished by the time the last of about ten pages had been sent, I lost the game. That seldom happened. And during the entire spring of '75, it *never* happened. I won every game, because the act of writing about this Rangers team, and its competition, came quick and easy. Those rose-colored dispatches from Florida weren't the customary spring training false propaganda that had been sent home in previous years, the artificial rah-rah, the stories crammed full of brightly colored crepe paper and "we'll be contenders *if . . .*" bullshit.

Everybody associated with the Rangers organization was convinced that the team would not only contend for the AL pennant, they were going to flat-out win the thing. That second-place finish from the previous year was no fluke. Hell no. It had been a sneak preview. World Series in Arlington. I'll bet I typed those four bizarre words every other day, at least. With Billy the Kid Martin at the helm, there would be no stopping these Rangers.

Why not? Most of the American League was a shambles, the end result of decades of oppression imposed by the New York Yankees. Before expansion, the AL had become nothing more than the story of the New York Yankees and the Seven Dwarfs. Then the Yankees, beginning in 1965, had gone into full-phase collapse. Without the Yankees marching through the season like the Roman army, with the New York media pounding the drums and blowing the trumpets, there simply was not a hell of a lot to look at in the AL.

The National League, always ahead of the curve in the employment of black and Latin American stars, was where the fan looked to find the talent. The National League had won 14 of the previous 16 All-Star Games. The most meaningful symbolic gesture of major league baseball of that entire era took place in the 1970 game at Cincinnati. When Pete Rose scored the winning run for the NL All-Stars by barreling over Ray Fosse at the plate like a professional bowler clipping off a ten-pin, that was the collision seen and heard around the baseball world. The National League was fast, tough, gritty, aggressive. The American League was something that got knocked on its ass.

So the notion that a team like Texas could win the AL title did not seem too outlandish. The team's only real obstacles appeared in the forms of Oakland and Baltimore. The Orioles appeared finally on the verge of deterioration, with age-related erosion of Brooks Robinson's grand skills and the departure of left-handed ace Dave McNally, who had gone to Montreal and played without a contract in order to further challenge baseball's dying reserve clause. As for the A's, they no longer owned their ace starter, Catfish Hunter. Catfish had been set free during the off-season, signed by the Yankees, but the Yankees were not going anywhere either.

I was as guilty as the rest in touting the splendidness of the Rangers that would surely unfold in the coming months. Everyone inhaled the euphoria and fell victim to the spell. Somehow, we ignored the glaring fact that the Texas pitching, beyond Ferguson

Jenkins and Jim Bibby, coming off a 19-19 season, remained thinner than Dust Bowl chicken soup. The Rangers were not the only ones who thought they would be going somewhere. *Baseball Digest* picked them to win the pennant. A done deal. The only suspense came with the question of which team would be the opponent in the World Series, the Dodgers or the Reds.

March 5

When many baseball players reached the major leagues, they were like brand-new convicts. The first thing they did was find the Lord and the law library. Jim Spencer never mentioned the Lord, but he damn sure perfected the role of the clubhouse lawyer. He represented himself in his case, and presented his evidence to a one-man sportswriter jury. He'd taken a salary dispute with the Rangers to arbitration.

"The dollar amount is less than significant," Spencer declared, "since the difference between me and the ball club has to be the smallest that's ever been brought to arbitration. At least, that was what I was told. But it reached the point where it was a matter of principle, and neither side was going to compromise." Bitch, bitch. Piss, moan.

Spencer's dour demeanor stood in mirror-opposite contrast to a man seated at a nearby picnic table, eating a hot dog. The picnic table sat outside a little lunchroom that adjoined the Rangers' clubhouse at the Municipal Stadium in Pompano Beach. The down-home setting resembled that of a country store in some place like Bleeding Gums, Arkansas, and the player with the hot dog was Jeff Burroughs, otherwise known as the Long Beach Long Baller.

The right fielder had won the American League MVP the season prior, and his universe seemed adorned with lilacs and orchids.

"I don't think fame has gone to my head. Not yet, anyway," Burroughs conceded. "It is not like I've been besieged by auto-graph seekers.

"But," Burroughs added, "last month, I was playing golf in Palm Springs, and this woman came up to me and asked, 'Aren't you Robert Redford?' How about that?" Burroughs turned his head, and tipped his chin upward, so that I could admire his noble profile.

Joe Lovitto, an outfielder of unrealized greatness, the living example of the Darrell Royal dictum—"potential means you ain't done it yet"—sat nearby, eavesdropping.

"Robert Redford, huh?" Lovitto said to Burroughs. "Well, that figures. Because I've seen Robert Redford up close and in person, and I can tell you for sure that he is uglier than homemade dog shit. The skin on his face is like the craters on the fuckin' moon."

Lovitto remained on his tear. He had a copy of a recent sports section from one of the Dallas papers. It contained a quarter-page ad run by Mr. G's Menswear of Arlington. The ad copy read: "Make a Big Hit. Leisure Suits. Solid Colors in White, Navy, Brown and Yellow. $39 to $59." Beneath the copy, the reader saw two male models—Burroughs and Toby Harrah, the Rangers' shortstop. Burroughs looked spiffy in a dark Western-cut leisure suit with white-stitched pockets. Harrah, with his perfectly coiffed and lacquered Prince Valiant hairdo, appeared even sportier, wearing a polyester leisure shirt, patterned with designs that appeared to be little horses. If ever there was a portrait of men in the 1970s, this was it.

"Get a load of those two!" Lovitto boomed. "Do they look like a couple of Golden Gate noodle smoochers, or what? They'll have to change the name of this team from the Texas Rangers to the Texas Rump Wranglers." Lovitto's remarks were cuttingly harsh, not to mention politically incorrect. In the case of the Mr. G's Menswear ad, I had to admit that Harrah bore a striking resemblance to Mr. Joybox in the motion picture *The Loved One*.

I returned to the hotel to play Race the Six-Pack. As usual, the best quotes had been the ones that could never see print. But life remained swell.

March 9

Every major league baseball team employed a man who carried the job description "traveling secretary." But in the case of the Texas Rangers and Burt Hawkins, "good shepherd" would have been more apropos. Touring America with a band of drunken Gypsies, and tending to their galaxy of self-inflicted crises, was a staggering day-to-day, night-to-night job. Every ninety seconds, the phone in Burt's room would ring.

"Goddamn, Burt. I've got a problem. This hooker stole my luggage."

"Jesus Christ, Burt. I've got a problem. I'm in jail."

Et cetera, ad nauseam. And good old Burt, an ex–baseball writer from Washington who'd once been nominated for a Pulitzer Prize before he'd gone to work for the Washington Senators and who took no bullshit from anybody, always fixed the difficulty.

As I arrived at the Pompano Beach ballfield, Hawkins approached me, and he did not look happy. One member of the Texas press corps was alleged to have "misbehaved" on a blind date. I was stunned. *"HIM!"* I wailed. "Impossible. Sweet little mild-mannered guy like that. Why...he wouldn't rape a fly!"

(Turned out, I was right. What happened was that the journalist had gotten a little clumsy trying to help a young woman out of a car, and the whole thing blew over.)

Coincidentally, the player that I'd scheduled to interview that same day had established national notoriety for a troubled love life of his own. Mike Kekich, a left-handed pitcher making a long-shot bid to return to the majors after being exiled to Japan, had been involved in the trade of the decade. Two seasons previous, while playing for the Indians, Kekich and teammate Fritz Peterson had traded wives. The transaction went badly for Kekich. When Mike's new wife found out that Mike earned about half of what Fritz was making, she gave him his unconditional release. With every turn in Kekich's life after that, Sister Fate continued to kick him in the balls. Kekich, approachable and bright as hell, was bummed and did not mind saying so.

"My emotional problems involved a lot more than my domestic situation," Kekich explained. "The most troubling thing happened when Cleveland cut me last year. I was having one of the best springs of my whole career, and the next thing I knew, I was standing in line at the welfare office. Until you have experienced total rejection—and I mean total—then you have no idea what that does to your confidence. It feels like a whirlpool sucking you under."

For an encore, Kekich had gotten kicked out of Japan. I asked him about that, and he grinned. "Okay. This was what happened. This Japanese sportswriter is interviewing me, through an interpreter, and he had the usual questions about comparing Japanese baseball to what went on over here. And I said, sort of in passing, that the Japanese umpires were not quite as consistent as their American counterparts. So the next day, in great big Japanese letters, a headline appeared that said 'Kekich Doesn't Like Japanese Umpires.' Next time I'm on the mound, I threw 13 straight strikes, the ump called 13 balls. After the 13th, I charged the umpire and tried to strangle him. End of story."

After the Kekich interview, I went to Billy Martin for some follow-up comments. In regard to the wife swapping, Billy said, "I don't care if he married a koala bear. If Kekich can pitch, he is more than welcome here."

I mentioned to Billy that Kekich seemed to still be grappling with his worldview. Billy responded: "Tell Kekich that if he is looking for sympathy, he can find it in the dictionary, right there between shit and syphilis."

March 11

Exhibition play had begun. Since the readers back home had already been assured that the Rangers were not a baseball team but rather an irresistible force, their 12–4 win over the Atlanta Braves should hardly have come as a surprise. The magnitude of the victory was tempered by the true nature of what took place on the field, not in this event, but in every exhibition game ever played. In a competitive sense, those games were not competitions at all. Not when players ran wind sprints in the outfield throughout the game, while others took pitching wedges and worked on their short game just outside the foul lines, or took naps on the dugout roof. Games played at the Pompano Beach stadium had as much big league atmosphere as a grade school carnival. The grandstand reminded me of a bullring constructed of bamboo that I stumbled across in the Yucatán jungle. Due to the absence of restroom facilities, the bullfight aficionados peed in beer cups.

And, lest the political leadership in Dallas–Fort Worth prematurely announce the route of the Rangers' World Series victory parade, it was noted that the team hadn't knocked off the '27 Yankees, and that the middle of the Braves' batting order had some guys named Nordhagen, Asselstein, and Pocoroba. The Atlanta team's only identity throughout the history of the first-ever big league franchise in Dixie had been Hank Aaron, doggedly pursuing the Babe's career home run record. Aaron surpassed that when he belted Number 715 in 1974. Now Hammerin' Hank was gone, gone back to Milwaukee where his career had begun, to finish off what remained of it. Naturally, that created a huge void in the baseball scene in Atlanta. The Braves without Hank Aaron generated all the appeal of a Mardi Gras parade with no drunks.

The highlight event of the Rangers' spring home opener occurred when a small boy hopped over the fence onto the playing field to grab a foul ball. Joe Macko, the Rangers' equipment manager, accosted the trespasser and confiscated his baseball. The crowd viewed that as an act of bullying, and a hearty avalanche of jeers arose from the stands. Macko felt chagrined and returned the ball to the youthful offender. He thus incurred the wrath of the Rangers' bullpen coach, Charlie Silvera. Charlie had been the third-string catcher for the Yankees in the glorious yesterday of the 1950s and was retained by Billy Martin as, if nothing else, a memento of the years of his natural prime. While Charlie served in Texas, I never heard him say a damn thing that was worth quoting—except now. "Imagine the nerve of that kid, snatching the ball off the field like that," Silvera seethed. "It's like going into somebody's house and stealing a loaf of bread off the table."

March 12

Baseball barnstorming in Florida was underway full time. In 1975, sixteen of the twenty-four major league teams trained in the orange juice provinces. The Orioles were headquartered in Miami, and the

Yankees trained just up the coast in Fort Lauderdale. The Expos and Braves shared a facility in West Palm Beach. The Twins stayed in Orlando, the Astros at Cocoa, and the Dodgers languished impressively in their storied facility at Vero Beach.

On the Gulf side, the Royals worked out at Fort Myers, the Pirates holed up in Bradenton, and the White Sox sunned in Sarasota, while the Mets, Cardinals, Reds, and Phillies were clustered in the Tampa–St. Pete–Clearwater area. The Tigers parked their spring act in Lakeland, while the Red Sox got their livers in shape for the long season at nearby Winter Haven. All these teams played exhibition games in minor league ballparks. Over the course of my baseball writing tenure, I rolled across the state in a new Chevy station wagon, a spring training rental, that had become known as the Gonzo Wagon (not my idea) and saw at least one game at all these facilities. In some ways, each was the same—yet each contained some idiosyncratic feature that set it apart from the rest. They radiated a special, peaceful charm, although, after enough exposure, a person became sick of looking at palm trees.

Kansas City's facility in Fort Myers was rather ordinary, but what set the place apart from the rest was the drive over, along the highway known as Alligator Alley, a long strip of road that cut through the primeval, reptile-infested swampland. It was spooky out there; no place to ever get stranded. I always iced down an extra chest of beer for the contingency that something like that might happen. The highlight of the journey came at Immokalee, a village largely inhabited by Seminole Indians, on the outskirts of the swamp on the Fort Myers side. Immokalee was quaint—quaint in the aspect that the little town stood out as the most remote, godforsaken, and depressing shit heap I had ever seen. Coming from a person who has toured most of West Texas, that's no small compliment. Immokalee consisted of a collection of mud-colored clapboard shacks with front yards stacked with rusted plows and hot water heaters. Really, the place resembled the site of an airline disaster.

It turned out that Immokalee had the lowest per capita income of any municipality in the entire United States. Yet I envied those Seminole Immoka-lites. They managed to get by on $475 a year, and they didn't have to kiss anybody's ass to get it. Once, I saw an Immokalee woman changing a tire on a pre–World War II pickup truck, while the love of her life sat in the cab, drinking wine from a 1.5 liter bottle. That image would linger with me forever, and the man in the truck was my idol.

After absorbing the Immokalee experience, anything that happened at the ballpark at Fort Myers came as an anticlimax. The Rangers' exhibition contest against the Royals, in this one case, contained some qualities that resembled an actual regular season game. Texas scored the only run of the game in the top of the 11th inning, when Cesar Tovar crossed the plate all the way from first base on Mike Hargrove's single to right field.

Tovar's career highlight came in his days with the Minnesota Twins, when he played all nine positions in a game. His versatility spilled over into his off-the-field life as well. Had Tovar ever written a baseball autobiography, the title might have been *I Led Three Wives*. Tovar said that because his fame as a major leaguer was of international magnitude, his domestic life history had been eventful and sometimes complicated. "I guess that's why Tovar is so trim," reasoned Steve Hargan. "He never has time to sit down and eat."

Of Cesar's dash to score the game's winning run, I wrote that "Tovar took off from first base like a man chasing a mechanical rabbit."

That morsel of prose had been the product of an experience

the night before, at the greyhound track in Hollywood, located down Highway A-1A between Pompano Beach and Miami. A friend of a friend, a person down on his luck in Texas, had somehow secured a job at the dog track. He dressed up like a circus ringmaster, complete with the top hat, red jacket with tails, and black boots, to lead the procession of greyhounds into the starting gate. Since I didn't know a damn thing about handicapping the greyhounds, I wagered on the dogs that looked most relaxed in the post parade. That strategy produced spectacularly dubious results. For five consecutive races, my exact picks, instead of running first and second, actually finished next-to-last and last. Five straight races!

Afterward, I learned the awful truth. The man in the circus costume confessed that his duties further entailed patrolling the kennel area to keep an eye on the trainers, who, when the opportunity presented itself, would jerk off a rival dog in order to neutralize its competitive edge.

March 15

Most of the Rangers who arrived at the ballpark for their game against Baltimore looked as if they had arrived via freight train. They were drawn, pale, and needed a shave. Actually, they were fresh in from a three-day, three-exhibition-game trip to Mexico City. I'd wisely stayed behind in Florida, nursing a sore back. Jim Sundberg, the Rangers' catcher, admitted that the trip had been a drag, and that he was exhausted.

"I fell asleep on the way to the field this morning," Sundberg said. "That's hard to do when you're on a bicycle."

The slumber party continued on the field, as the Rangers batters stood mesmerized by the offerings of an Orioles trio of

Ross Grimsley, Dyar Miller, and Jesse Jefferson. All those heavy hitters who were pegged to take the Rangers to the World Series had, in fact, been quiet most of the spring.

Some of the averages going into the Baltimore game: Jeff Burroughs, .115. Jim Sundberg, .091. Mike Hargrove, .200. Willie Davis, .164, and that would plummet even more after an 0-for-5 showing against Baltimore.

Davis lived next door to me at the team hotel. He arrived at Pompano Beach accompanied by his Doberman, d'Artagnan. I went to pat old d'Artagnan on the head one morning, and the son of a bitch tried to take my arm off.

About his spring slump, Davis presented a "so what?" posture. "As far as I'm concerned, spring training is a waste of time," Willie declared. "Exhibition games don't turn me on at all. I can't get up for 'em. I just go out there and try to get my legs in shape. Of course, when the regular season comes, it gets fun again. There's plenty of fun to be had with this team. There's a happy atmosphere around here, and that's what life's all about."

And with that, Davis proceeded to disappear for a couple of days, and Billy Martin didn't have the slightest idea where he had gone.

March 17

The good old Gonzo Wagon rolled into Vero Beach and historic Dodgertown, a converted military base that was the fabled spring home of the defending National League champions. The facility was superior to any other in Florida.

About 3,000 fans were there. Many of them watched the game in lawn chairs set up on the beautifully terraced landscape; they all wore blue Dodgers baseball caps, and on this occasion, green shirts, since it was St. Patrick's Day. L.A. put most of the regular pennant-winning lineup on the field against the Rangers. Its lineup included Bill Russell, Steve Garvey, Dave Lopes, Jim Wynn, and Joe Ferguson, with Andy Messersmith on the mound, followed by the chain-smoking knuckleballer, Charlie Hough. That same day, the Associated Press announced the results of a nationwide poll of sportswriters (they didn't poll me) who found that while the Cincinnati Reds had a swell ensemble, the Dodgers would "wear again the National League crown" at the end of the 1975 baseball season. The person who wrote the story about the AP poll left lipstick all over the Dodgers' face. "Great lineup from top to bottom. Home run blasters, singles hitters, speed. This team has every appearance of being a manager's dream." Gush, gush. The Dodgers naturally won their exhibition against the plebeian Rangers, 5–2, and after the game I wrote:

> The Rangers got a close-up look at some real uptown living. They call it Dodgertown, but Rockefeller Heights would be more appropriate. The place is a tiny paradise, with swimming pools, golf courses, individual villas for the players, and a tree-shrouded stadium that looks like the San Diego zoo. The Rangers might have been awed by the opulence. They didn't hit and weren't too sharp in the field. They lost, and then departed for their Pompano Beach headquarters, fondly known as Iwo Jima, where they feel more at home.

For my P.M. feature story, I interviewed a recent addition to the Rangers' pitching staff, left-handed veteran starter Clyde Wright, who once pitched a no-hitter when he was playing for the Angels. Wright told me that when he was on his game, he had the best control in the major leagues. "I can knock a gnat off a barbed wire fence from sixty feet, six inches," Wright bragged.

As the Gonzo Wagon headed back to Pompano, I drove and sipped, engulfed with contentment. Baseball was in full bloom everywhere. In Lakeland, the Tigers' Ron LeFlore, fresh out of the Michigan state penitentiary, tripled and scored on a wild pitch for the final run in a game against the Expos that ended in a 10–10 tie. In Arizona, the Indians were in midseason form, beating themselves, 4–3, against the Angels, when Duane Kuiper let a run come in when he made a perfect throw to first base, which was uncovered at the time. In California, Billy Graham was visiting Richard Nixon, perhaps there for a laying-of-hands fundamentalist salvation of the former president's tortured ankles. That morning, I had been immensely cheered by a headline in the Fort Lauderdale paper that read: "Intestinal Bypass Surgery Gives Fat Men a Better Outlook."

Those were the days, those 1970s. Americans were happy then, although they didn't know it.

That was not merely the springtime of 1975; it was the springtime of our lives.

Chapter 4

March 20

B illy Martin had placed himself on the one-day disabled list. He did not suit up for an exhibition game against the Expos. With a thin and sarcastic smile, Martin said that he had pulled a muscle the previous day playing golf. So one of two things must have happened. Either Billy was suffering from a prodigious hangover, which was unlikely because people aren't supposed to get hangovers in Florida, or he was butt-sprung after getting into a fight with somebody.

After the workout, it was confirmed that the latter scenario had taken place. I suspected that might have been the case, since the starboard side of Martin's head appeared slightly swollen, and a little bit lopsided. Jim Fregosi, the smooth veteran, confirmed it. He told me that Martin had gotten much of the worst of a fray that happened at a cabaret in Boca Raton late the night before.

So, in the Banyan Room at the Surf Rider that evening, I approached Martin and said, "Heard somebody put it on you." It was still early enough in Billy's nocturnal adventure land to get a civil response.

Billy shook his head. "Here's what happened. This smart-mouth son of a bitch from Detroit comes up to me and tries to pull my chain. Tellin' me how I fucked up when I pulled the pitcher too early in some game when I was managing the Tigers. He figured I'd go spinning off, and he'd tag me quick, before the bouncer could jump in, and then maybe get his name in the paper for kayoing the mini-guinea here. Be the big event of his miserable-ass life. You can't believe how much of that crap I have to take, and since I was trying to get something going with a friend, I wasn't in the mood to jack with him. Even offered to buy the prick a drink, and get rid of him.

"But he was waiting for me in the parking lot. So I thought, 'What the hell? I'll crack him good.' But I was wearing a pair of brand-new Florsheim shoes. You know what a problem it is when you fight somebody when you're wearing new shoes."

"Yeah, sure," I said, lying. I didn't get into fistfights and, being a sportswriter, never wore new shoes. Because of salary limitations, sportswriters usually purchase previously owned shoes, ones that are nicely broken in.

"So," Billy continued, "I aimed for his jaw—the sweet spot—and my feet skidded right out from under me. I struggled to get up, and that was when he nailed me. Then I slipped again, and he nailed me again. I tried to kick the shoes off, but they were too damn tight. And then he was gone. What a nightmare."

That Banyan Room, which served as Billy's nighttime office, was filling up fast. Art Fowler, as usual, was faithfully stationed at Billy's right elbow. Wherever Billy went to manage, Art went, too. Art was Billy's pitching coach. He weighed about 250 and about a third of that was in Art's face. Fowler was one of those "traditional" pitching coaches that Mike Marshall liked to attack. Art wasn't just old-school, he was Precambrian. Basically, Fowler's chief job obligation entailed sitting beside Martin in saloons, nodding his head and saying, "Tha's right, B-e-e-e-ly." And, when the occasion presented itself, and somebody in the bar had pissed Billy off, Art's job then became to pin the offending party's arms back while Billy beat the shit out of him.

Later in the evening, Martin was glad-handing vacationing Northerners and engaged in a cheerful conversation with a tall, beyond middle-aged, and heavyset Canadian man. A retired Mountie, probably. The topic was boxing. Billy knew more facts about boxing than even Dr. Joyce Brothers, who had won the top prize on the old TV quiz show *The $64,000 Question*. Martin was especially fond of recalling the exploits of Joe Louis, and the Canadian talked about having seen Louis fight once in Toronto. Billy went into a recitation of the date of the fight, all of the details.

"Oh, it was hotter than hell that day. I remember it like yesterday," the Canadian guy said. "Ninety-five degrees, eh?"

"It was 102, you stupid fuck," Billy shot back.

"Eh?" The proud old Canadian suddenly looked disturbed. His wife looked appalled.

"Are you deaf?" Billy was yelling now. "I said it was 102 fucking degrees, and if you were there, like you claimed you were, you would have known that. So I don't think you were there. I think you're a fucking goddamn liar!"

Billy probably was seeking atonement for his parking lot humiliation the night before. I looked at Billy's shoes. They didn't appear new. The Canadian wisely sensed what was about to happen. He took his wife by the arm and, sputtering dark oaths under his breath, hustled out of the bar.

"Hey, you walked your check, you gutless old fuck," Billy screamed after him.

Billy wasn't quite done. He was still fuming over remarks made about him in the Fort Lauderdale newspaper that morning. Elliott Maddox, an ex-Ranger then playing for the Yankees, told a reporter that Martin had misled him about his role for the season. Maddox, in print, said that Martin was well known for lying to his players. Texas was playing the Yankees the next day in Fort Lauderdale. Jim Bibby, who was six-foot-seven and armed with a Godzilla fastball, was scheduled to pitch for Texas.

Cesar Tovar stood with Billy at the bar. Tovar read the newspaper and laughed. "T-h-e-e-s-e guy, he be fucking with you," Tovar said to Martin. Tovar was plastered. "Maybe you tell B-e-e-bby to h-e-e-et him in the head! Ha-ha-ha-ha."

Martin endorsed the proposal. He outlined his plan to a nearby tableful of drunk Texans.

"If he shows up tomorrow, I promise you one thing. He's going down on his sorry black ass." At that point, Martin suddenly noticed that one of the persons seated at his table, a news cameraman from Dallas known as Quinn the Eskimo, happened to be black himself.

Martin looked at Quinn the Eskimo somewhat apologetically and declared, "Hey! Don't get me wrong. Everybody in baseball knows I've always bent over backward to be fair to the blacks. Them and the fuckin' Cubans."

So the next afternoon, at the stadium in Fort Lauderdale, Jim Bibby plunked Elliott Maddox on the shoulder with a curveball. Before the game ended, a full-scale brawl took place. Afterward, Maddox said, "I knew I was going down. I had two things in my favor. I knew it was coming, and I knew Bibby wasn't going to try to knock my head off. Otherwise, the ball would have hit right here." He pointed at his left temple.

Only Billy Martin could instigate a bench-clearing rumble in an exhibition baseball game, which, after all, was supposed to be as down-and-dirty competitive as a tea dance. Still that was a natural consequence of who the man was.

Alfred Manuel Martin, his father Portugese and his mother Italian, was born May 16, 1928, in Berkeley, California. (The birth date was significant to the extent that it was at a party celebrating Billy's twenty-ninth birthday when a brawl erupted at New York's Copacabana nightclub that ended his playing career with the Yankees.)

Because Billy's dad couldn't keep his hands off various University of California coeds, his mother Joan divorced Alfred Sr., raised the boy, called him Bello (Italian for beautiful), and thus the origin of the name Billy. The father's flair for fooling around was meaningful, because most shrinks insist that if the father chased the chippies, it was a slam dunk that the son would follow suit. During Billy Martin's lifetime, he might well have been known as the Sultan of Twat.

Simply stated, as a player, Billy Martin was a poor man's Ty Cobb. He played every game like he was Crazy Horse chasing down Custer. His fervor for winning baseball games was unexcelled. Casey Stengel, who had managed Martin with the Oakland Oaks in the Pacific Coast League, insisted that the Yankees acquire the infielder as one of his first managerial acts in New York.

In 1950, Martin joined a lineup that was in the process of winning an unprecedented five consecutive World Series championships. Mickey Mantle had replaced Joe DiMaggio as the team's centerpiece icon. With Yogi Berra behind the plate, Phil Rizzuto at shortstop, Hank Bauer and Gene Woodling flanking Mantle in the outfield, and hurlers like Whitey Ford, Allie Reynolds, and Eddie Lopat, he joined what was an invincible ensemble of baseball talent.

Because baseball is an activity in which natural instinct can prevail over sheer athletic ability, Martin was able to function among a galaxy of some of the game's immortals. When the Yankees' regular second baseman, Jerry Coleman, was drafted into the service in the Korean War in 1950, Martin got his opportunity to perform as a regular. Before his first start, Martin noticed that Stengel listed him eighth in the batting order. Stengel, who once had noted, "The Yankees don't pay me to win every game. Just two out of every three." So only Billy Martin would muster the temerity to approach the legendary manager and demand, "Are you kidding? I guess that tomorrow, you'll have me batting behind the groundskeeper."

"Where do *you* think you should hit?" Casey responded.

"Third," said Billy.

It was the famed Cleveland general manager Frank Lane who said, "When you play against Billy Martin, he is somebody who you absolutely hate, but deep down inside, you wish you had about ten guys like him on your own team." Martin was the essence of fearlessness. He told me that once, after getting beaned, he put on a hockey goalie's padding and stood in the batter's box while a pitcher drilled him with pitch after pitch, in order to avoid becoming gun-shy.

Martin's career batting average was .257. But when the chips on the table were stacked to the ceiling, Billy could transform himself into a Hall of Famer. In the seventh game of the 1952 World Series against Brooklyn at Ebbets Field, the Yankees were clinging to a 4–2 lead in the bottom of the seventh inning when the Dodgers loaded the bases with two outs, and Jackie Robinson at the plate. On a 3-and-2 count, Robinson popped the ball up. Ordinarily the first baseman, Joe Collins, would have made a routine catch. But Collins apparently lost sight of the baseball. The other player closer to the ball, reliever Bob Kuzava, seemed confused, and remained frozen on the mound. With two Dodgers, Carl Furillo and Billy Cox, already crossing the plate and Pee Wee Reese rounding third with the potential winning run, Martin sprinted in from second base and made a desperate, miraculous, diving catch, snaring the ball just inches from the ground, thus winning the Series for the Yanks. That stands out as the greatest clutch catch in World Series history. Willie Mays's sensational over-the-shoulder grab of Vic Wertz's long drive in 1954 was more spectacular, but that happened in Game 1 and ultimately didn't much matter as the Giants swept the Indians in four straight.

A year later, in a World Series rematch against the "wait'll next year" Brooklyn bums, Martin put on a rousing impersonation of Joltin' Joe DiMaggio. With the Yankees winning in six games, Martin batted .500, with two homers and a slugging percentage of .958, and was named MVP of the Series.

Impersonating Joltin' Joe was one thing. Impersonating Rocky Marciano was quite another. After the birthday rumble at the Copa, Yankees GM George Weiss, fearful of Martin's off-the-field influence on Mickey Mantle and Whitey Ford, shipped Billy off to the Kansas City A's. That was the cruelest of possible destinations for the fiercest little Yankee, since the Kansas City franchise was largely regarded as little more than a New York farm team. To a small extent, Billy got the last laugh on Weiss. One of the players the Yanks got in return, relief pitcher Ryne Duren, turned out to be one of the most prolific drunks in the annals of the big leagues. But it was the darkest day of Martin's life, since he based his entire identity system around wearing the Yankee pinstripes. He felt as if he had been blackballed from the most exclusive fraternity in the world.

The remainder of Martin's playing career was characterized by his fists more than his baseball abilities. In 1960, then with the Cincinnati Reds, Martin responded to a brushback pitch from the Cubs' Jim Brewer by throwing his bat at the pitcher. Then Martin charged the mound and delivered a punch that shattered Brewer's cheekbone. The Cubs, having lost their ace, sued Martin for $1 million. (Later, the team dropped the suit, but Brewer brought his own case, and Martin settled by paying Brewer $10,000. Martin didn't seem to mind all that much, since he pursued a fist-driven life style for the remainder of his days.)

After his retirement, Billy Martin initiated a managerial career, first in the minor leagues at Denver, and from then on, it seemed that Billy was like the Human Cannonball—hired and fired on the same day. At every stop on the ride, Martin built winners. But his ferocious resentment of authority figures—any and all—inevitably led to his unending chain of dishonorable discharges.

A capsule summary:

- In Minnesota, Martin's first major league managing post, he had beaten one of his pitchers, Dave Boswell, to a gore-stained pulp in a bar fight. "Knocked Boswell stiff as a straw hat," in the words of the New York sportswriting goliath Red Smith. Though his decking of pitcher Dave Boswell was a headline maker, it was a smack to the jaw of Twins traveling secretary Howard Fox that led to Billy's receiving his marching orders at Minnesota. Martin did not help his cause by referring to Twins owner Calvin Griffith as a "pumpkin-headed idiot."
- Though he was fired at Detroit in 1973, he incurred the wrath of owner John Fetzer in 1972. During a losing streak, Martin placed the names of his eight position players (prior to the designated hitter rule in the American League) in a hat and produced a batting lineup based on the order that the names were drawn. Al Kaline, for the only time in his career, was the lead-off hitter, and shortstop Eddie Brinkman, hitting .205 at the time, batted cleanup.

The Tigers won the game anyway, 3–2, and afterward Fetzer said, "Maybe I should fire the manager and hire his hat." Meanwhile, Martin maintained a running feud with the general manager, Jim Campbell. The relationship between them deteriorated to the extent that whenever Martin would get up to use the restroom, he would say, "Excuse me. I've gotta go take a Jim Campbell." That was the same Jim Campbell who'd gotten himself so wasted at the winter meetings he couldn't remember making a trade. Why would Billy pick on a great guy like that? Because in Billy World, bosses were to be despised and defied.

It was in Detroit that Martin, at the recommendation of bar owner Jimmy Butsikaris, helped Ron LeFlore get a release from Michigan state prison so that he could play center field with the Tigers. Martin played himself in the made-for-TV movie about the LeFlore story. He did the best job of acting by a baseball player since Babe Ruth in *Pride of the Yankees*.

The first time I encountered Billy Martin, he sat in his office after the Tigers had butchered the Texas Rangers in the season of '73. "Billy, your team just beat the Rangers, 17–0. Do you think the Rangers are the shittiest team you have ever seen?" I asked him.

"Seventeen–two," he corrected me.

The next encounter took place on a hot September Texas Saturday the same year. Billy had been hired as the new manager of the Rangers, replacing Whitey Herzog, who had been fired essentially because Martin himself had recently been fired in Detroit and was therefore available.

Martin wore a pair of Wrangler jeans that were so new the sales tag remained stapled to the back pocket, and a pair of chocolate-colored lizard skin cowboy boots. It was tempting to tell Billy that with this franchise, he was joining the circus, not the rodeo. But I knew his reputation, of course, valued my front teeth, and wisely kept my yap shut.

I introduced myself to Martin, and told him I'd be one of the persons who would be covering his latest team. We stood face-to-face. "Nice to meet you," Billy's mouth said, while his eyes said, "If we ever have any work-related disagreements, I hope, for your sake, that you're not a hemophiliac."

Martin's voice belied his fire-brewed persona. It was a voice with a soft and almost gentle quality, like Mister Rogers, the kiddie show host.

"One question, Billy," I said, as we were exiting the elevator. "This Rangers team, bad as it is, still has some controversial personalities on it. How do you plan to deal with that?"

He didn't hesitate to respond.

"Who do they have who's more controversial than I am?" Then he beamed and walked away. The man oozed charisma, and with that simple rhetorical question, probably uttered the greatest understatement in four decades of major league baseball.

Once on board in Texas, Billy right away began to demonstrate his exceptional skills in the fine art of managing a baseball team, the tactics that made Martin the one-of-a-kind commando in the dugout and in the clubhouse. He cajoled, badgered, manipulated, intimidated his players, his coaches, and the media.

The result, wherever Billy went before wearing out his welcome, was an "us-against-them" mentality that drove his teams to championships. Martin maintained a sixth sense when it came to understanding his opponents, perhaps even better than his understanding of his own ball club. In terms of baseball strategy, Martin played chess while the guy in the opposite dugout was playing Chinese checkers. He was manic over detail. While managing at Minnesota, he attempted to teach one of the greatest natural batters the game has ever seen, Rod Carew, the intricate art of stealing home. So, during his career with the Twins and later the Angels, Carew would successfully steal home seven times. Of the Rangers' near-miracle run at the A's during the '74 season, Martin told me the one shining moment that stood out in his mind over the whole 162-game campaign happened in late August, when Texas infielder Dave Nelson reached base, then proceeded to steal second, third, and home. "Now *that*," Martin said, "was Billy Ball."

March 21

A week before, a new signee from the Rangers' amateur draft had arrived in camp. That was Bump Wills, son of Maury Wills. He could not run the bases like his father had done. But then, nobody else could, either. Bump swung a pretty good bat according to the scouts, was handy with his glove at second base, and could strum a guitar and sing pop tunes in a delicate tenor voice. He was the product of one of the best college baseball programs in the United States, Arizona State, where they seemingly had a machine that minted major leaguers.

Bump Wills looked a lot like his father. He had been in Pompano Beach about a half-hour, and was still wearing street clothes. He carried himself like somebody who'd been in the big leagues for ten years. I'd approached him and asked if he was satisfied with his first professional contract. Really, I didn't care whether he liked the terms of the deal or not, didn't think the readers would, either, and inquired about the contract just so that I could get his name in a story, since he was Maury Wills's son and all. Bump looked at me and said, "I took journalism in college, and that's a leading question."

So, on first impression, Bump came across as a young man with ego issues. A snot, in fact. Time would prove that to be anything but the case.

Now it was a week later, and Billy Martin had announced that he'd trimmed his roster, and that a handful of prospects were being shipped to the Rangers' minor league camp. That constituted a bad deal for the evacuees, not so much because their big league ambitions would have to wait for another year, and maybe forever. The more deflating aspect for fellows who were being cut meant no more of the fun-in-the-sun trappings of major league life at Pompano Beach, the Atlantic neon that accompanied that. The place they were headed then was the bush league camp in Plant City, Florida, rural and stone dead, far from the beaches, about as nowhere as Nothingsville can get.

The motel where the team lived in Plant City contained all the vitality of a nursing home. Minor leaguers, after their baseball workout, sat in the lobby, watching *The Flintstones*, and wore glum, "I'd rather be anyplace else but here" expressions.

Greg Pryor, an infielder who'd just received his ticket to the toolies, walked out of the Pompano ball yard with a taut face, suitcase in hand. "Well, I'm off to the halfway house," he muttered when I'd bade him farewell.

"You know what bugs the hell out of me?" Pryor added. "I'm leaving, and Bump Wills, who's never even played an inning of minor league baseball, is still here." Pryor pointed to the field, where Bump, in his Rangers uniform, fielded ground balls.

"I'll guarantee you one thing," the young man declared. "If my name was Greg Mantle instead of Greg Pryor, I wouldn't be headed out to any damn Plant City."

If Pryor had been bothered by Bump Wills's lingering presence on the big league field, he probably had even more cause to question the presence of a tall man, also in a Rangers uniform, who was trotting around in the outfield. He had the look of a veteran—a veteran of World War II. The man in right field was Eugene McCarthy, a former presidential candidate and then still a U.S. senator from Minnesota. The senator had been a fan and friend of Billy Martin's from his days as the manager of the Twins. Now, the big guy was killing a week in Florida, shagging fly balls by day and middle-aged cocktail waitresses by night.

A man such as Eugene McCarthy served as a typical example of the assortment of personalities that Billy Martin carried in his entourage. Politicians. Entertainers. Ex-prizefighters. Judges. They arrived from throughout the land, a Fellini-like procession of the odd and colorful, all there to share a cold one with their dear old Billy.

Good old Billy was in top form that night at the Banyan Room, about to leave for a ride down to Miami with Charley Pride, the country singer. Pride, who had actually played baseball in the Mets' farm system in the distant past, was scheduled by his record company to make a surprise appearance at some big C&W club where LaCosta, the younger sister of Tanya Tucker, was also appearing.

Billy Martin surprised me by asking if I wanted to go along. Once in the car, I found out the true purpose of the invitation. Billy wanted somebody to occupy a place in the back seat so that the blond Sun Coast sweet potato he'd befriended would have to snuggle up in his lap on the ride down and back.

March 22

The Rangers returned to Fort Lauderdale, scene of the Elliott Maddox fracas. Serenity had been restored.

Inside the New York clubhouse, I chatted with the Yankees' new outfielder, Bobby Bonds, the former National League star now about to sample life in the Apple. The topic of the chat with Bonds was Willie Davis. Bonds had competed against him in dozens of games, could deliver an accurate scouting report, and, most importantly, quotes from a star of the game always impressed the readers back home.

Bonds came through nicely. "Willie will be the most colorful player Texas ever had," he said. "Playing center field, running the bases—Willie does it all, and does it with a flair." Then Bobby interrupted himself. His little kid was running around inside the clubhouse. "Barry, where are your shoes? Go put your shoes on," Bonds told the boy. If I'd had any sense, I'd have asked the kid to autograph some memorabilia for me.

After the game, I accompanied a small group down to Miami for dinner at Joe's Stone Crab, the famous restaurant. The group included the traveling secretary, Burt Hawkins, and his daughter Joy, an actress who used to dress in a tiger costume and interact with Dean Martin every week when the singer had his TV series on NBC. Another person with show-biz credentials invited himself along. That was Jimmy Piersall, the subject of the movie *Fear Strikes Out*, the true story of how the Red Sox outfielder had flipped out, then had come back and played some after a visit to the madhouse. Anthony Perkins of *Psycho* fame portrayed Piersall, a man who probably would have been comfortable and very much at home in the Bates Motel.

The year before, Piersall had done some PR work for the Rangers, and had been fired after he'd approached me with the preannounced intention of providing bodily harm over some stuff I'd written. Brad Corbett, the new Rangers owner, had felt sorry for Jimmy and given him a job. Piersall had no recollection of the event in which he attempted to murder me, but I sure as hell did.

During the dinner, Jimmy talked about another bitter experience from his past, when he'd tried to manage a minor league team. "Awful. Just awful. All of the players were on dope. All the time. Every one of them."

"What kind of dope," Joy Hawkins wanted to know.

"I dunno," said Piersall. "Marijuana I guess. Is there any other kind?"

March 23

For the second time that spring, the Gonzo Wagon rolled across Alligator Alley to Fort Myers with a game against Kansas City. Ever since the old Philadelphia A's had moved the franchise to the Midwest, the Kansas City baseball fans never really watched what might have amounted to a contender. After Charlie Finley made himself so hated in the heartland by moving the franchise westward to Oakland, the American League replaced the A's with an expansion franchise in 1969, and the Royals still struggled to achieve .500. That much seemed destined to soon change. The Royals' lineup began to include promising talent like the third baseman, George Brett.

They had a sense of humor, too. In '74, against the Rangers, K.C. starter Al Fitzmorris gave up nine runs in two and two-thirds innings, and the Royals staged a brave rally but eventually lost, 12–11. After the game, Fitzmorris sat on a stool in front of his locker, sipping a cold Coors, and said, "There I was, pitching my fucking guts out, and then those guys [gesturing toward the rest of the occupants of the clubhouse] let me down."

In Fort Myers, the Rangers got stomped. Steve Foucault, the Rangers' closer, got tattooed like a Hell's Angel. Hal McRae poked a long home run off Foucault, and John Mayberry hit one even farther. Foucault was funny-looking, for a baseball player. He was just about bald, and though he was built along the circular lines of Mike Marshall, he maintained more the bearing of the Maytag Repairman than the resident Ph.D. on the Dodgers' bullpen. And unlike the Dodgers' ace closer, Steve Foucault (who would eventually become a cop), he seemed to have no theory whatsoever when it came to the mechanics of pitching. Foucault threw overhand, sidearm, and from all points in between.

He explained that his alarming showing against the Royals should be no source of concern. It was part of Billy Martin's master plan.

"Those two long homers were hit off fastballs," remarked Foucault, who, of course, was otherwise known as Fookie. "Billy wants me to throw fastballs against American League teams this spring. Because in the regular season, I'll be throwing them curveballs. That way, I keep 'em off balance."

Afterward, reporters circled Billy and inquired if he had, indeed, given Fookie written permission to give up Atlas missile shots to K.C.

"Uh, yeah, yeah. Sure," said Billy.

"Fookie's been hit hard all spring. Are you concerned?"

"Concerned? Nope. Why should I be?"

"You seem upset, though, Billy. Are you mad about something?"

"Nope."

March 24

Time now ran short on the Florida springtime experience of 1975. Even though I had some doubts about this Rangers' World Series fantasy notion, nobody would have known it from the tone of my newspaper articles. Every day, I cranked up the bullshit machine and pumped it back to Texas.

Yankees general manager Gabe Paul appeared in Pompano Beach, and that triggered trade rumors. The Rangers needed another left-handed pitcher, and the Yankees had one to spare, Mike Wallace, who'd posted a 6-0 record the previous season.

"Nope. Not going to happen," insisted Danny O'Brien, the Rangers' GM. "To get Mike Wallace, the Yankees want us to give back two of our best prospects, [pitcher Jim] Umbarger and [third baseman Roy Lee] Howell. I am not going to prostitute our organization with a trade like that."

In the entire time I covered baseball, I'd never heard the word "prostitute" used in such a context.

With the exhibition schedule drawing to a close, the best Rangers hitter in camp had been Jeff Burroughs, the league MVP, or Mike Hargrove, the Rookie of the Year, back for an encore. Outfielder-DH Tom Grieve maintained a spring average that teetered around .500. Grieve seemed mystified by the splendid showing. "Never in my career have I ever had so much trouble making an out," he professed.

March 25

The Rangers' spring residential headquarters in Pompano Beach, the Surf Rider Resort, provided rooms with color schemes designed to induce seizures and had walls like rice paper. Throughout the spring, I had been perplexed about a weird noise that emanated from the room next door in the wee-wee hours, the room occupied by Willie Davis and that vicious Doberman of his, d'Artagnan.

"H-u-u-m-m-m-m. O-o-o-m-m-m-m-m." Sounded rather like

an old-fashioned electric fan. Finally, the mystery became solved. In Orlando, before a game against the Twins, while most of the players killed time listening to hillbilly music on their jam boxes or playing hearts, Willie Davis sat in a lotus position on the floor and hummed his Buddhist chants. Orlando, home of the Magic Kingdom, might have been the best place for a man like Willie Davis because he came across as something not of this earth. Davis had the body of an extraterrestrial, for sure. Zero body fat. Absolutely none, and Willie had the most equine-looking legs I'd ever seen on an earthling.

During the baseball game, signs emerged that the chanting might be working. Davis had his most promising game of the spring. He hit a home run, and Bobby Bonds had been right about Willie's flair for running the bases. With Willie on first, Mike Hargrove stroked a single to right field, and Davis flew to third—*whoosh*—in about six breathtaking strides.

"I realize that I am a pretty good showman on the field," he conceded afterward. "But I never think about it. People tend to get sunk in praise sometimes. It hasn't happened to me, but I have seen it going on around me."

I asked him about the chanting routine. Maybe Davis could initiate a new Rangers fad. "I've been chanting two and a half years—in this lifetime," he explained casually. "I know that I chanted in a previous life, though. My ex-wife began chanting a year before I did, and I began to see some important, happy changes in her and decided to explore it myself." Now this had been the same woman who had chanted Willie's ass right into the L.A. jailhouse just a month earlier.

The conversation took place in the visitors' dugout at Orlando's Tinker Field, in the shadow of the big football stadium then known as the Tangerine Bowl. Two years hence, two years to the day, I would see a future Rangers manager laid out in the same dugout, dazed and bloodied, after having been punched out by one his own players, Lenny Randle.

Yet that scene ranked as no less strange than the stuff Willie Davis was about to throw down after the game with the Twins that the Rangers had won, 8–5.

Earlier, Willie had complained about what a drag those boring exhibition games were. "Oh, yeah, spring training has a way of dragging down my karma," he declared. (Karma? I wish Willie's karma would run over his goddamn dogma, I was thinking.)

Now, he insisted, cosmic forces would soon come into play. "I know that everything is going to be all right this season," he promised. "I go through the whole season in advance, and I use all phases of time—past, present, and future.

"It's important to do that. That's why crooks get caught. They leave out some of the phases."

So I sat there, scribbling notes, nodding, and pretending to understand what in the hell Davis was talking about. Willie continued to talk. "It's the Universal Law. Cause and effect. The theory of relativity was always there. It just took an Einstein to figure it out."

So that perhaps explained how Willie had dropped those easy fly balls against the Orioles in the 1966 World Series. Even the commissioner's office had been curious about that. Now we know. The Universal Law. Cause and effect.

Davis also explained about how life with the Rangers, he felt sure, dovetailed nicely into his personal theology, because of what Willie perceived as Billy Martin's "live free or die" attitude. "There is no greater feeling than being in a tight pennant race, and I was in plenty of those during 14 seasons with the Dodgers. Everybody goes out and plays like it is the last game they'll ever be in. And it's

a cinch this team will be in the race. A lot of that comes from Martin. He's used to success patterns and has almost always won, as a
player and as a manager. This is an entirely different atmosphere
than what I lived through last year in Canada.

"At Montreal," he continued, "after we lost, everybody would
sit for an hour like this," he said, affecting a pose where he stared
somberly at the dugout floor. "I wondered why, and they'd say,
'We can't be happy because we lost.' I couldn't go along with that.
I've got no time to be sad. If we lost, then somebody must have
won, so I just feel happy for them."

Now I thought, "Sure, Willie, go tell that to Billy Martin the
first time this team loses four straight."

With the regular season of 1975 very close at hand, it became
all too evident that some entertaining vignettes lay just ahead in
the ill-suitably arranged shotgun marriage of Billy Martin and
Willie Davis. It would not be pretty. But it would be entertaining.

April 4

Spring training was about over. It was getaway day. I sat with
Billy Martin in his office and asked, "Who has been the most impressive player in camp this year?"

Martin said, "What the hell is this? Awards night?"

"No. But I got some quotes from [rookie infielder] Roy Smalley Jr. He's the guy I'm writing about."

"Okay," said Martin. "The most impressive player in camp
was Roy Smalley Jr. Does that satisfy you?"

"Yeah. Thanks."

And who said that Billy Martin was an ass to deal with?

I retreated to Surf Rider and, for the last time that spring,
played Race the Six-Pack.

Then I packed and rode to the airport. The team was flying to Houston for a couple of more exhibition games, but I wasn't going with them. Randy Galloway, who covered the Rangers for *The Dallas Morning News,* sat next to me at the gate in Miami, waiting for a flight to DFW.

Galloway was deathly afraid of air travel, and he was drunker than Sam Houston. He stared at one of our fellow passengers, a nicely dressed man who carried an attaché case. Then, Galloway spoke, loudly enough to be heard all over the airport.

"I'm not getting on the goddamn plane. That motherfucker has a bomb in that briefcase," Galloway shouted. "Just look at him. Shit, anybody can tell that he's a fucking madman!"

The man with the briefcase smiled. The gate agent smiled. Randy Galloway had flipped out, and everybody seemed tickled. That was why those 1970s were a superior time to be alive. People were less uptight, and airports were fun.

Chapter 5

April 8

*W*hen the bell rings...

Throughout Florida and across the Arizona desert, that four-word mantra served as the catch-phrase of players and managers involved in the activity of baseball spring training. The bell they all talked about symbolized the opening of the regular season, when things mattered. In fact, during the month of March, "when the bell rings" rivaled "have a nice day" and "this is a stickup" as the most frequently spoken four-word utterances in the United States. It resonated with happiness and goodwill, like "Praise the Lard!" at a Baptist church Wednesday night potluck supper.

Come September, we'd all know for whom the bell had tolled, but nobody wanted to think about that in the brash and joyous mind-set that accompanied the arrival of the season, the longest and most arduous and adventurous journey in all of sports. Doris Day and Lorraine Day, who'd married Leo Durocher, were pretty faces, but nothing or nobody ever rivaled the loveliness of Opening Day.

So the diamond horses climbed into the starting gate across the land. Six entries were poised to hear the clang and sprint toward the first turn in the American League West. I surveyed the field. Most horse players, as they handicap a race before selecting the probable winners, must identify and cull the ponies that would not withstand the 162-game pace but would fade as the finish line approached.

After I studied the form, a big X got applied to three teams— California, Minnesota, and Chicago.

The Angels presented the most dynamic one-two punch in the league when it came to starting pitching. Nolan Ryan brought stuff to the mound that no pitcher in baseball could match, and Frank Tanana had been even better than Ryan. The remainder of the lineup, with the exception of Mickey Rivers in center field, consisted merely of an assembly of names... Jerry Remy... Leroy Stanton... Rudy Meoli... that were unforgettable only because nobody knew them in the first place. The one, single player of note and value from the previous season, Frank Robinson, had moved on to Cleveland to become the big leagues' first black manager. So the Angels would be going noplace.

How about the Twins? In 1965, God's Frozen People had ruled the league, and only Sandy Koufax at his fiercest best had prevented the Twins from winning the World Series. It had been a great lineup—Earl Battey, Don Mincher, Zoilo Versalles, Jimmie Hall, Bob Allison, Harmon Killebrew, Tony Oliva, and a pitching ensemble headlined by Mudcat Grant, Jim Kaat, and Camilo Pascual.

The problem in Minnesota came with the gnawing reality that the calendar identified the upcoming season as 1975, not 1965. The names from the past were gone. Harmon Killebrew had hung it up after '74, and I'd been there in Bloomington on a chilly October afternoon to watch his last game. The stands had been vacant. Only Oliva remained from the Twins' glory era, and Oliva had the legs of a cheap antique love seat. He practically needed a walker to make it from the dugout to the batter's box. Minnesota had two outstanding players. Bert Blyleven possessed the best curveball in the game, and no player in either league could match the poetry-in-motion swing of Rod Carew. The remaining twenty-three players on the Minnesota opening day roster had AAA written all over them, and the shortstop, Danny Thompson, had been diagnosed with leukemia. So put an X next to the Twins.

Chicago looked to be all but bedridden, suffering from the chills and coughing up green stuff. The White Sox had a bad case of American League–itis, the epidemic that had spread among so many of the franchises. The only player with much oomph, Dick Allen, had left. Wilbur Wood, a beer keg dressed in a baseball uniform, ranked as the Sox's best player. Wood had been a reliable knuckleballer who carried the workload of a gold prospector's pack mule. Over the previous four seasons, Wood had averaged right at 357 innings. Next to the coach's son on a Little League team, nobody in the realm of the sport had logged so much overtime. So the analysts in the fine art of moundsmanship, the people who really understood the occupation of pitching, calculated that sometime in mid-June, Wilbur Wood's arm would fall off. At least, good old Harry Caray would be behind the microphone to describe that event. I could just hear Harry, the glorious old gasbag: "H-o-l-y Cow!"

The best player for the White Sox by 1975, far and away, was Nancy Faust, who played the organ with style and verve at the otherwise dismal and ancient ballpark where the team performed on the South Side.

Okay, that left three teams that had the capability to be running for the money at the finish line. The Kansas City Royals showed promise. George Brett and company provided some tangible indications that K.C. might mesh nicely as the league's only

Turf team. Manager Jack McKeon thought, and with some justification, that his pitching staff might be the best in the league. "Not my top two guys, necessarily, but from top to bottom, nobody is as deep as we are," McKeon had told me a week or so earlier in Fort Myers, after John Mayberry and friends had teed off on the Rangers. The Royals might still be a year away.

Then there was Oakland, shooting for its fourth straight World Series championship. But Catfish Hunter, baseball's celebrated $3.5 million man, had bid a fond adieu to the Bay Area, sprung from pugnacious Charles O. Finley's baseball jail, courtesy of bail money supplied by arbitrator Peter Seitz. Among the belongings that Catfish Hunter had carried with him to New York had been the 25 regular season wins he had accumulated during the 1974 regular season. Who was supposed to make up that deficit? Besides, the A's all hated each other, didn't they? The newspapers all said so. Therefore it must have been true.

That left the Rangers. From 1973 to 1974, the Rangers' record had improved 28 and a half games. All the contributors were back. The backbone of the lineup consisted of players on the sunshine side of age twenty-five—Mike Hargrove, Jim Sundberg, Jeff Burroughs, Toby Harrah, Lenny Randle. Those players, fortified by seasoning and confidence, could only get better. The off-season had added two veteran pieces—Willie Davis, the center field antelope, and Clyde Wright, the much needed, reliable left-handed starter. With the savage genius of the dugout, Billy Martin, cracking the whip, why shouldn't this team win at least 100 games? Ah, the intoxicating vapors of springtime. If Arlington Stadium had been Gulfstream Park, I'd have gone to the window, boxed the Texas-Oakland-K.C. trifecta, and plunked down $12.

The Rangers would celebrate opening day, actually opening night, at home in Arlington against the Twins. A crowd of over 28,000 showed up, which was not as modest as that might sound since the ballpark could only accommodate 35,000. Ranger Mania had not entirely gripped the region, but interest was palpably expanding. In the early days of the franchise, the team's desperate marketing personnel offered everything but Genie in a Bottle Night—"the first 25,000 fans will receive three wishes!" The franchise had at least risen above that. And during the previous autumn, just months earlier, the God-almighty Dallas Cowboys had failed to make the NFL playoffs.

Charley Pride, the man I'd identified in my season opener pregame story as the North Dallas Nightingale, sang "The Star-Spangled Banner," a tune that had confounded him on some previous embarrassing occasions when the lyrics evaded him. "Yeah, I've been known to mangle the spangles," he had candidly admitted back at Pompano Beach. This time, Pride worked his way flawlessly though the anthem. Then the Rangers tanked on opening night, and the opera was over by the fourth inning, as the fat lady hit all the high notes. Minnesota pounded Fergie Jenkins, 11–4.

Jenkins was his customarily composed self after the game. He looked at me evenly and said, "You write any bad shit about the way I pitched tonight, and there won't be any more quotes from the Pope, you know?" By "the Pope," Jenkins was referring to himself. Obviously, I required access to whatever insights he wished to share with the public.

"Don't worry about any of those stories," I assured Jenkins. "They are only words. And what are words after all? Words provide the net through which all truth escapes."

"That's right, but the box score never lies, and I don't guess you can do anything about that," Jenkins conceded. "They might not tell the truth, the whole truth, and nothing but the truth, but day in and day out, the box score keeps its story straight."

Billy Martin complained that in all the residual euphoria from the spring in Florida "the guys seemed a little keyed up for this one, and then came out flat."

So what? Just one game out of 162, right? "Uh–uh," revealed Steve Hargan, who had come in to pitch five innings' worth of relief for Jenkins, after Tony Oliva had belted a home run and hobbled around the bases. "Billy never said anything, but I knew that he had to be boiling on the inside, in the dugout," Hargan said. "For the whole game, I was afraid to look over there at him."

April 9

Good ballgame. Bottom of the ninth. Twins on top, 3–2. One out, and Willie Davis singled to right, bringing Lenny Randle, nice clutch hitter, to the plate. Hot damn. This was more like it. Fans were on their feet. They stomped and clapped. Then, without warning, Davis took off for second base. Glenn Borgmann, the Twins' catcher, threw Davis out by least four feet. Goodbye, rally. So long, ballgame.

Willie Davis, seemingly, took off on his own. When Davis returned to the dugout, Billy Martin was there to greet him. Through binoculars from up in the Arlington Stadium press box, I watched Billy and Willie engage one another in earnest conversation. Billy didn't look angry, but perhaps concerned. Yes. Concerned. Concerned and sincere.

Naturally, after the game, everybody wanted to talk to Billy since Willie had already split the scene. So, was it true? Had Willie ad-libbed and hauled ass on his own un-sanctioned trip to second base? Billy was evasive. Game 2 of the season came way too early for any boiler room explosions. "Let's just say that Willie got a sign," Martin said.

Huh? So Willie had gotten a sign. Knowing Davis as I then did, the obvious question, one that remained un-asked, could only be, "What was the source of the sign? The dugout or the planet Neptune?"

As the media left the clubhouse, Martin summoned first base coach Merrill Combs and third base coach Frank Lucchesi into his office and slammed the door.

I trotted over to the Twins' locker room and talked to their manager, Frank Quilici. He played on the Twins' pennant winner in '65 and demonstrated that he had managerial tools when he hit .208. Quilici had given me a ride to the ballpark at Oakland before Game 1 of the 1973 World Series (all the big league managers usually attended the Series) and accidentally slammed the lid of the trunk of his rental car on my head while I was getting out my typewriter. The guy manning the press gate had been a real turd. Hadn't he ever seen a sportswriter enter a ballpark with blood dripping down his face?

"Hey, Frank," I said. "Were you surprised when Willie took off like that?"

Quilici grinned. "Not as surprised as Billy seemed to be," he said.

April 11

Friday night brought the Oakland A's to the ballpark for an early season showdown. The Rangers had salvaged the last game of the Twins series, but were getting beat again by Oakland, and fans had started to wonder about this so-called Rangers nuclear power plant that I'd been touting all spring. Billy sensed another lost cause in the bottom of the seventh inning, and vented some of his frustration on the home plate umpire, Rich Garcia.

Martin had grown peevish, and finally, in the seventh inning, expressed too much aggravation to suit home plate umpire Rich

Garcia when he'd come out to argue a call. Garcia said he gave Billy the rest of the night off because Billy had used profane language. (Like the author of this book, Rich Garcia and Ted Kaczynski, the notorious Unabomber, were both born May 22, 1942, and both evidently maintained a low tolerance for what they regarded as cheap shit.)

With Martin gone, Frank Lucchesi managed the rest of the game for the Rangers. Frank, himself a master of self-promotion, staged and produced an umpire protest of his own in the ninth inning. He dropped down to his knees and made little sand castles out of the dirt at home plate.

After the game, since the Rangers' clubhouse would be all ice and no worthy quotes, it made more sense to venture over to the visitors' side on third base and talk to Sal Bando, the Oakland third baseman. I had gotten used to talking to Bando. At Arlington, Bando's locker was next to Reggie Jackson's. Jackson had a way of being aloof, and when I asked a question, he usually shrugged his shoulders and said, "I dunno. Ask Sal. What do you think about that, Sal?"

And Sal would always try to offer a reasonable response. So I bypassed Reggie and went to Sal for a critique of Lucchesi's show at the plate. "Crazy goddamn Italian. That's what Lucchesi is," Sal said. "Of course, Frank knew that the game was on TV back in the Bay Area, and that his whole family would be watching."

April 12

Now more than the Bay Area was watching. This time, the whole country, or at least a portion of it estimated at six million. Texas vs. Oakland appeared as the season's opening episode of the NBC *Game of the Week*, with Joe Garagiola calling the play-by-play. Texas had been selected for the big stage for the second time in the history of the franchise, and the game marked the first occasion where people from coast to coast could witness the true nature of what a half-ass, backwoods, pissant little ballpark Arlington Stadium truly was.

Those Rangers players realized, and had known for a few weeks, they would be scrutinized by the patrons of every airport bar in America, not to mention every corner tavern—from Harvey's Good Booger Lounge in Altoona to the Dead Skunk Saloon in Eureka Springs—so they came down with stage fright.

Oakland dominated most of the game. Then Texas staged a rally. They trailed, 7–5, with two outs in the last of the ninth, but Jim Spencer was at bat with guys on first and second. This, the same Jim Spencer who had so bitterly bewailed the south winds that customarily blew in Arlington. Now the flag on the pole at the right field corner, sure enough, flapped hard, toward the plate.

Spencer swung, the ball took off, headed for the seats, a game-winning homer on the game of the week! Yee-haw! The whole town was gonna get laid tonight! Then, as the ball neared the stands, it appeared to stall in midair, just hung there, suddenly out of petrol, motionless, and finally fell straight down into the waiting glove of Reggie Jackson, who stood on the warning track.

Repo men and IRS collection agents have confronted happier faces than what I encountered from Jim Spencer after the event. Usually loquacious, Spencer spat out a few words: "I gotta play in this ballpark, and I guess I'll make the best of it. That's the only comment I wanna make."

April 15

God had smiled on the Rangers and let it rain on Sunday. So the final game of the series with the A's had been postponed. Billy's boys had already dug themselves an early, shallow grave and hit the road at 1-4.

Round Two of baseball's opening day celebration found the Rangers in Chicago. As usual, I stayed off the team bus and rode the commuter train from the Loop down to the south part of the city where White Sox Park was located. People used to warn me, "Don't go down there yourself, you fool. Do it enough, and one day somebody will find you in an alley, and all that will be left will be your Lone Star beer belt buckle and a pair of socks."

Perhaps, but the allure of mingling with sons of the soldiers who used to battle Eliot Ness intrigued me and was impossible to resist. These South Side Chicago toughs had "Real Deal" stamped across their low-brow foreheads, not like those weasel-faced pimps who masqueraded as goons in the honky-tonks of Texas. Most normal people got their adrenaline rush riding on roller coasters. My choice of heart-rate-boosting recreational thrills came with sharing the sidewalks with Nick "the Wood Chipper" Baldocci and Carmine "Piano Wire" Mosca, their cold, uncaring hit-man eyes unfocused, void of any feeling or emotion, yet so all-seeing and deadly. At least, that was what I liked to imagine. The local chamber of commerce had been touting the South Side's two great growth industries, breaking and entering. The managing editor of one of the great old Chicago scandal sheets that dominated the Midwest media in the 1920s once declared that "a good newspaper should be like a screaming woman, running down the street with her throat cut." By 1975, there were no more good newspapers, although damsels in varying stages of distress remained available on every street corner in South Chicago.

White Sox Park, so old that it had ear hair and a nut sack that sagged down to its knees, was mostly packed for the home opener, predominantly with hoods and goons. Mayor Richard Daley sat in a box right behind home plate, surrounded by a collection of gentlemen who might have been off-duty professional wrestlers. One of them was a dead ringer for Haystacks Calhoun, and they all packed heat.

During the three years I'd been coming to Chicago, it was the first time I'd seen more than 10,000 people assembled in what I'd described in the paper as a "grimy old pavilion." The Rangers were not a big draw in Chicago.

In the mid-innings, a rumble started in the stands, and that soon escalated into a riot. The season before, it had been my honor and privilege to be on hand for what will be remembered as the historic and celebrated Ten-Cent Beer Night Riot in Cleveland. But that was no riot, but rather a bunch of giddy party people who toasted the arrival of summertime. Hardly anybody got hurt, even though some shrill and sanctimonious do-gooders demanded and got a lifetime ban on beer-night promotions.

That opening-day folk dance in Chicago, now *that* was a riot, rougher than an Italian wedding reception. Festivities began when fans in the upper deck began dropping lighted firecrackers and buckets of beer down upon the people seated underneath. That began along the left field line. People beat the crap out of each other. After the cops moved in to gently perform the patented public service protocols that gained such fame at the Democratic convention protests of 1968...in which Mayor Daley himself, the master of the malapropism, had assured citizens that the "Chicago police are always on hand to preserve disorder"...the combat shifted to the right field area, and when the cops advanced to quell that disturbance, the hostilities renewed on the left field side.

As for the game, the Rangers won that, 6–5. Tom Grieve provided the winning edge with a home run off Claude Osteen. The ball didn't make it all the way over the left field wall into the stands, but a fan, establishing what would become a Chicago tradition, screwed the home team as he reached from the first row of the cheap seats and grabbed the ball, while the home plate ump ruled it a homer.

Grieve's comment: "I know that it's the job of the players to concentrate on the ballgame and nothing else, but those fans...that was something. There will be some sore jaws in Chicago tomorrow."

Some sore brains for ballplayers and one or two sportswriters as well. All three games for the Rangers series in Chicago were daytime affairs, meaning the nights had been free for the full exploration of the happy bistros of Rush Street.

I stood at a bar with Steve Hargan, the pitcher, who had been approached by a stranger. A woman. Hargan had some quality about him that attracted women, and this was in the 1970s, when liberated women were so generous that I would later learn that any sex you got in that decade didn't count.

Hargan's friend commented on the liquor intake. "Why do you guys pack it away like that," she wondered. "You think it makes you feel good. It doesn't. Alcohol is not a stimulant. It's a depressant."

The pitcher looked at the woman, did not respond for a couple of seconds, and finally said, "No shit?" Then Hargan addressed the bartender. "I'll take a glass of depressant on the rocks, please. With a lime twist. Wait. Make it a double."

So the season of 1975, the dawning of free agent baseball, was now at full gallop. The free agent of note, Catfish Hunter, had just made his second start for the Yankees, and absorbed his second loss. The New York fans, being what they were and always would be, saluted Catfish with a barrage of boos.

The winning pitcher had been Bill Lee of the Red Sox. Lee had been dubbed Spaceman. Baseball writers, on the whole, thought that any player who did not express himself in one-syllable grunts, while he squirted tobacco juice onto the floor and passed wind, had all the traits of a psycho and was not to be trusted. Bright people like Bill Lee exceeded the comfort zone of the sportswriter.

Lee addressed the Catfish situation. "Every time he goes out there, fans don't see a 20-game winning pitcher. They see a $3.5 million pitcher," Lee declared, thereby uttering the most profound summation of baseball's soon-to-come epoch.

"He is a nice guy," Lee continued. "I hope this doesn't ruin his life. He shouldn't have to have that burden. I wouldn't want to have that burden. You only need so much to live on."

That begged the question "how much is 'so much'?," and somebody asked it.

"About $1.89 and all you can eat," Lee replied.

April 19

The Rangers swept the three-game series at Chicago, went to Arlington, where they'd been awful in their first home stand, and returned to stone. That Royals' pitching staff that Jack McKeon had promoted so ardently at spring training gave meaning to the manager's words. Steve Busby, Paul Splittorff, and Al Fitzmorris took turns at making the Rangers' batting order look like cotton candy. Willie Davis, the team's great black hope, appeared particularly—almost alarmingly—befuddled with a bat in his hands. Willie's adjustment from the sheer-heat National League pitching to the off-speed, breaking ball offerings that characterized the American League pitchers showed no indication of progress. In the batter's box, Davis seemed out of sync, out of tune, out of his mind, as if he were not swinging at a baseball, but rather a swarm of insects. Nothing was going right for the Rangers at their home park, where they were 1-7 after the Royals had breezed through North Texas.

The final game of the set was a daytime affair in Arlington, and I was serving my term as official scorer, the poor, dumb shit-head in the press box who is required to determine whether a play should be termed a base hit or an error. The league paid the scorer $50 a game in 1975 bucks...that would have been a raw deal at ten times the amount. My share of the scoring load was twenty-six games, and since I was the chairman of the writer's association, I scheduled my turn for the earliest part of the season, just to get it done and over.

Often, a game would go without mishap or controversy. That wasn't the case in the Sunday finale against Kansas City when the Royals' shortstop, Freddie Patek, fielded a routine grounder. For reasons unknown, after picking up the harmless two-hopper, hit directly at him, the shortstop's legs mysteriously gave way, and he sat down on his butt without making a throw. Well, when a fielder falls down, the scorer must customarily give him the benefit of the doubt and rule the play a base hit. This was different. I'd never seen a player just sort of collapse as Patek had. I gave him an error.

The scorer was given twenty-four hours to reverse himself—if warranted by oral testimony from players or umpires who had a better view of the play than the turkey in the press box. After the game, I went to the Royals' clubhouse and consulted Patek, a little fireplug of man. Patek was congenial, but could offer no explanation for his pratfall. "I guess I fell down on the job literally," he said. "Or *sat* down on the job. Hell, I'd call that an error."

Good. Wonderful. Case closed. Until I mounted the team charter for a trip to Oakland.

Boo. Hiss. The Rangers expressed universal contempt for me and the "E" that had been flashed on the scoreboard after the Patek mishap. In their view, the scorer had robbed one of their own of a well-earned base hit. "Assholes like you ought to be sent to the electric chair," announced Dave Nelson, the base-stealing infielder.

Ah, but the airplane soon left the ground, the booze began to flow, and the Patek incident became forgotten soon enough. The flight was commercial, an American Airlines 747 jumbo jet, and the team bought out the two-story first-class section. There was room to mingle. Billy Martin was doing his share of the sipping, but was in a surprisingly benign mood, considering the team's sluggish start. He was looking forward to playing the A's on the road.

Billy ordained that the A's were eminently beatable. The topic of Reggie Jackson was raised. "Jackson is an overrated right fielder, which goes along with his overall package as probably the most overrated player in the game today," Martin said. Then he drank deeply from his glass . . . and it *was* a first-class glass, not one of the crappy little plastic cups they serve 'em back in the cheap seats, where the proletariat drank. He warmed to his topic.

"Reggie Jackson," Martin decided on the airplane to California, "is as useless as tits on a Chinaman."

April 20

Not wanting to incur the wrath of the American Tit Anti-Defamation League, I left Billy's scouting report on Reggie Jackson out of the public print. Against Fergie Jenkins in a frigid night game at the Oakland Coliseum, Jackson hardly resembled a Hall of Fame candidate. Neither did any of the other A's, though.

Jenkins out-pitched Ken Holtzman, 2–1, and yielded only two hits, both to his former teammate with the Cubs, Billy Williams, who was then winding down his career working in Charlie Finley's three-ring baseball shop.

Maybe there was hope for the Rangers after all.

April 22

Before a night game against the Angels at Anaheim, I nursed a Bloody Mary in the press lounge, my eyes surveyed the room, and... *there he was!* Gene Autry, the owner of the Angels, sat alone at a table, eating a sandwich. Autry himself, the only performer to win a star in every available category on Hollywood's Walk of Fame—movies, records, life performance, radio, TV—sat placidly minding his own business. He'd been born just north of the Dallas–Fort Worth area, in Tioga. Hollywood offered the town of Tioga some money to change its name to Gene Autry, Texas. The people of Tioga told Hollywood to get bent, but the little town where Autry had spent his teen years had been more willing. Thus: Gene Autry, Oklahoma. This man sang "You Are My Sunshine." He sang "Rudolph the Red-Nosed Reindeer." And Autry's own nose was pretty red, too, as he sat like the biggest and proudest bullfrog in the pond in the lounge, when I walked over and introduced myself.

"The good old *Fort Worth Star-Telegram*," Autry boomed. "I still subscribe. Read it almost every day!" I refrained from telling Autry about a rich woman in Fort Worth who forbade the mention of his name in her house. As a little girl, she idolized Gene, until she'd approached him for an autograph at a rodeo where he'd performed in Louisiana. According to her, the legendary performer was pickled and made a remark that nice men don't make to adoring fans who happen to be little girls. Autry no longer looked like the singing cowboy of the black-and-white screen, since he was then built like a roasted marshmallow, but he damn sure sounded like the man who sang about Rudolph.

Gene said that he hoped his Angels team might finally contend. He loved the game. "But for the last few seasons, we keep having all these goll-danged [yes, he actually said goll-danged] injuries. Always somebody on the disabled list. You know, for all these years, the Sons of the Pioneers never missed a day's work."

After meeting the likes of Gene Autry, the game itself seemed to lack significance. The Rangers won. The key moment occurred when rookie third baseman Roy Lee Howell ambled to the plate with the bases loaded against Nolan Ryan. Howell, redheaded and bespectacled, owned a potent left-handed swing. His movements afield, however, showed all of the dexterity of Gort, the robot in *The Day the Earth Stood Still,* and that factor prevented Howell from realizing a long big league career.

As Howell dug in against Ryan, Burt Hawkins, the traveling secretary, seated next to me, said, "I'll bet you $20 against $100 that Howell hits a grand slam." He pulled out a $20 bill and placed it on the long press box worktable. I reached in my wallet and produced the $100—all that was left in there after a week-long trip to the West Coast.

Ryan, the crossbow artist, came with a fastball. Howell swung. KUH-RACK! Oh, sweet Jesus, I could practically hear the Rangers' radio play-by-play man, Dick Risenhoover, saying, "A long fly ball! Deep to right field! It's going…it's going…it's off the top of the right field fence! Three runs are in, and Roy Lee Howell missed a grand slam home run by six inches!"

Atta boy, Roy Lee. I snatched up Burt's $20 bill faster than God makes poor folks and said, "Too bad."

In the clubhouse, Howell sat in front of his locker. "Ooooo-weeeee!" the rookie sighed. "When I first hit the thing, I was damn certain the ball was headed out of the park."

I looked at Howell with a half-smile and said, "So was I," and hoped that nobody noticed the little urine stain in the front of my Levi's.

April 23

After an all-night charter flight from L.A. to the Twin Cities, on which, as usual, I was lulled to sleep by the peaceful melodies of tinkling ice cubes and shuffling cards, the Rangers checked into the Leamington Hotel in Minneapolis. The Rangers were the only team in the American League to stay there, because Bob Short, the former owner of the Rangers who had transferred the franchise from Washington, D.C., to Arlington, Texas, also owned the Leamington.

The hotel was not a five-star joint. Not a four, nor even a three. But at least the guests didn't catch the crabs from the bed linen. Also, the Leamington was in easy walking distance to not only one of the best bars in the big leagues, the Blue Ox, but also a massage parlor that one player had dubbed Nikki Nguyen's Hand Job Haven. It was a great place to go and just...relax.

Rain that was about to turn to sleet poured down on the Twin Cities, so the Friday game with the Twins was scrubbed early. I had to write the hardest story that confronts the baseball writer—the rainout story. I knocked out an optimistic little number that hinted that things weren't as bad as it might have seemed for the Rangers at the end of the first month of the season of '75. Yeah, they'd lost five of their last seven games, but had won two of the last three and were riding a winning streak—one straight.

They played the game on Saturday, and the only thing more miserable than the weather was the attendance: 4,400. In the land where people said "yah" and "yur durned tootin'" with each sentence, fans were ignoring the Twins in droves. Minnesota had drawn only 660,000 in 1974, far and away the worst number in the major leagues.

At Metropolitan Stadium, which featured a PA announcer with a voice like a Black & Decker chainsaw, the humble assembly of fans sat silent as the Rangers won, 7–2. The only noise from the stands were the cries of the vendors—"Grain Belt! Ice cold Grain Belt beer!"

The Sunday game was iced-out, too. That meant the drudgery of covering a doubleheader would happen later in the season, but I was glad anyway. Nikki Nguyen had taken the last of my financial resources, and it was time to get the hell back home to Texas.

Chapter 6

May 2

The smoking lamp, as usual, was lit in the Rangers' club-house, and the iced-down keg of Coors was the object of heavy patronage. Texas had beaten the Chicago White Sox in the bottom of the ninth with a Billy Martin Special, the run that was manufactured from a variety of features that did not include a well-hit ball. The team was cresting the wave of a five-game winning streak. After a close win, the postgame locker room setting for any professional baseball team always presented a scene of pastoral inner peace, where twenty-five naked men walked among one another in a display of communal fellowship, feeling good about themselves. As the effects of those friendly little green pregame pepper-uppers wore down, spirits were being rejuvenated by the suds in the cup.

Samantha Stevenson, one of the first woman journalists allowed into a big league clubhouse, was in there, quivering with joy as she beheld the Turkish bath action. *Blazing Saddles* was a movie box office hit in 1975, and I could see Samantha mouthing the words, "It's twue! It's twue!" Samantha worked for some way-down-at-the-end-of-the-dial radio station. She was a slender blonde and sexy, and had a flirtatious air about her. She was a rising personality in the then limited ranks of women in sports journalism. They all were confronted with sneering barricades of sexism erected by the male establishment. (Samantha would later gain some national notoriety when her daughter, the love child of NBA great Julius Irving, became a world-ranked tennis player.)

Billy Martin himself had sanctioned Samantha's presence in the clubhouse, angering some of the players' wives in the process. The last person on the planet to care about any sensitivities of baseball wives was Martin. He regarded each and every one of them as jealous, conspiratorial, and darkly manipulative, a menace to the team concept and the delicate balance of personalities necessary for a productive clubhouse.

Now Martin sat in his office, his feet propped up on his desk, and fired up a cigar. Every position player in his lineup had made a contribution to the win over the Sox, and Jim Bibby and Steve Foucault provided clutch pitching. So who did Billy want to single out as the key person in that night's success story? Why, Billy himself. He implied that his strategy in the ninth inning was the vital element in the outcome.

Bill Parcells, the football coach, once cussed a sportswriter and called him a jerk for asking if he thought he'd out-coached his opponent. Big Bill was right. The writer had been a jerk—for trying to suck up to Big Bill. And Big Bill had been a jerk, too, for pretending that he didn't get off on the notion that he'd out-coached somebody.

Billy Martin wasn't like that. Whenever Martin was convinced that he'd out-managed the guy in the other dugout, he felt it expedient to yodel it from the mountaintop. In this case, he insisted that he'd not allowed himself to be out-foxed by the White Sox' Chuck Tanner. In the ninth, Tanner had removed his pitcher, Goose Gossage, in favor of a left-hander, Terry Forster. The Rangers had a left-handed batter at the plate when Forster entered the game. "He [Tanner] was trying to put me in a bind, personnel-wise," Martin said. "But I made up my mind I wasn't going to let him, even if I had to go with a left-handed hitter against their left-handed pitcher." Martin's batter, Roy Lee Howell, struck out, but everything turned out nicely when Lenny Randle hit a two-out trickler down the third base line. Chicago's Bill Melton charged the ball, then couldn't get it out of his glove as Joe Lovitto scored the winning run for Texas.

Now Martin's Rangers were challenging the Oakland A's for first place in the AL, just like I'd assured the readers they would. If Oakland missed Catfish Hunter, nobody noticed in the first month of the year. Vida Blue had regained his 1971 form, when he had been the most dominant pitcher in the American League. After Blue had blown away California in a shutout, the Angels' (and ex-A's) manager, Dick Williams, said that, "Blue now has pinpoint control of all three of his pitches. He will win a minimum of 25 games this year."

In the AL East, the game's first free agent star was struggling, and so was his team. The Yankees had been settling into the AL basement, with rumored ambitions of turning the cellar into a condo, and Catfish Hunter had been hard pressed to produce many Ws. In an udder-nonsense pregame stunt at Minnesota, Hunter had even lost a cow-milking contest to the Twins' Danny Thompson. Perhaps Hunter had forgotten that he wasn't working for Charlie Finley anymore, and therefore no longer had to call himself Catfish. Hunter had just lost a close game to Baltimore, which had another manager who didn't mind tooting his own horn, Earl Weaver.

With the game on the line, Weaver had signaled Paul Blair, his whippetlike center fielder, to try to bunt his way on base. "It had rained the last two nights, the infield grass was soggy, I thought it was a good gamble." It worked. The next hitter, Bobby Grich, got the same sign from the dugout as Blair. Hunter fielded the ball, and threw it into right field as Blair dashed around the bases to score what became the winning run.

The only player in George Steinbrenner's Yankees lineup with anything going at all was Ron Blomberg, the first baseman. Blomberg was appearing as a before-and-after model in a national ad campaign for a hair clinic. In the before picture, Blomberg was seen frowning, with a craterlike bald spot on top of his head. In the after shot, Blomberg showed off his cute bangs and was grinning. He looked like one of Herman's Hermits.

If the AL race was producing any surprises, it was the Cleveland Indians. Gaylord Perry threw a five-hit shutout at Boston to run his lifetime record to 14-1 against the Red Sox. Everybody in baseball thought that Perry, in essence, was cheating, throwing a grease ball loaded with the lubricants that he might have concealed in his glove, or under the bill of his cap, or elsewhere on his uniform. Everybody thought it, all right, but nobody could prove it. In 1973, when Whitey Herzog managed the Texas Rangers, he said, "Every time Gaylord Perry picks up a win, they ought to give a save to his wife's doctor." Whatever the circumstances, Perry's pitches had been dancing like Fred Astaire. "My slider was moving in three different directions," Perry said cheerfully after blanking the Bosox.

Frank Robinson was still adjusting to his new role as the manager. As the first black skipper in the big leagues, he had been assigned extra duties. Like being the DH occasionally. After Perry's win over Boston, he said, "I'd prefer not to, but I'll play tomorrow." Hell, Robinson was lucky that the Indians didn't make him drive the bus and tote luggage as well.

Cleveland was my least favorite team. The Indians had fallen victim to the Charlie Finley syndrome, and were wearing a ghastly, all-red uniform ensemble. Boog Powell, an ex-teammate of Robinson's at Baltimore who was winding down his career at Cleveland in 1975, said of appearing in public in the uniforms: "I feel like a massive blood clot."

Over in the National League, the Houston Astros introduced a look that was just as offensive, with horizontal rainbow stripes across the shirts. Charlie Hough, the Dodgers' knuckleballer, described the Astros' motif as resembling "a Hawaiian bowling team."

May 5

On a Sunday afternoon, the Gillette razor people set up a baseball-wide promotion. It had been calculated that somebody, on that particular day, would score the one-millionth run in big league history. The press boxes throughout both leagues were connected in a sort of twelve-unit conference call, to set up the dramatics of the millionth run. Gillette needed some marketing help. This was 1975 and hardly anybody in the United States had shaved for a couple of years. Mel "How About That, Sports Fans?" Allen, New York's venerable play-by-play house man, expressed amazement at what was about to take place. "I thought the Yankees had scored a million runs by themselves," he marveled. So the player who scored Number One Million would receive a year's supply of Gillette blue blades, or some such bullshit.

The countdown came quickly. Throughout the majors, a runner crossed the plate about every twenty seconds. At Wrigley Field, run number 999,998 crossed the plate. In Milwaukee, here came run number 999,999, and, then, the winner was: Bob Watson, of the Astros, playing at Candlestick Park in San Francisco.

Another cornerstone event would happen in San Francisco that same day, one that Gillette hadn't anticipated. In a doubleheader, Giants and Astros pitchers combined for 44 bases on balls, a major league record, and nearly eight hours had been required to set it.

May 8

Valerie Perrine had just won the best actress prize at the 1975 Cannes Film Festival for her portrayal of Lenny Bruce's wife. Perrine said that was her biggest thrill, ever, in show biz, surpassing the moment when Frank Sinatra invited her to be among some dinner guests at his hotel suite in Las Vegas. The actress said that when she arrived at the party, Sinatra had already self-embalmed himself. He called room service and demanded an order of "wieners and kraut" for his entourage. The order arrived in a washtub, and Sinatra began throwing the wieners at his guests until they took the hint and left.

I read that story, and that was when it struck me. For going on what was almost two years, I'd been traveling the country with baseball's answer to Frank Sinatra. That, of course, was the tempestuous Bantam Billy Martin, man of many mood swings.

Billy had been fond of telling the media that his clubhouse door was always open. "It might not always be warm and friendly, after a tough loss, but the door is always open."

After a 6–5 loss to Kansas City at Royals Stadium, a game in which Steve Busby prevailed over Clyde Wright and a variety of Rangers had done just enough of the little things wrong to cost the team the game, Billy's clubhouse door was not open. He could be heard addressing his team inside, though, and from the tone of his oratory, it sounded as if he was about to start throwing some wieners.

Then Martin's voice went up another octave.

"I've got the floor! I'm doing the talking here!"

Then another man's voice could be heard from inside, the unmistakable voice of Willie Davis:

"GET YOUR FUCKING HANDS OFF ME!"

Now Martin again:

"TURN LOOSE OF HIM! LET HIM GO!"

Another chorus of curses and threats came from the clubhouse, indecipherable, and then Martin made himself loud and clear again:

"THAT'S THE WAY THINGS ARE GONNA BE. IF YOU DON'T LIKE IT, GET YOUR ASS OUT OF HERE!"

When Whitey Herzog managed the Rangers, he was always afraid that the visitors clubhouse in Kansas City was bugged. Well, no hidden microphones were necessary on this occasion. In their own clubhouse, situated across a hallway, the Royals players said they could hear the shouting.

Once the writers were finally allowed to enter Martin's grim locker room domain, they found Billy in a Code Red frenzy, steaming and hissing like a burned-up radiator.

Someone tactfully asked the little scrapper about his postgame interchange with Willie Davis.

"You guys must have had your ears glued to the door, huh? Guess you're starving for a good story. Well, you're not gettin' it from me. Now GO! Now and forever. You want a story, maybe the opposing manager will give you one someday. I mean it. Get the goddamn fuck out of my office."

That incident perfectly framed the life and times of Billy Martin. Baseball's marathon season, the 162-game grind, left most players and managers stoic, and a little blasé, over the outcome of one, single game. Just another day or night at the office. Not

Billy Martin. He took every loss hard, regarded defeat as a personal insult. He usually responded with shock and dismay, blaming the world while, inside, he tormented himself. *Where did I screw up? Where did I go wrong?* None of Billy's players relished his company after a loss, which was the primary reason his teams so often won.

As a sportswriter, it was supremely entertaining to watch Billy Martin, the sporting life's version of Mount Saint Helens, explode.

The next day, the Rangers beat the Royals, and Billy Martin seemed to have undergone an emergency personality transplant. Not only had he apologized to me for flipping out, he said he'd actually gone to Willie Davis and made peace with his outfielder as well. "I won't say that I actually told Willie that I was sorry," Billy said. "I told him I basically liked him, but when I was talking to him, to just keep his goddamn yap shut." Davis confirmed that. His room was next to mine at the Sheraton Royal Hotel. I could hear him in there, chanting. "O-o-o-o-m." It was enough to drive anybody nuts. I banged on Willie's door, and he talked about how he and Billy had kissed and made up. "I ran into him in the hotel bar, and we had a drink or two. Actually, more like six or seven. We got it all straightened out." But I had serious doubts about Davis's stability by now, and sure as hell knew that Martin did as well. As far as the comments regarding the new manager-outfielder détente, the on-the-record statements of both men involved seemed saturated with insincerity. I returned to my room, had a smoke, settled into something akin to yoga posture, though it was more fetal than lotus, and began to chant.

After the game that night, Steve Cameron, the baseball writer for the *Kansas City Star*, was kind enough to take me to a place that he swore was a mob joint that dated back to the days of Machine Gun Kelly and Pretty Boy Floyd. They called it the Virginia Tavern. Kansas City, in my estimation, was the most underrated city in America. But the Virginia Tavern took on the atmosphere of an old boardinghouse, and I told Cameron that if the patrons were mobsters, they were pretty nondescript. Soon, I would get something in the mail from Cameron, a front-page clipping from his newspaper's Metro section. A couple of nights after our visit, the Virginia Tavern had hosted a shootout, with six dead. There was a photo. The tavern was drenched with blood, the deceased people covered with sheets. Good, solid, unbiased journalism at work there. Several years prior to being appointed publisher of the *Kansas City Star,* Jim Hale, had been running the paper in Clearwater, Florida, he had hired a sportswriter directly out of the state pen in Texas who had served a lengthy stretch for murdering his date. "The guy said that he was a first offender," Hale conceded. "He just didn't tell me what he'd done."

The paper also ran a diagram of the death scene that detailed the exact whereabouts of the victims when the shooting occurred, and Cameron had gleefully circled the two bar stools we had occupied on the night of our visit.

May 10

Joe Falls, the *Detroit Free Press* columnist, was on hand at Tiger Stadium to watch the Rangers beat Detroit, 3–1, before a nice crowd of about 25,000—too nice, in Falls's harsh estimation.

"God almighty," Falls wailed. "We have 25 percent unemployment in Detroit! The city is broke! They just laid off 830 cops! And yet, they had 40,000 out here for opening day, damn near 17,000 showed up for the last game of the season for the horseshit Red Wings, the Globetrotters pulled in 29,000, and about 10,000 psychopaths showed up for some fucking karate match! If everybody's so damn broke, where do they find the money to go to all these stupid ballgames? What the hell is the matter with these people?"

The anti-jock had spoken.

That same day, down in Cincinnati, the New York Mets beat the Reds, 3–2. A utility man in his 15th full big league season, Joe Torre, knocked in the winning run. Torre was a catcher when he broke into the majors. My old friend from Texas, Bobby Bragan, had managed Torre when he played for the Braves. "Sometimes, you see guys who aren't confident at the plate, afraid of getting hit by the ball," Bragan said. "Joe isn't like that, and that's too bad, because otherwise, I could call him Chicken Catcher Torre."

May 12

Billy Martin was cooing, Willie Davis had four base hits, and the Rangers were hot. They swept the Tigers, with Ferguson Jenkins winning over Mickey Lolich in the Sunday finale of the road trip. Texas had won four straight, had pulled itself out of its early season tailspin, and moved past the Oakland A's for first place in the American League West.

Catfish Hunter had gone to Oakland and humiliated his old boss, Charlie O. Before the game, Hunter had expressed concern about returning to his old ballpark. "I'll probably leave the mound after the first inning and walk into the wrong dugout," he said. Instead, Hunter went out and pitched a two-hit shutout. Afterward Reggie Jackson seemed to be taking a cheap shot at his owner, Finley, for letting Hunter drift off to New York. "It was weird, trying to hit against him," Jackson declared. "It was like a bad dream."

Meanwhile, across the Bay, the Big Red Machine from Cincinnati showed signs of getting into gear, and all that the rest of baseball could do was watch and tremble. Wes Westrum, the San

Francisco manager, had watched Joe Morgan single-handedly dismantle his Giants with three singles, two stolen bases, and a trio of gems in the field.

"I have nothing against Johnny Bench or Pete Rose, but Morgan is the best player on that team," Westrum declared. "There isn't any part of his game that he doesn't play as good or better than anyone else in the league."

On the other side of the tracks, the Atlanta Braves were making their case as being the worst team in the National League, although the Houston Astros would be hard to overcome for that designation. The Braves' best player was Ralph Garr, of whom Expos manager Gene Mauch had said, "He'll swing at anything. Falling leaves. Paper airplanes. Peanut shells. The problem for our pitchers is Garr always gets his hits." Well, not always. Garr, who'd won the NL batting championship the year before, noted, "When I don't hit, the Braves don't win. I hate to say it, but that's the way it looks."

At least the Braves had it better than Evel Knievel. In London, he'd attempted to jump his motorcycle over thirteen double-decker buses. He cleared twelve. Afterward, with "his costume in tatters and his face blackened," the stunt artist told the crowd, "I'm through." To which his manager said, "Nonsense. Once you're out of that body cast, you'll be good as new." Baseball players might not have realized it, but compared to the rest of the world, they had it made.

May 16

Billy Martin's lineup had incurred some casualties. Dave Nelson, the second baseman, was out for two months after ankle surgery. So the team summoned reinforcements and called in Roy Smalley

Jr. from the AAA team at Spokane. This was the arrangement: Lenny Randle would move from third to second, replacing Nelson. Smalley would play his natural position, which was shortstop. Toby Harrah would be shifted from shortstop to third base. The loser in the proposition was Harrah, who was establishing All-Star credentials at shortstop. In another era, a player such as Harrah would, via his agent, inform the team that he was refusing the transfer, and go home to his seaside palace for a long pout.

But this was 1975, and Harrah had said, by golly, if it helps the team, I'll play third. "In the end, it could mean $25,000 for every man in our clubhouse." The twenty-five grand that Harrah referred to was the winner's share of the World Series, and it seemed like all the dough in Fort Knox to baseball players of the time.

Smalley Jr., the rookie, made three sensational plays against the Tigers that earned him a standing ovation at Arlington Stadium. Thus Smalley became the third man in stadium history to earn such an accolade. The others had been phenom pitcher David Clyde, when he won his major league debut at age eighteen in 1973, and another man, that same season, a drunken fan from Grand Prairie, who'd whipped four ushers and three Arlington cops before being hauled away in chains.

After the game, in the clubhouse, players discovered a cake on the table in the middle of the room. In the paper, I described the cake as "big enough to cover half of the infield, and ornate enough to serve as a permanent lobby display at Caesars Palace."

It was Billy Martin's birthday. Billy was touched. "I love celebrating my birthday," he admitted. "And I never had a birthday party until 1969."

Aww. Poor Billy. But he'd forgotten about that birthday celebration of his back in 1957, the one that ended up in the drunken conflagration at the Copacabana in New York, the rumble that caused general manager George Weiss to trade Billy to Kansas City and banish him from the Yankees' garden forever.

— ◉ —

Finally, after all those years, Billy seemed to be drinking from the deep goblet of sweet revenge. He retreated into his office to talk to a writer from *Sports Illustrated*. The guy was preparing a cover story on Martin, one that would appear in the June 2, 1975, issue, that came adorned with the headline that read, "Billy Martin: Baseball's Fiery Genius."

I had reminded the fiery genius that making the cover of *SI* was the kiss of death—the ultimate jinx, and asked Martin if he was concerned.

"Yep," he said.

May 21

Like most baseball teams of the 1970s, the Rangers had been family-oriented. In fact, a family was there to greet one of the players in the lobby of the Pfister Hotel in Milwaukee when the team arrived for a three-game series. The family consisted of a blond schoolteacher from Ohio, who'd developed a strong friendship with one of the players while on vacation in Florida during spring training. So had her mother and little sister, and all three had traveled to Wisconsin to renew the warmth.

Another player had an entourage awaiting his Milwaukee arrival as well. These were three teenage girls from Minneapolis who followed him to certain American League cities. This had been going on for at least two years. I told the player, jokingly, that if he didn't start sharing the wealth, I might have to inform my Texas readership that he was lacking in big league skills.

The phone rang in my hotel room at the Pfister. It was the player, insisting that I come to his room. Curious, I knocked on his door. He shoved one of the three out into the hallway. "She's all yours," he said, and slammed the door. The girl might as well have been wearing a T-shirt inscribed... "If You Even Think About So Much As Touching Me, You'll Get Thirty Years." Plus, the girl was completely wrecked on drugs, my guess, L.A. turnarounds and horse tranquilizer.

Well, as a representative and officer of the Baseball Writers' Association of America, my first responsibility was to uphold the organization's canon of ethics. I thought fast, and then did the honorable thing. I located a freight elevator, escorted the girl down into the basement of the Pfister Hotel, and left her there, babbling.

After an experience like that, the ballpark seemed safe and inviting. I went to County Stadium early the next day, which was a rare thing for me. I wanted to interview Hank Aaron, back in Milwaukee, where his home run hitting career had started when the Braves were still headquartered in Suds City. Hammerin' Hank was the toast of baseball in 1974 after surpassing Babe Ruth's career home run record. Now, a year had passed, and Aaron was sliding toward the finale of his career in a Brewers uniform. Milwaukee was plainly utilizing the old star, a relic from County Stadium's proud past, as a gate attraction. The Brewers had an acute shortage of those in 1975. The only man other than Aaron on their roster with any fan recognition value was Don Money, who, with a name like that in the dying days of baseball's *pre*-agent era, was clearly ahead of his time. He and Norm Cash.

Hank Aaron no longer offered much on the field. In fact, since the Brewers played in the American League with its designated hitter rule, Aaron seldom made it onto the field. Aaron had become a ceremonial fixture, like the battered old boxing champ, hired to glad-hand the customers in some Atlantic City casino, and sign autographs.

The week before, he had surpassed the Babe's career record for runs batted in (2,217), an event to which most of the national media had assigned one and a half column inches, at the bottom of page 9, under the little heading of "Elsewhere in the Majors."

Aaron had gained a reputation late in his career for becoming terse and abrupt with the reporters, limiting his remarks to as few words as possible. So, when I asked him about what the RBI record meant to him, he said, "It doesn't mean anything. Look, I'm batting .214 right now. Robin Yount is batting almost .400, and when I was playing here with the Braves, he wasn't even born. So go talk to him." End of interview. End of story.

May 24

Two wins in Milwaukee put the Rangers in first place. What a time to be rolling into New York City, where the lights are pretty. On the team bus ride from La Guardia to the Essex House, on Central Park South, Cesar Tovar shouted out the window, "Tex-eees Rangers Number One! We the best!"

From outside the bus, a voice shouted back: "Kiss my cock!"

Billy Martin was not on the bus to witness the frivolity. The manager revealed that two months earlier, during spring training in Florida, he had received a letter from someone who threatened to kill him when he arrived in New York. So Billy was met at the gate at La Guardia by a bodyguard, and he was zipped off to an undisclosed hotel for his protection.

Some sportswriters had described the letter writer variously as a nut case, a kook, a psycho, and a sick-o. And since I suspected that Billy had written the letter himself, they were probably right. Knowing Billy like I knew him (which wasn't much, but enough), I figured he'd arranged a social situation that required some seclusion, now that he was here in the city that he loved the best.

The Rangers lost the Friday night opener to the Yankees. The Yanks, for the second straight year, played their home games at Shea Stadium, and the men in pinstripes seemed totally out of place there. It was like holding the Oscar awards at the La Brea Tar Pits. After Shea Stadium had opened in 1964 adjacent to the New York World's Fair, the novelty had worn off quickly. The ballpark had all the charm of a stainless steel toilet seat. The constant roar of jet traffic directly overhead made it impossible to keep what was left of my mind on the activities down on the baseball field.

A few hours after the loss to the Yankees, after midnight, I saw Billy at his favorite oasis, Danny's Hideaway in midtown Manhattan. He did not seem too concerned about the homicidal man who'd sent the threatening correspondence to Florida. Martin was accompanied by a woman wearing a polka-dot dress and red shoes. Mickey Mantle and another woman also sat at Billy's table. Mickey and Billy—siblings of the sauce. Mantle, as usual, was dispensing punishment to his proud old liver. (A Dallas surgeon at Baylor Hospital, years later, told me he had looked in during Mantle's ill-fated organ transplant operation, and the doctor had said, "Mantle had the most horrible-looking liver I have ever seen. It resembled an old, dried-out sponge." Exactly one day after the surgery, Mantle had insisted on being released from the hospital. He'd told his doctor, "Look, you and I both know that this isn't going to work, and I've got a piece of ass down in New Orleans that won't wait.")

Mantle had a history at Danny's Hideaway. According to a story that Billy liked to tell, it was in the Hideaway that Mickey had been approached by a woman who told him, "Mr. Mantle, my son Kevin absolutely idolizes you. Kevin would be so thrilled if you autographed this menu."

The mightiest Yankee of baseball's modern times gave the woman a big, winning smile and said, "Imagine how thrilled Kevin would be if I fucked his mother."

May 29

The Yankees won all three games at Shea Stadium, and the Red Sox enjoyed similar success against the Rangers at Arlington Stadium.

Not only had Boston beaten the Rangers in the series opener, they had done it rather insultingly. Boston pitcher Rick Wise, just for kicks, had drilled Willie Davis in the ribs.

Peter Gammons, aka Peter Ball Game, who covered the Sox for the *Boston Globe*, laughed and said, "Wise [an ex-Cardinal and ex-Phillie] is a typical National Leaguer. He's got no problem with throwing at guys. Plus, he doesn't like Willie Davis worth a damn."

The humor of the whole thing seemed to escape Davis. He expected retaliation. When Steve Hargan, pitching for Texas, did not aim at the head of any Boston hitters, Davis staged a sit-down in center field. He squatted—not his standard lotus position for chanting, but close enough.

Hargan expressed bemusement. "I'm familiar with that movie *Angels in the Outfield*," he said. "But Buddhists in the outfield? I dunno."

As a postgame Memorial Day fireworks show blasted away, the Rangers' clubhouse vibrated with the concussive BOOM sounds from above. It was eerie in there, like being inside a submarine under a depth charge attack. The room was made even eerier by the sullen Willie Davis. He refused to explain his bizarre show in center field. "Sometimes," he said rather mysteriously, "things go on in the dugout that the writers never see, and nobody tells them about it afterward."

May 30

Boston, for the first time that season and quite a few of the ones that had recently come before it, showed signs that this team might be in store for a uniquely positive destiny.

Rick Wise and Luis Tiant were at top form in the starting rotation, and Bill Lee, the Spaceman, had made an even more ample contribution. Lee was moving in on Don Drysdale's record for consecutive scoreless innings. Lee beat the Rangers, but the scoreless string was broken at 29 innings.

"I'm pitching a lot better this year for two reasons," he explained after the game. "First, I lost twenty pounds over the off-season. And second, I switched from French to California wine."

Lee added that he really hadn't cared about beating Don Drysdale's scoreless inning record. "My dad used to play on a softball team with Drysdale in Burbank, and when I was a kid, Drysdale and I used to chase rabbits together."

I found that statement odd. Drysdale had been a color announcer for the Rangers' TV crew in 1972, and was well known for chasing fuzzy things. But they weren't rabbits.

Chapter 7

May 31

George Steinbrenner ventured beyond the boundaries of civilization to visit the primitive territory known as Texas, and was duly introduced to the idiosyncratic cultural habits of its natives, so rustic and untamed. The Grand Cyclops of the Knights of the Royal Turtleneck had traveled out to the rugged frontier amid terrain that was rougher than the sex on 42nd Street in his own hometown, ostensibly to watch his baseball team perform. But—as in everything he did—George maintained ulterior motives. Steinbrenner had come to Texas to lobby his Rangers counterpart, Brad Corbett, into voting to get rid of baseball commissioner Bowie Kuhn at the upcoming owners meeting. Ever since Kuhn had exhibited the temerity to suspend Steinbrenner as managing general partner of the landmark franchise in the Bronx for making illegal contributions to Richard Nixon's campaign, George's vengeful heart ached with the urge for retribution.

The Yankees' owner put in an appearance at the Texas Rangers' off-the-field habitat. That was the Red Apple, almost within crawling distance of the ballpark, a den of delight and laughter. The Red Apple was a first-tier meat market where young women went to break in their new birth control pills. Billy Martin was a late night fixture in there, as were most of his single players and some of the married ones, when they could sneak off.

A bartender named Joe (aren't they all?) recognized Steinbrenner at once, and treated him to a local delicacy called a Mexican flag. That consisted of three ingredients—dark rum, tequila, and absinthe—poured gently into a shot glass over an inverted spoon to produce tri-colored tiers. Then the concoction was set ablaze and inhaled through a straw, inducing a condition sometimes known as the blind staggers. According to the bartender's testimony, and bartenders never lie, Mr. Steinbrenner had seemed dubious at first, then became downright congenial and ordered another.

There used to be a saying, from back in the Casey Stengel days, that it's great to be young and to be a Yankee. What was even greater was to be not-quite-middle-aged and *own* the goddamn Yankees, and that being the case, George Steinbrenner was the happiest man alive. Also, the most celebrated investment in baseball, Catfish Hunter, had been starting to justify his so-called market value. Hunter was winning, and Steinbrenner looked shrewd.

The concept of wealth fascinated Americans everywhere, but nowhere as much as in Texas, where a legion of dumbass white trash hicks who picked their noses with salad forks had rolled the dice and gotten filthy rich in the oil patch. In the domain of long Cadillacs and bad art, people like that were worshipped. So naturally, somebody who could cash in by simply throwing a baseball also became the object of widespread fascination.

Nobody in Texas gave a flying flip about Catfish Hunter when he was winning the Cy Young Award with the Oakland A's. Now that he had become the amazing $3.5 million man, people were all but tearing down the gates of Arlington Stadium to watch him perform.

For a decade, the Yankees' position in the American League standings had teetered between second division and intensive care. Yet the mystique lived on. Before Hunter's Saturday night start against the Rangers, I visited the New York clubhouse and discussed the issue with an expert on the topic. That was Elston Howard, now a coach, and a holdover from the time when the Yankees seemingly held a monopoly on all things that were great in baseball.

"It's funny how people talk about the Yankees' uniform, like it is some kind of magic. But the uniform didn't make Mickey Mantle hit all those home runs, or make Joe DiMaggio the kind of player he was. The same with Babe Ruth," the old catcher said. "The Yankees won because we had better players. We were a happy bunch of guys, and we had a lot of fun on the field. We went out every day with one thing in mind, and that was to beat the crap out of the other ball club."

Howard blamed the team's on-the-field deterioration on the ownership of CBS. "The farm system went to hell. But you know, people still come to see the team, just because we're the New York Yankees. On the road, the hotel lobbies are always full of people, just there to see us up close and personal."

I transferred Howard's comments to the clubhouse on the other side of the field, the one behind first base, just to get a rise out of Billy. "The Yankees are just another team," Billy sniffed. "Just another team we have to play and beat."

People in the grandstand suggested otherwise. Over 38,000 of them piled their way into a stadium designed to hold 35,000.

Right away, Catfish Hunter established that he was the man in charge. I was wrapping up my allotment of games as the official scorer, and hated every moment of it.

In the third inning, Toby Harrah slapped a hard grounder into the gap between Graig Nettles at third and the shortstop, who was Jim Mason that night. The ball bounced off Mason's glove, and I didn't hesitate to call the play an error because I had a feeling that Catfish Hunter might throw a no-hitter, and I sure as hell was not about to put my ass on the line as the guy who screwed it up for him. Just that very morning, I'd read a magazine story that identified the worst job in Texas: chicken sexer, whatever that was. No, having to work as the official scorer at a major league baseball game was even worse than screwing chickens.

Cesar Tovar led off the sixth inning with a hot, seeing-eye bouncer up the middle that was a clean hit. That was the only one that Hunter would give up that night. Tovar's hit and Mason's error were the only two plays that prevented a perfect game from Catfish Hunter.

If the heat that came with being baseball's richest star was grinding on Hunter, he certainly concealed any feelings of stress. He maintained a happy and unaffected Gomer Pyle demeanor. "When I was going bad earlier this year, I asked Whitey Ford [a pitching coach] and all three catchers to go out with me to the bullpen and watch me throw," Hunter said. "Every one of them noticed that my arm was out in front of my body, and there is no way you can throw a ball low like that. I am a control pitcher, not a strikeout pitcher, and when I don't have my control, I might as well not be out there."

Jim Mason, the shortstop I'd charged with the error, was a former Ranger. He was an Alabama boy, endowed with all the dirt-floor sophistication of a NASCAR jack handler. I asked him about the joys of playing for a marqee franchise like the Yankees. "The clubhouse is always crawling with reporters," Mason said, "and shit keeps disappearing from my locker. So you figure it out."

June 3

A few million copies of Billy Martin's *Sports Illustrated* cover story had arrived in mailboxes and newsstands, and with that, sure enough, had come the notorious jinx. Just to be on the safe side, I avoided the team charter flight to Baltimore, and traveled commercial. The Rangers had developed every indication that despite being managed by "baseball's fiery genius," this was a choke team. In games at Arlington Stadium that had attracted crowds of 20,000 or more, Texas was 0-7. Now they had waded into deep quicksand against the American League East. The Rangers had lost eight out of nine games against the Yankees and Red Sox, and had dropped from first place to fourth in the West, six games out of first place, which was by then occupied by the Kansas City Royals.

Even more alarming was the nonperformance of the Rangers' key pitcher, Ferguson Jenkins. Not only had Jenkins been banged around like a one-legged rodeo clown in the series finale against the Yankees, he had committed three errors. Over the course of his last three starts, Jenkins's earned run average had swollen to a plus-eight. Jenkins had been professionally philosophical about his malaise. "Like they say. When things start to go horseshit, they don't go in half-measures."

Martin was pissed off at his team, and he was pissed off at me because I had written: "*As a strategist, Billy likes to compare himself to Napoleon, but with that funky little trimmed mustache of his, from a distance, he looks more like Hitler."* He was beginning to act like him, too. After his team had tanked in the home stand, Billy was hotter than a pissed-off postal worker. Martin's trademark had always been keeping his players alert by jabbing them in the eye with a sharp stick. He started to rag on his players, catcher Jim Sundberg in particular. That so-called concept of clubhouse chemistry was out of whack. Some of the test tubes bubbled over, and Billy Land was becoming toxic in a hurry. With Jenkins trapped in the latrine for nearly a month, Martin had resorted to a six-man starting rotation, and the pitchers had begun complaining, off the record naturally, that the notion of working approximately once every nine or ten days was handicapping their performance standards. On-the-field performance substantiated that. All six had been running hot and cold. "So what am I supposed to do?" the frustrated Martin responded. "Ask for two of them to raise their hands and volunteer to drop out?" Billy knew that the situation would have to be corrected, and soon.

What Billy needed, and badly, was a guy like Nolan Ryan, whose manager, Dick Williams, had said, "When he gets his fastball over the plate, he'll beat you, and when he gets his curveball over the plate, he'll no-hit you." Ryan had done exactly that against the Orioles on June 1, and was in the process of pulling a Johnny Vander Meer act against the Brewers in his next start until Hank Aaron got a single in the sixth inning. As the man who managed in the opposition dugout for this upcoming series, Earl Weaver, had pointed out, "The only thing that matters in baseball is that little hump in the middle of the infield."

Martin's mood had been soured even more by Willie Davis. The man who was advertised as the center field savior and final piece in the Rangers' pennant-winning jigsaw puzzle and being compensated with a whopping 1975 salary of $105,000, was not on the team's flight to Baltimore. On two occasions earlier in the season, Davis had requested an advance on his paycheck, and Rangers owner Brad Corbett had accommodated him. The third time had not been the charm for Willie. "The eagle shits on the first and fifteenth, and you'll get the check, like everybody else," Corbett told his disgruntled veteran. So Davis evidently had formed a one-man picket line. The only person laughing had to be Gene Mauch, who'd managed, or *tried* to manage, Davis in Montreal the season before.

In a baseball game played not too far from the site where Francis Scott Key wrote "The Star-Spangled Banner," the lights of Memorial Stadium gave proof through the night that the Rangers still sucked. I'd been out to see Fort William McHenry a couple of times, always the highlight of any trip to Baltimore. Edgar Allan Poe's grave site was also a must-see for any tourist. I would not necessarily imply that Baltimore was a dull place in 1975, but on this trip, on the ride from the airport to the hotel, the cab driver asked me if I knew where he could find some action.

Since Johnny Unitas had retired from the Colts, the people of Baltimore had turned more and more to the baseball team for hope and support. So the summer of '75 found the city more downcast than usual. The Orioles had not been faring well, either, and remained in last place in the AL East. "I'm not worried," Weaver remarked after the game. "The fans here don't start booing until July." After this latest loss at Baltimore—the homeland of humidity and a population depressed because they suspected that there was more to life than crab cakes—somebody asked Martin when Willie Davis might show up again.

"It doesn't make any difference whether Davis reports or not. We're going to trade him," Billy announced. That begged the question: To whom and for what? Martin shrugged. "Two teams had shown a mild interest," Martin said, sighing. "Really, Willie has been fair to me, but if something is bothering him, then that's his problem.

"But I'll be frank with you. This mess, along with the losing streak, is making me uptight."

The next night, just to change his luck, Martin replaced Frank Lucchesi in the third-base coaching box. So Texas won, and afterward the manager's outlook seemed to have changed dramatically.

"I've got a feeling that from now on, things are fixin' to go our way," Martin smiled. (*Fixin'*. Billy had been turning Texan with alarming speed.)

"So how long have you been feeling that way?" someone inquired.

"Exactly two minutes," Martin came back. "I just got a phone call. Willie Davis has been traded to the St. Louis Cardinals."

Later that night, I reached Davis on the telephone. He had just learned of the trade. "This is exceptionally good news," Willie said. "Now I am gone like a cool breeze, and headed to St. Louis on a burning jet."

Not being the manager, I was going to miss old Willie.

June 10

You know that you're in for a long flight when the pilot tapes a suicide note to the cockpit door. En route to Cleveland, the Rangers' chartered 727 bounced and jolted its way into the jaws of a Great Lakes gale, the kind that sank the *Edmund Fitzgerald*. In preparation for my impending doom and journey into the hereafter, I knocked down about thirty of those little airline bottles that contained J&B

scotch. My only initiative in life in those days was the pursuit of the San Francisco pleasure ethic: if it feels bad, do it.

The next morning found me in the coffee shop of the Hollenden House hotel in downtown Cleveland, along with my two loyal companions, hash browns and a hangover. In the morning paper, the *Cleveland Plain Dealer*, baseball writer Russ Schneider was in a crappy mood. Reading Schneider's material, one could practically hear him grinding his teeth. The writer was distressed because his Indians had traded two starting pitchers, Jim Perry and Dick Bosman, to Oakland, in exchange for John "Blue Moon" Odom. A raw deal for Cleveland, the writer fumed, and, as the final insult, Charlie Finley, the prick, announced that both Perry and Bosman would start for the A's in an upcoming doubleheader in Cleveland.

After breakfast, I returned to my hotel room. Outside, the skies above Cleveland were the color of ash, as usual. In '75, the only thing more lacking than nightlife in Cleveland was day life. The highlight of the long and dreary hours that preceded the baseball game happened at 11 A.M., when *The Price Is Right* came on. No existence is worse than a nighttime traveling job, because sleeping in a hotel during the daylight hours is an impossible situation. For some reason, my room was always, *always* within spitting distance of the hallway ice machine. *Thunk! Thunk!* All day, all night. Why hadn't somebody invented a muffler for the hotel ice machine, the most despicable piece of machinery ever devised by mankind? And that "Do Not Disturb" sign that the guest foolishly hung on the doorknob served as an open invitation to the fiendish and sadistic housekeepers to go next door and create a racket that sounded like the Tennessee–Alabama football game. Bang. Thud. They even vacuumed the ceiling and the walls. Didn't they know that *I just wanted to be left alone!* No.

Let me amend that. I just wanted to sleep. Being left alone was never a challenge. My roommate was the room service tray, and what remained of the cheeseburger, and the un-eaten french fries that lay there on the plate, glaring at me with a cold and greasy stare. And everybody thought that this baseball writing gig was a dream job.

Finally, six o'clock arrived and the cab carried me over to Municipal Stadium. That place was big enough to seat the entire population of China. The problem was that the entire population of China didn't give a damn about the Cleveland Indians, and nobody in Cleveland did either. The 5,000 people who typically showed up for a night game against the Texas Rangers might as well have been invisible in a structure so vast as that ballpark.

Cleveland was where baseball careers went to die. The Indians' 1975 roster was made up of the usual assembly of names that resonate through time only with the fans of the deepest, darkest baseball trivia. George Hendrick, Rick Manning, Jack Brohamer, Charlie Spikes, John Ellis, John Lowenstein, Alan Ashby. Fritz Peterson was on the roster, his ticket to Cleveland being the reward for his infamous wife-swapping stunt of 1973. The guys were baseball's answer to the Ghost Riders in the Sky, specters in cleats, galloping along the eternal path to nowhere.

The Indians were a manager's nightmare. Not just the Cleveland manager, but also the manager of the American League All-Star team who was required to choose an Indian since every team in the league was supposed to have a representative at the "mid-summer classic."

If Russ Schneider had been upset by the trade that brought Blue Moon Odom to Cleveland, the transported pitcher was even more steamed than the sportswriter and didn't mind saying so. In a pregame interview in the Tribe's clubhouse, Odom said he'd like to be retraded to Texas, then qualified his desire to wear Rangers blue. "Actually, I'd like to play anywhere where they'll pay me."

Odom was furious with Cleveland general manager Phil Seghi. When the trade from the A's had been confirmed, Blue Moon had demanded an eight-grand bonus on top of his $40,000-a-year salary to make up for the lost playoff check that he'd been used to receiving in Oakland and sure as hell would not receive as long as he was in Cleveland. Seghi refused. So Odom went out and pitched a two-hit shutout over Kansas City in his Indians uniform, then indicated he would not pitch again until his financial concerns had been satisfied. Odom's snit defined his times, a long-lost baseball mentality when the winning team concept and the postseason financial incentive reigned as the player's foremost motivation. To the latter-day operatives of open market baseball, the World Series check might buy platinum lug nuts for the kid's tricycle. To the barons of the free agent game, despite what they said in print and on the airwaves, winning and losing became a secondary matter. They lovingly tended to their individual stats like hothouse orchids.

"So what's next?" I asked Odom. "There isn't all that much you can do about it."

"I'll stay here and suffer until something gets worked out."

"With an attitude like that, won't it affect your pitching?"

That was the question that seemed to truly irritate an already chapped butt.

"Affect me? I didn't say it would affect me on the mound. I always give 100 percent on the mound. Who are you with anyway? You better quote me right on that. Rico [Carty] is standing right here, and he heard what I told you. You misquote me, and I'm gonna come looking for your ass."

As long as I had him good and steamed, it seemed reasonable to finish the job.

"In Denny McLain's book, he said that you were Charlie Finley's clubhouse snitch in Oakland. How about that?"

"Here's my answer to that. Get the hell out of here."

I thanked Blue Moon and left, as requested, and made a mental note that when in search of a happy-face story, stay the hell away from the Cleveland Indians. Blue Moon Odom obviously realized that, too, and the next day, he got his wish and was traded to Atlanta.

Still, the tattered and battered Indians had enough to beat the Rangers, 7–5, in the series opener. It was yet another troubled outing for Ferguson Jenkins, who lost to Cleveland's immortal Dave LaRoche. The Texas team was slowly being bled to death. This was the team's 10th loss in 12 games, and the Rangers had slid down to fifth place in the American League West. That was their problem. The Stroh's beer in the press box was cold and refreshing, and that was all that mattered to me.

Billy Martin sat in his cramped office in the visitors clubhouse, engaged in a serious telephone conversation with the Rangers' owner, Brad Corbett. That indicated that the Rangers' management was about to fulfill the traditional baseball tactic—when in doubt, panic.

Obviously, a trade was in the works. Probably something big. That meant one thing: more work for the sportswriter. I returned to the hotel and wrote a story for the afternoon edition of the next day's *Star-Telegram*, about fifteen paragraphs' worth of sheer speculation. I told the readers to get ready to see the departure of two members of Billy Martin's funny-looking six-pitcher rotation. This time I was right.

The next morning, it was back to the coffee shop. Casey Stengel might have been renowned for speaking in terms that were largely incomprehensible, but he had made the most profound statement perhaps in the history of the sport when he'd said, "I don't have any problem with a player being up all night with a woman. I have a problem with a player being up all night *looking* for a woman."

I shared a booth with a Rangers player, an infielder by trade, who bore the truth of Casey's pronouncement. The player's eyes were the color of the rising sun on the Japanese flag, and his hands trembled so badly that he could scarcely read the menu. The player confided that the night before, he had patronized an establishment called the Hairy Buffalo and had picked up a woman.

"She climbs poles for the telephone company," he said. "She also said that she was a heroin addict and liked to sweat. I'm going back there tonight. Maybe I'll get unlucky again."

With men such as this taking the field for the Rangers, I then knew for sure that the material being generated for my newspaper regarding this team being headed to a World Series had amounted to the greatest fantasy since *The Creature from the Black Lagoon*. Later in the day, I read a quote in one of the Cleveland newspapers. Muhammad Ali was discussing his upcoming bout against Joe Bugner. Ali said that he had told Joe Bugner the following: "If you beat me, they'll make you a movie star. If you beat me, the queen will invite you to the palace, President Ford will give you a private audience, and Governor George Wallace will invite you to Alabama and say, 'Good. You whipped that nigger.'"

I was tempted to show that to Billy Martin. Since Billy insisted that he could do to Ali what Joe Bugner could not, perhaps he should schedule a bout. Whatever the result, Martin would no doubt have been more content than he appeared to be in Cleveland, trying to manage these Rangers.

June 13

Doubleheaders were always soul-draining events on travel day, especially when the second game lasted 17 innings. At least the Rangers had finally beaten Cleveland. When the team bus arrived at Hopkins Airport, Burt Hawkins, the traveling secretary, cautioned the players that the plane would be leaving in only ten or fifteen minutes, and to head for the gate right away. Naturally, the entire group stampeded its way into the airport saloon. There was still time for a quick pop before getting down to the task of serious drinking on the plane. The players were amply lubricated after the flight and bus ride from Logan Airport to the Sheraton Boston hotel when they arrived after midnight. Infielder Ed Brinkman, the player that Texas received in exchange for Willie Davis, said of his new teammates, "My God, these guys are wasted. They need to tone it down."

Two of the Rangers' younger and brighter talents, Jim Sundberg and Mike Hargrove, were so giddy that they utilized the long metal strip that separated the up and down sides of the hotel's two-story escalator as an amusement park slide. Zoom! Down they went. Sundberg was traveling about eighty miles an hour when he hit the floor at the lobby level, then catapulted forward, blindsided some poor bastard wearing an airline flight crew uniform, and sent him tumbling in a backward somersault. The guy was not a good sport about it. Not at all.

The Boston Red Sox loyalists carried a reputation for being the most knowledgeable in baseball. If they were so damn analytically insightful, how come they were completely ignorant of the reality that their cherished Old Towne Team was poised to become destiny's children, come the climax of the season of '75. Even though Boston sat atop the American League East leader board, albeit precariously, only 13,000 turned out to watch the Sox play the Rangers at Fenway Park. Not only was the gathering paltry in numbers, nobody seemed to be paying much attention to the game. The focus of attention was the right field stands, where the spectators amused themselves by flinging Frisbees back and forth.

In fairness, there was not much for them to watch that night. The Rangers belted four homers, including a Sundberg grand slam, and the Sox got socked, 12–4.

Billy Martin was asked how much fun it had been to enjoy a laugher after his team's difficult June Swoon. "Are you kidding?" Billy snapped. "I was in this ballpark in 1950. Boston was leading 9–0 in the ninth inning, and we wound up winning, 15–10. No lead is safe in this ballpark."

Really, a person would have to have the soul of a South Texas sheriff not to feel saturated by the charming mystique of Fenway Park. Among its eccentric delights was the stadium announcer, Sherm Feller, who sounded like his mouth was stuffed with peanut butter and Ritz crackers. For instance, the Rangers' Jeff Burroughs came through on the Fenway PA as "Burrzzz." His delivery was enhanced by long pauses. "Now batting for the Red Sox" . . . (then Sherm would give it about eight seconds) . . . "Rico" . . . (and then the count might reach two-and-two before he would get around to saying) . . . "Petrocelli."

Another source of cheer, one the fan in the stands missed out on, was the press box presence of Boston sportswriter Cliff Keane, an old man who was shocking in his sarcasm. Keene called me "Mah-lon" because, for some strange reason, he thought I looked like the actor, which I didn't. As the Rangers were beating the Sox, Sherm Feller, between innings, announced that the upcoming Saturday game at Fenway would be Latin American Appreciation Day. "Oh Jesus Christ," moaned Keene in a classic display of New England tolerance. "I hope somebody sets up a machine gun nest."

In the Red Sox clubhouse afterward, I interviewed one of the Sox' hotshot rookie outfielders, Fred Lynn. He and Jim Rice were providing the needed catalyst to get Boston off the ground, and pennant-bound. Lynn had been a teammate of the Rangers' slick shortstop rookie Roy Smalley at Southern Cal. They shared the same confidence and cool that is rare in first-year major leaguers.

"Since I left USC and worked my way up through the Boston minor league system, I have been successful at every level," Lynn said. "That's for four reasons. The hotels are better, the travel arrangements are better, the crowds are bigger, and as you move up, you see more strikes."

Yes. The poise and polish of the major league baseball player. While Fred Lynn was talking, his teammate, outfielder Juan Beniquez, had patronized the clubhouse snack table, and walked about laughing to himself with his seven-inch un-circumcised dick inside a hot dog bun, covered with Dijon mustard and relish. Beniquez was packing one and a half pounds of home-wrecking sausage. At the winter that followed the 1975 season, Beniquez was traded to Texas. I asked a Boston writer for a "scouting report" on the outfielder, and the writer said, "He's a degenerate."

After the Rangers beat Boston again to complete the two-game series, the team boarded the charter for the flight back to

Texas. En route, Lenny Randle had taken out his tennis racquet and was batting around a cold dinner roll, and challenged Mike Kekich to a match. "The winner gets Roy Smalley's magic glove," Randle said. Ed Brinkman, the newcomer, watched and then sat with his face covered with his hands. The real kicker about that episode was that Lenny Randle regarded his body as an obsidian temple and was the only player on the Rangers' team who did not consume alcohol. Lenny had gotten goofy on the fumes.

Chapter 8

June 10

The All-Star ballots had been printed and were being distributed at Arlington Stadium as well as at the rest of the ballparks. The voting process, by 1975, had become the only item of marginal interest as far as the All-Star Game was concerned. Baseball in that time contained two absolutes. One: At some point in any game, a pitcher would scratch his balls. Two: The National League won the All-Star Game, frequently racking up runs in the late innings to complete the job. This had been going on for nearly two decades, and contributed so greatly to the negative image of the American League that it had declined to the extent that it was essentially a glorified version of the AAA American Association. Attendance reflected that.

Earl Weaver, the Orioles' manager, had determined that the cause of the AL All-Star slump had little to do with on-the-roster inferiority. "The National League has better biorhythms in July," Earl had deduced.

The decade of the 1970s was characterized by a nationwide search for the inner self, and that was being accomplished with a large inventory of devices that ranged from Scientology to Transcendental Meditation to est. By 1975, the rage du jour had become biorhythms, a study devised by some Swiss Mister who figured that it was easy to predict an individual's highs and lows by adding the number of days the person had been alive by either 23, 27, or 33, and thereby determining who was hot and who was not in three areas: physical, intellectual, and emotional. Good God. If Einstein had been so damn smart, why had he not figured that out? Advocates of the study had enthusiastically noted that Marilyn Monroe and Judy Garland (who'd told people that they'd have been messed up, too, if they'd been gang-raped at age fourteen by a bunch of drunk midgets in monkey costumes) both registered record-low biorhythms on the days they had OD'd, and that Ted Kennedy's were double-dose bad the night he had driven off the bridge.

If only they had known. By 1975, Teddy would have been in the White House, and Marilyn would have been first lady. So the leaders of business and industry were applying the study of biorhythms to personnel management and, as a result, Aetna's profits had risen by 9 percent, and in the province of Punjab, they hadn't experienced a train wreck that killed more than 1,000 people in almost a year.

Now, Earl Weaver had applied the theory to his roster and had achieved spotty results, and reverted to his more proven tactic—Earl's Law—which stated that whenever he didn't smoke a cigarette between innings, the opposition always scored.

Earl was a hoot, and his team had won the American League East five of the last six years, going into '75. Brooks Robinson, Baltimore's ultimate fielding machine at third base, explained to me why. "Earl insists that we make all of the routine plays on the field. We don't try to make the spectacular play, because when we do, that's when somebody winds up throwing the ball into the dugout. As far as the outfielders are concerned, Earl thinks it is more important to hit the cutoff man than hit a home run. Also, we don't take chances on the bases."

Robinson might have been oversimplifying Baltimore's success formula. Also, with players like outfielder Paul Blair, shortstop Mark Belanger, and Robinson himself, the Orioles had been blessed with defensive artists endowed with the stylish grace of matadors, men who made the great plays look easy. One of the game's promising third basemen, George Brett, marveled at Robinson's artistry with the glove. "He appears to know where the ball is going to be hit even before the pitcher throws it," Brett said. Brett was right. Robinson, like Larry Bird and Wayne Gretzky, owned a rare sixth sense when it came to anticipation.

Earl Weaver and Billy Martin were the two big league managers of their time who approached baseball as a dice game, like backgammon or Yahtzee, in which you play the short odds with every roll, and over the course of 162 games, you come out ahead.

Earl and Billy went head-to-head the night after Texas's hiccup-y flight back from Boston, and Weaver came out on top, 9–8, in an atypical Oriole win. "Yeah, yeah, I know. Pitching and defense is what wins," Weaver said afterward, "But somewhere along the way, you also have to hit the goddamn baseball, and that was what we hadn't been doing. I ordered extra batting practice, and that didn't work, so we began avoiding batting practice altogether, and that didn't work, either. But maybe we're starting to come around." (Earl was right, as usual. His Orioles, stuck in last place for most of the first two and a half months of the 1975 season, would eventually win 90 games.)

In the other clubhouse, Billy Martin was not particularly concerned by the latest loss. Billy was preoccupied about an impending player transaction, and a significant one at that. His owner, Brad

Corbett, was eager at work playing puppet-master, the ego-driven practice that compelled men such as he to own baseball teams. Brad, a New Yorker who'd found his fortune in Texas where he manufactured plastic drilling pipe, was a large, round man who loved fine wine, fine cigars, and fine food. He loved his private jet, and he loved getting drunk and making midnight player transactions. He loved life about as much as any person I'd ever seen.

Corbett had been on the line to his Southern California counterpart, Gene Autry. Since it had become apparent that the 1975 Angels were dungeon-bound, what, Corbett had inquired, would be required to send Nolan Ryan over to the Rangers. Autry told Corbett that any trade for Nolan Ryan would have to include Corbett's red hot and ever-so charming Scandinavian trophy wife. Corbett had anguished over the decision, then chickened out and called Cleveland.

June 14

Burt Hawkins, the Rangers' traveling secretary and media liaison man, called me at home and said I needed to get my "hippie ass" out to the ballpark for a 2 P.M. press conference. I resented that. I had a 1970s look all right, but I was damn sure no hippie. Usually I wore a Mexican wedding shirt with cheerful embroidery on the collars and cuffs, and Mexican straw sandals, huarachas, that were comfortable. Hell, if somebody had handed me a guitar, I'd have strolled over to your table and sung "Guadalajara."

I knew the purpose of the press conference was to announce a big trade. I also knew that Gaylord Perry, the old grease-baller himself, was coming to Texas. What I did not know was what the Rangers would give up in return. As it turned out, two members of Billy Martin's strange six-man rotation, Jim Bibby and Jackie

Brown, would be going to the Indians. The Bibby part of the deal bothered me. He was my best friend on the team. Bibby had a fastball that nobody could hit, but Art Fowler, the pitching coach, had screwed him up, stressing changing speeds and pitch placement and throwing the ball American League pussy-style.

So big Jim accepted his fate with a philosophical "business is business" attitude. Brown, an Oklahoman who liked living close to home, took the news of the trade a little more personally, realizing that a posting in Cleveland was the equivalent to an assignment to the Alcatraz of baseball. "I'm stunned," was all that Brown said.

The deal also included a minor league prospect, Rick Waits, along with $100,000, which Corbett forwarded to Cleveland after selling the newly acquired Ed Brinkman to the Yankees for that exact sum.

Billy Martin seemed ecstatic. "This puts us back in the pennant race," he said. "Gaylord is thirty-six, but he's a young thirty-six. He stays in shape and has good personal habits."

Perhaps that was the case. But what little hair that was left on Perry's craggy cranium was turning gray, and he looked older than most trees. "I'd been hearing stuff about a trade for weeks," the pitcher said. "Everybody had. Some of those rookie kids over there [at Cleveland] would see me in the clubhouse and say, 'You're still around, old man?'"

Perry stopped just short of saying that the news of the trade was the best news he had gotten in his entire life, but the reason had more to do with simply being able to evacuate second division baseball's most loyal tenant. I think old Gaylord was just relieved that he didn't have to wear those all-red Indians uniforms in which the most fitting fashion accessory would have been an orange wig and juggling balls.

In baseball, just as it always seemed that after a fielder made a great play to end an inning, he led off the next one at the plate, a player involved in a big trade made his debut in the new uniform against the team that had just traded him. So naturally, the Indians had come to Arlington as Perry joined the Rangers.

Cleveland Manager Frank Robinson refused to openly concede that he and Perry had not gotten along. "If there had been any friction between us, then why would we have waited so long to trade him?" Robinson wanted to know. "We parted on friendly terms."

Bob Sudyk, a Cleveland newspaper guy who had ghostwritten Perry's autobiography *Me and the Spitter*, asked Robinson what he'd said to Perry when the trade came down. "Actually, we have not spoken since the trade. The only factor in the trade was that this year, on the mound, Gaylord was not pitching like Gaylord had pitched in the past."

With the Perry deal complete and the Great Lubricator officially a Lone Star resident, the mood at Arlington Stadium's postgame party room took on an air of genuine festivity. The room was always open to key Rangers' front office people, media, the owner and his guests, but also wives, mistresses, and children. Billy Martin, energized with optimism that the season of '75 might not be a lost one after all, stood laughing at the bar. I hadn't seen him so happy since spring training. His wife, Gretchen, was there, too, along with Martin's son, little Billy Joe, who was grade-school-aged. Gretchen was not the type of woman that one would expect to be married to a man with the innate hell-raising proclivities of Nightlife Billy. Mrs. Martin was no Milkshake Mademoiselle. Rather, Gretchen came across as demure, educated, and serenely self-possessed.

Billy Joe, on the other hand, was clearly an apple very close to the tree. While the grown-ups enjoyed their cocktails in the clubroom, Billy Joe and a couple of other kids, including Brad Corbett

Jr., played baseball, swatting a Nerf ball. Billy's kid decided that a table full of Big Brad's corporate fat cats should be the plate. So Billy Joe decided to steal home, just like his father had taught him to do. He took a running start and slid headfirst—knocking over the table and sending drinks flying and fat cats sprawling.

June 15

The Rangers were the only team in the majors that played Sunday home games at night, for the obvious reason that as summer approached, in the afternoon you could bake gingerbread on second base at Arlington Stadium. A much larger than usual Sunday night crowd, over 27,000, came to watch the famously controversial Gaylord Perry make his first start for Texas. Cleveland hit him hard, and Texas lost. Maybe, in his haste to get the hell out of Cleveland, Perry had forgotten to pack his petroleum jelly.

Dennis Eckersley started for the Indians and got the win. "We wanted to beat Gaylord bad, and now that we have done it, it's kind of sad."

From Perry's viewpoint, the loss did not equate to the end of the world. "That kid [referring to Dennis Eckersley] is going to be a pretty good pitcher one of these days," he said. Perry, who obviously recognized talent, was tactful enough not to add, "Of course, he'll have to get his ass out of Cleveland to accomplish that."

June 19

Texas rallied to beat the White Sox and Goose Gossage to complete an eventful home stand. Afterward, Joe Macko's equipment boys in the clubhouse were furiously at work loading suitcases, duffel bags, balls, bats, gloves, training room necessities, and all the rest of the supplies for the major league baseball arsenal onto a truck for delivery at the airport. The behind-the-scenes mechanisms necessary to move a team from city to city involved a to-do list that was longer than the auto supply listings in the Detroit yellow pages. The logistical challenge of getaway day rivaled the one that the roustabouts faced when the circus left town.

Less than an hour later, the players and the rest of the Rangers' traveling troupe boarded a late night commercial flight to LAX that preceded the long bus ride down to Anaheim, where a series against the Angels awaited the team. The plane was a Delta 747, and the flight had originated in Atlanta. Because of a reservations snafu, one of the Atlanta passengers had a first-class ticket for the whole trip to California, and now he made a stink about giving up his seat. He was a Coca-Cola executive. Burt Hawkins, the team's traveling secretary, said "to hell with it," and the guy was allowed to ride up front. I sat next to him. The baseball people fascinated the executive traveler, and he asked me all sorts of questions about the details of my job. He was friendly as hell.

Two hours into the flight, with a full glass of scotch on the tray table in front of me, I nodded off. Then I was bounced awake when the plane hit an air pocket, and was alarmed to see the glass coming off the tray. There was only one thing to do, and in an amazing display of dexterity, I swatted the glass over into the Coca-Cola man's lap. The humor of the moment totally escaped him. Ordinarily, I might have felt some chagrin. But hell. He wasn't supposed to have been sitting there in the first place.

June 20

Bam! Bam! Bam! Eight o'clock on an Orange County morning and a member of the Texas press corps was at my hotel room door.

He was getting ready to go kill most of the day at Disneyland and wanted to know if I had any dope. Ha! About a week earlier, one of my spiritual advisors from Texas had supplied me with a killer joint, and he'd told me to use it only for a special occasion, and to share it with somebody unsuspecting as a practical joke. This was Sumatran temple dope, strong enough to cripple a baboon.

So we fired the thing up, and I watched with a modest degree of alarm as my media friend's mental capacities vanished completely. I wasn't doing all that great, either, and had lost the use of both my hands. It was all I could do to punch the down button on the elevator. I followed my crazed companion as he reeled into the coffee shop, filled with happy families from places like Keokuk, Kankakee, Kokomo, and Kalamazoo, eager to visit the park, ride the rides, and have their photos taken with Mickey Mouse and Donald. Boy, were they surprised when Goofy barged in.

The Texas journalist moved from booth to booth, demanding, "Hey, man. Can I borrow your car?" While he was putting on his bizarre performance, I stuck my tongue out, in a salacious manner, at a pretty girl working the cash register. She laughed, and I did the same. Such was life on the road with a baseball team in 1975.

That night at the stadium sometimes known as the Big A, the Rangers staked Gaylord Perry to a 6–0 lead, and from what happened after that, it would not have been unreasonable to suspect the Rangers were passing around some of that mind-warping smoke in the dugout.

If there was ever a team in 1970s baseball that would have benefited from the use of steroids, it would have been those '75 Angels. By the end of the season, one player would reach double digits in the home run column, and the entire team would hit only 55 balls over the fence. You could tell the Angels had no power just by looking at them. Most of the players in the lineup looked anorexic. They really could have used a player like Fred Lynn, who that week had knocked in 10 runs in a game against the Detroit Tigers, with three homers, a triple, and a single. His 16 total bases tied an American League record held by Ty Cobb, Lou Gehrig, and Rocky Colavito. "Ten RBIs! That's a month's work," Lynn said, and for the Angels, it would have been.

And yet—those Angels had enough offensive muscle to over-come the six-run deficit—and after the Rangers scored three runs in the top of the 11th inning, California scored four of its own runs in the bottom portion of the inning to win the game.

Billy Martin was devastated after the game, and described the outcome as the most frustrating loss of the season, if not his entire career. Martin seemed to be unraveling. So was his team. Rangers batters were hamstrung and helpless the next afternoon against the Angels' Frank Tanana. By the time he was through with Texas, Tanana had struck out 17 Rangers, a league record for a left-handed pitcher. He had that many by the eighth inning, and was gunning for the major league record going into the ninth. So here were the Rangers, with an oppor-tunity to participate in a game that might be remembered in the annals forever, and they blew it. Lenny Randle, Leo Cardenas, and Roy Smalley came to the plate and instead of whiffing like they should have, the same way they'd been doing all day, two of them flied out to short right and the last guy grounded out to third.

At least that *Sports Illustrated* cover jinx that afflicted Billy Mar-tin had worked to benefit the Rangers as well. Nolan Ryan had made the cover issue after Martin appeared, lost his next three games and missed his scheduled start against Texas with a pulled groin muscle.

After a day game in Anaheim, I accompanied a small group who drove up to L.A.'s Palomino bar to watch a performance by singer-songwriter Doug Sahm, one of my heroes in the so-called progressive country movement that was my favorite music genre in the mid-1970s. During the course of the evening, I sat for a while next to some deep-voiced dude with a beard.

On the ride back, somebody asked me, "So, what all did Waylon have to say?"

"What in the hell are you talking about?"

"Waylon Jennings, you asshole. You were sitting right next to him."

The next day, in the visitors clubhouse at the Big A, Jim Spencer, the first baseman, gave me double fistfuls of crap. "So how fucked up could you have been?" he laughed. "Sitting there in a nightclub next to your idol—and not even know it." Spencer really cracked up over that one.

(Enter, *Twilight Zone* theme tune. In February 2002 I picked up the morning paper and read that Waylon Jennings had died. Then I turned to the sports section, and at the bottom of page 2, saw a story that said that in Florida, former major league infielder Jim Spencer had died suddenly of a heart attack.)

June 24

After Texas had stunk up the California coastline, the team climbed onto yet another wee-hours flight halfway across the United States. It was 8 A.M. Chicago time when the players got off the bus from O'Hare at the Executive House hotel. In a few short hours, they were back on the field at White Sox Park. They dragged around like the cast from *Night of the Living Dead*, and lost the game, 7–5.

"I didn't feel tired at all," first baseman Mike Hargrove said. "I felt numb."

Uncharacteristically, the manager issued the team a pardon for its uninspired effort. "They were out on their feet," Martin declared. "Call it an alibi, call it an excuse, call it what you want. But the schedule cost us the game tonight. I'd like to get my hands on the guy who devised that. It's inexcusable."

Yeah, but it was the same scheduling outrage that every other team in baseball would confront on multiple occasions in that or any other season. More than the ability to throw strikes or hit split-finger sliders, the key to longevity in the big leagues was the capacity and the will to endure the relentless agenda of migrating through airports and hotels for six exhausting months.

After the game, I drank a couple of vesper cocktails with Steve Hargan, the pitcher. The hand that held his drink seemed to be slightly unsteady. Alcohol fatigue?

"Nah," said Hargan. "It's not the drinking that's getting to me. It's the tab."

Times were tough, and the Rush Street bars seemed a little less like "that toddlin' town" of song fame. Chicago was mourning the passing that week of one of its most treasured citizens, Sam Giancana.

The Washington columnist Art Buchwald wrote that, "Sam died quietly in his sleep, after being shot one time in the mouth and five times in the neck." Buchwald claimed to have attended a wake held in Sam's honor at the Cloak and Dagger Bar and Grill that was attended by some of his old CIA companions who'd employed Giancana to murder Fidel Castro. Buchwald quoted one of the CIA men: "One thing about Sam, no matter what we asked, he never demanded anything in return. Oh, once in a while he might ask us to have the Justice Department drop an indictment or he might ask us to have the FBI lay off him. But outside of that he considered it an honor to serve his country."

June 27

James Walker, who covered the Rangers for the *Dallas Times Herald*, wrote a story in which he contended that Jeff Burroughs, the league MVP from 1974, had been dogging it in right field. He'd written the piece to impress his boss by stirring up some controversy. The story was completely unfair to Burroughs.

Billy Martin had hot lava squirting out of his ears when he'd read the piece and promptly banned Walker from the clubhouse. Burroughs, naturally, wasn't pleased, either.

"If it makes you feel any better," I said to Jeff, "Martin called Walker a double cunt."

"A *double* cunt?" said Burroughs. "God. That's awful. One's bad enough."

Around the league, baseball writer abuse had become the American pastime.

According to a wire service report, Detroit manager Ralph Houk had gotten angry with a writer from the *Baltimore Sun* and "dragged him out of the clubhouse while his players cheered." The writer, Phil Hersh, then took the extreme step of filing criminal assault charges against Houk. Later, Houk sent the writer a letter of apology. "I was very upset about your story," the letter said, "but I admit this did not justify the physical measures which I used to eject you from the clubhouse." Hersh quickly dropped the charges, but added that, "No working journalist should be submitted to that kind of treatment." I started to write Phil Hersh a letter that read, "Shit, at least

Houk didn't have some Puerto Rican prostitute come and kiss you on the mouth, with a photographer standing by, in case he needed to blackmail your ass at some point *like some managers I know.*"

On a later trip to Detroit, Houk did not seem all that apologetic over the episode. He told me and some others his version of what took place. "I tried to kick the guy in the ass, but I was wearing my spikes, slipped on the concrete floor, and damn near fell on my ass," Houk said. "It was like some scene from the Keystone Kops. And the players weren't cheering, either. They were laughing at me."

June 28

On the flight from Chicago back to Texas, the players, fresh from losing three games to the woeful White Sox, seemed even drunker than usual. Every baseball team that was traveling that day probably shared the condition.

An Eastern Airlines jet had crashed in New York while trying to land at Kennedy Airport. Nets forward Wendell Ladner was among the hundred-plus dead. That was the kind of news that scared pro athletes stiff. Red Sox pitcher Bill Lee, whose team was in a little slump, said, "The way our luck is going, our plane will crash, and everybody will live."

An amazing number of them were absolutely terrified of flying. One of them was Cesar Tovar, who sat next to me on the two-and-a-half-hour ride back to DFW. I tried to take a nap, and Tovar slapped me across the face and said, "You no sleep! We talk!" So we talked, the sole topic being the women in Tovar's life. When it came to girls, Tovar preferred the full-figured variety, and he expressed a particular fondness for one of his old friends who, in the player's own words, had "an ass like a washing machine."

June 29

In the steaming summer of 1975, most of the teams in both the major leagues had sailed into the midseason doldrums. The San Francisco Giants had lost five straight games, and Wes Westrum, the manager, said, "We're not in a rut. We're in the Grand Canyon."

On the other side of the continent, people in New England were bummed as well. Baseball's best human interest story, the comeback try by Tony Conigliaro, had taken a downward turn. Tony had been nearly blinded when hit with a pitch in 1967, and as his vision had deteriorated, he'd quit the game in 1971. In 1975, Tony was back with the Red Sox, attempting to make it as a designated hitter, with a big league contract worth $70,000— generous for the time. But Boston GM Dick O'Connell was giving up, and shipped Conigliaro to the team's AAA farm in Pawtucket. Tony wasn't happy. "It's a strange feeling that I am starting all over again," he said.

The only team in the big leagues with much traction going at all was Sparky Anderson's Big Red Cincinnati Machine, and guess who else? Charlie Finley's Garish Green and Gold Machine in Oakland. The A's had been making me break a preseason prom- ise to my readers. Their gravy train was going to jump the tracks, remember? Now, as the All-Star break lay just ahead, the A's had been enjoying life without Catfish Hunter. As usual, they rode in a hot air balloon, and gazed down upon the groveling assembly of baseball's proletariat arrayed beneath them. Kansas City was closest at five and a half games back, and rumors were floating that Royals owner Ewing Kauffman was about to get rid of the manager, Jack McKeon. Kauffman was in Charlie Finley's league when it came to colorfully eccentric behavior. But one story about him was *not* true, that being the canard that Kauffman had married his maid, presumably so that he could get his ashes hauled.

Every other team in the AL West, as the halfway point of the 1975 season approached, was cooked, and in Texas, Chicago, Minnesota, and California, the fans could smell the burnt smoke from the ovens. But things were going so well in Oakland that backup Ray Fosse, the man who'd immortalized himself by getting knocked on his hindquarters by Pete Rose in that 1971 All-Star Game, got a key hit that helped the A's beat the Twins for their 11th win in 12 games. Fosse was only hitting .047 at the time. He said he wanted more playing time. "But the only way that's going to happen is if Gene Tenace gets hurt or something, and I wouldn't want to see that happen...necessarily."

That was one element about Charlie Finley's menagerie that made them so oddly functional. Players could tell the truth and get away with it.

Chapter 9

July 2

Journalism's most demanding job, and I had it, was covering a major league baseball season wire-to-wire. The work was tantamount to writing a soap opera with 162 subplots, using a cumbersome all-male cast. Eventually the grind compels the brain circuits to play some mean-spirited practical jokes.

I sat in the Arlington Stadium press box, surrounded by the sights and sounds of the American game, but feeling isolated and alone. Then, out beyond the big scoreboard atop the left field stands, in the shimmering darkness of the summertime Texas sky, a vision appeared—the Gates of Heaven, which represented the end of the regular season. Ah—but that was merely a mirage, a false and fleeting illusion. The tormenting truth was that the finish line lay concealed in the haze, lingered three months off in the distance, and I was completely out of words to describe the events on the field.

Also, a problem had occurred at the newspaper that employed me to do this life-risking assignment. A girl who worked the switchboard had asked me to fix her up with a baseball player, and I'd told her that she would need to successfully complete a diet program before that would occur, unless she was interested in Cesar Tovar. As a result, not only was she no longer speaking to me, whenever I phoned into the paper to transmit a story, she transferred the call to the want ad section.

The team that was the object of my daily chronicle had been stacking up a substantial inventory in the loss column, and still had picked up two places in the American League West standings. The Rangers were riding a treadmill of desperation. Billy Martin had been behaving like, as they say, a saber-tooth tiger with hemorrhoids, and his personality was becoming infectious with the players in his dugout.

Texas's game against Kansas City had entered extra innings, and the body language of the men in the white home uniforms suggested that they were about to lose. I stroked the keys of my faithful and mercilessly overworked Smith-Corona portable typewriter, wondering what to say, and bewildered by the notion that about a quarter of a million ravenous-for-baseball-insight subscribers might read the twisted narrative that I was poised to prepare. What the writer needed was inspiration, motivation. Fortunately, plenty of that was available in the little emergency room that adjoined the press box, and so the writer went and got some. A sixteen-ounce cup of Jose Cuervo, on the rocks.

Jose gave me a damn good pep talk. "Hey, amigo," he said with a thick Spanish accent. "Qu-e-e-t feeling sorry for yourself. If B-e-e-e-l-y give you any sh-e-e-e-t, you tell B-e-e-e-ly to k-e-e-e-s your ass."

"Thanks Jose, I'll remember that," I said, and went back for a refill. Then I returned to the typewriter and went to work, setting the scene.

John Mayberry, foster parent of three home runs from the night before, knelt in the on-deck circle in a tie game. If Alfred

146

Hitchcock had been directing, he would have had Mayberry decked out in a black hood, and carrying an axe. With Mike Kekich on the mound, Billy Martin hastily directed a summit conference that was also attended by a catcher and three in-fielders. Later, Mayberry would say that he didn't care about the nature of the discussion. "My only thought was to get the fat part of the bat on the ball." The part of Mayberry's bat turned out to be so fat that the ball landed in the center field seats, about 420 feet from home plate.

There. That wasn't so bad, after all. Besides, baseball writers throughout the big leagues were experiencing worse grief than mine, for various reasons. One writer from a Midwestern city that I'll call Chicago had experienced an evening of romance with a woman he'd met in a dark restaurant. "Next morning, she was in the bathroom and naturally, I went through her purse," the jour-nalist confided. "I looked at her driver's license. She was seventy-two years old! I haven't been able to get it stiff since."

Yet another writer, also from a Midwestern city, was experi-encing some domestic stress. "I got home about 6 A.M. I'd been to a cockfight and was covered with mud and shit. My wife was sitting on the sofa," said the writer. "She'd gone into labor and was sobbing. 'You've ruined my life!' Then I pulled a wad of fifty- and twenty-dollar bills out of my pocket that I'd won the night before, threw that down on the coffee table, and she wiped aside her tears and said, 'How much did we win, honey?'"

Oh, and in the Southern California city that I will call Los Angeles, a sports columnist was driving late, accompanied by a woman. The writer had enough alcohol churning through his bloodstream to anesthetize an entire company of Marines. A cop in a patrol car noticed that the columnist's vehicle was following the pattern of a seismograph needle when the Big One hit, and pulled the driver over. When the writer presented his driver's license, he was presented with a once-in-a-lifetime, God-given gift-wrapped miracle. The cop told the writer that he was a fan of his work, and let him drive on with the admonition to be careful the rest of the way. The columnist, as he drove off, turned to his woman companion and said, "Ha! Did you see that cop kiss my ass? In case you didn't know it, I'm *somebody* in this goddamn town. Now, where'd you say you live, baby?" The columnist was too gassed to realize that the woman with him in the car was actually his wife. "So she belted me," he told colleagues afterward, "and I drove into a telephone pole."

In the face of events like that, the stories of heroism and sacrifice performed by my brothers in the sportswriting battlefields of America, there was no place whatsoever for self-pity in my agenda, complicated as it was. Hell, I'd just received a card that entitled me to free meals at certain Dallas–Fort Worth Dairy Queen outlets, because of my distinguished citizen status as a postgame guest on the Texas Rangers radio network. An editor at my paper instructed me not to accept the largesse of the fast food people, pointing out a potential "conflict of interest."

"Yes. Of course. I understand," I told the editior, but, since the words "dairy" and "queen" seldom appeared in my baseball stories and never in tandem, I continued to take advantage of the card at least two times each day. So Blizzard cups had replaced empty beer cans on the floorboard of my Olds Cutlass. If only we could have realized how good life was in the 1970s. The women were never prettier, the young ones, at least. They all wanted to look like a folksinger, and wore their hair straight and long, all the way down to their butts, and parted in the middle. The music was good—lyrics and melody mattered back then—and so was the food. They put gravy on everything.

July 3

The All-Star balloting was about finished. The leaders in the American League consisted of all the usual suspects. Catcher—Thurman Munson, New York. First base—Gene Tenace, Oakland. Second base—Rod Carew, Minnesota. Shortstop—Bert Campaneris, Oakland. Third base—Graig Nettles, New York. Outfield—Reggie Jackson, Oakland; Joe Rudi, Oakland; Bobby Bonds, New York.

Over in the National League, Danny Ozark, one of the players who was on the field for the Fort Worth Cats on the night of Maury Wills's Texas League debut, delivered the quote of the week. Ozark was managing the Philadelphia Phillies, who had been blown off the field by St. Louis Cardinals relief pitcher Al Hrabosky. They called Hrabosky the Mad Hungarian because you couldn't see his face for all of his whiskers and hair, and he stomped around on the mound like some crazy son of a bitch the mad scientist had kept locked in the cellar. In 1975, Al Hrabosky was the most colorful player in baseball.

A writer asked Ozark if he thought that Hrabosky threw harder than anybody else in the National League. "No," said Ozark. "Two other pitchers throw harder than Hrabosky. Tom Seaver and what's-his-name."

The identity of what's-his-name was never determined, but it probably was not Charlie Hough of the Dodgers, who threw a knuckleball. Charlie had made the headlines for instigating a rumble. After San Diego pulled a suicide squeeze against L.A. in a game in which the Padres were leading, 9–1, Hough took umbrage and plunked Dave Winfield on the shoulder with his next pitch.

"Why not?" reasoned Walter Alston. "Our team hadn't been playing well, and maybe a brawl might spur them on, and make 'em a better ball club."

I never understood that kind of logic. Alston might as well have said, "My wife hit me over the head with an iron skillet, so maybe that will make me a better husband." If the fight did anything to improve the Dodgers, it would have to be without the services of their catcher, Joe Ferguson, who broke a hand while attempting to restrain Winfield and as a result was headed for a two-month vacation on the disabled list.

As for the Rangers, I decided to take a bold but necessary stand. Keeping this team on life support, when the outlook was hopeless, had become an exercise in futility. The time had arrived to pull the plug, and get it over and done. Ali, the ruler of the boxing kingdom, after he'd beaten Joe Bugner, said that Howard Cosell was very popular among black people because "blacks like to see white guys make an ass of themselves." So I decided to swill down four containers of Mexican Courage, imitate Howard Cosell, and Tell It Like It Was.

This was what I told my readers:

Ferguson Jenkins still manages to win one every now and then. But Gaylord Perry, the new acquisition brought in amid desperate circumstances after Billy Martin's six-man rotation turned out to be a bust, clearly isn't going to cut it because he is twenty-five-pounds overweight.

With the pitching in total disarray and team morale at an all-time low, it appears obvious that last place is beckoning. It is only a matter of time.

Whatever happened to those happy lies that I'd manufactured back during spring training?

July 4

Despite the propaganda that was being cooked up in the most promising young growth industry that America had to offer in the 1970s—drug and alcohol counseling—drunks were like snowflakes. No two were exactly alike.

I'd just read a biography of English novelist Malcolm Lowry, who'd gotten so messed up one night that he'd fallen off a footbridge and into a sewage canal. And that had been on one of his good nights. Later, when Lowry was found dead, they couldn't figure out exactly whether he'd killed himself either accidentally or on purpose, or whether his old lady had done him in, so the coroner ruled his passing "death by misadventure." What a stud! And it turned out that Lowry wasn't alcoholic really. He was orally fixated, a condition that people get when their breast-feeding is prematurely terminated.

Why, that was me as well. The news came as a relief. In the press lounge at Arlington, I had been so gripped with my oral fixation that by the time I got home, I decided to take a nap on the hood of my car. I'd been experiencing some pretty tough back problems, the hood felt warm and firm, not like those cheap-ass mattresses, stuffed with cotton seed, that I'd been forced to sleep on in the American League hotels. The hood was so comfortable that I fell into a sound sleep and didn't awaken until nine o'clock the next morning. A man who had moved into the house next door the very day before was giving me some hard stares from a face etched with curiosity, concern, and buyer's remorse.

So here I was on Independence Day. In three hours, I was supposed to be at Metropolitan Stadium in Bloomington, Minnesota, for a doubleheader and did not have the slightest idea how I was going to get there. But I was resourceful as all get-out in those days. By mid-afternoon, carrying a suitcase, a typewriter, and the portable mojo wire, I was pushing my way through the crowd of Minnesotans congregated beneath the stands after the first game of the double-dip. This stadium was the home of the football Vikings, and the Twins had taken on the role of the off-season tenants who provided the concessionaires with year-round occupational activity. So a big crowd for baseball was a novelty that I hadn't expected. The people milling about the stadium between games seemed restless. Unlike the atmosphere at a Vikings game, it was not cold enough to drink out of a flask, and quite a few of the Twins fans appeared almost self-conscious as they did so.

I entered the Rangers' clubhouse, and embarked upon one of the toughest tasks that a sportswriter can face: asking professional athletes questions over details of a game that I not only hadn't seen, but had no idea who had done what, or which team had won or lost. But I was experienced at this, and good at it. Just avoid specifics and ask general questions...questions like "How does this game affect the team's pennant chances?" and "How's the family?"

Eventually, I worked my way up to the press box, and obtained a box score for the opener. What I saw filled my heart with joy. A Chevrolet TV commercial had been blasting the airways, and I had become sick of the thing. It was more obnoxious than "Jingle Bells." So the star player in the Fourth of July Minnesota stadium celebration offered an opportunity for retribution.

I sat down at the typewriter and wrote:

It was a festive holiday at the ballpark, featuring baseball, hot dogs, apple pie, and Ford. That was Dan Ford, a Minnesota Twins rookie who put on a power-hitting display that overshadowed the postgame fireworks.

After the nightcap of what had turned out to be a long and exhausting day, I treated myself to a visit to that downtown Minneapolis massage parlor, where the customer came first.

July 6

One of baseball's more charming myths involved Gaylord Perry. Perry, pitching in his second big league season with the San Francisco Giants in 1963, commenting upon his own futility as a hitter, said: "There will be a man walking on the moon before I ever hit a big league home run."

So...on a July night in 1969, only minutes after Neil Armstrong had emerged from his landing craft and stepped upon the lunar surface...Perry connected for his first career homer.

That was a wonderful story, except that Perry never made the remark in the first place.

Perry was also the object of another myth: That he did not throw a spitball. Baseball's anti-conspiracy theorists kept insisting that Perry was always tugging on his hat bill and licking his fingertips to *create* the impression that he was loading up the ball with some moisturizing agent. That routine made the batters nervous enough, or agitated enough, to lose a measure of concentration, thus playing into Gaylord's very large hands.

After the second game of a doubleheader, the second in three days at Metropolitan Stadium, Twins manager Frank Quilici was not among the anti-conspiracy people. Perry finally won a game in a Texas uniform, a 7–0 whitewash, and Quilici was furious. Frank had been edgy already—his team was sliding inexorably into an abyss, experiencing the torture of losing game after game by a run or two, and Quilici knew that his job status was teetering on the ledge.

On June 1, Quilici's team had been three games over .500, and after the bad day against Perry, they'd slipped to seven under, and he figured this game might have pushed his team's confidence beneath the diesel truck that the big league grind becomes when matters begin to go badly. His fears were not without substance. Quilici would be fired at the end of the 1975 season, his career as a big league manager finished.

"If we lose, I want it to be fair and square, and anybody could see that wasn't the case against Gaylord. Listen, when players like Rod Carew and Tony Oliva come back to the dugout, complaining about doctored pitches that jump around in every direction, you know something is wrong. Carew and Oliva do not make excuses! They do not make this stuff up! So what do the umpires do about that? Well, you saw it. They didn't do a damn thing!"

Billy Martin was benignly disingenuous in his postgame address. This was the same Billy Martin who, just two seasons earlier in Detroit, had ordered one of his pitchers, Joe Coleman, to throw a spitter at Gaylord and the Indians, in protest of what he had termed blatant and open cheating. Now Martin, in a state of obvious relief after Perry had finally won a game for Texas, said that Gaylord was sharp again after working with pitching coach Art Fowler to correct some mechanical flaws. Here was what probably had actually happened. Since arriving in Texas after the trade that sent Jim Bibby and Jackie Brown to Cleveland, Gaylord decided to experiment with a new pitch: the dry ball. If he had received any expert advice from Art Fowler, then Billy's most trusted lieutenant, he had simply instructed Perry to get back to the basics.

July 7

The Rangers had flown from Minnesota to New York and arrived at the Essex House hotel well after midnight. Among the plusses that came with traveling with a big league team—and there were few, other than free whiskey—was that players and support staff (such as media) never had to jack with luggage. On getaway day, have the bellhop carry your stuff to the hotel lobby. Then, upon arriving at the next city, the traveling party would find a room key awaiting at the lobby desk, and inside the room, the luggage was already there.

As I stumbled into my Essex House accommodation, my thought processes were profoundly befogged, as usual, but not to the extent that I didn't notice something amiss. There was a guy already in the room, snoring away. The hotel staff had assigned me the wrong room.

So I did what any normal person would have done under the circumstances. I climbed up on a chair, leaped on the mattress, bounced up and down, and yelled, "Who's this sleeping in my goddamn bed!"

The poor bastard came awake, and seemed startled. "Holy shit! What is this? You get your fucking ass out of here!" The look on his face was the personal highlight of my entire 1975 season. I'd never felt better about myself in my life. Following the hotel guest's suggestion, I departed quietly. The hotel manager awaited me in the lobby. The man upstairs had already called down to complain about a madman inside his room.

"Sir, my name is Craig Stretch [that was how he pronounced it, anyway], and we'll have your room ready in another few minutes, and I wish to apologize, and in the morning, we'd like to offer you a complimentary breakfast," he said, appearing fearful. My impression was that deep inside his chilly hotel manager's heart, he did not feel apologetic at all.

"Breakfast, my ass. The bar is still open, ain't it?"

Craig Stretch nodded. He didn't like me worth a damn, and under his breath, as he turned briskly and walked off, I heard him whisper to himself: "Texan."

I wondered how he knew. Must have been my accent.

July 8

Billy Martin's Rangers were heavily involved in a simmering pennant race as the All-Star break approached. That was the one that seemed to be developing in the American League East between the Yankees and the Red Sox. Texas's only real participation in that competition had been a heavy contribution to the New York cause. Doc Medich had beaten Texas in the opener of a three-game series at Shea Stadium, and Catfish Hunter had shut out Texas in the second installment.

So the Yankees' presence in the chase for first place had been entirely through the courtesy of the Rangers, who had lost eight of nine games to New York. Still, the Yanks were having difficulty keeping pace with their New England rivals. The Red Sox had beaten the Twins (Minnesota had dropped 10 games under .500 by then) on a home run by Bernie Carbo.

Carbo, like the overwhelming majority of baseball players of 1975, was not getting rich, but nobody participated in the game for the sheer enjoyment of it more than Bernie. His home run had cleared Fenway Park's Green Monster left field wall by mere inches, and Carbo admitted, "That ball I hit would have been a home run in no other ballpark in baseball but Fenway Park. But it was a homer here and I am proud as hell.

"We're winning. We are in first place, the fans are in hog heaven, and I haven't got a care in the world."

They don't make 'em like Bernie Carbo anymore.

July 13

Bernie and his brethren had enjoyed a four-course meal over the weekend at Fenway Park, each one prepared and served at the table by Texas Rangers pitchers. During a four-game series in Boston, Rangers pitchers yielded an average of nine runs a game, and lost all four.

Gaylord Perry had experienced some more difficulty with his "mechanics," and Boston had won the first game, 8–7. Billy Martin did not know, but Perry's outing would be the strongest showing by any Rangers pitcher through the series.

Billy complained about his pitchers, while Billy's pitchers complained about him. "He bitches about us, rips us behind our backs," Clyde Wright said with a sigh. "How does Billy know? He's always pickled by the fifth inning."

Fans can always tell for sure that their team had turned to pig shit when, in the local papers, the word "merciful" appears just before "All-Star break."

The Rangers boarded their charter flight back to Dallas fresh from losing seven out of eight games amid the big media exposure that came with trips into the mysterious East. Now their record was 41-49, the team was gasping at 15½ games out of first place, and life with Billy would be at its turbulent worst for the remainder of the campaign. Billy didn't accompany the team back home. Instead, he traveled directly to Milwaukee for the All-Star Game where he had been appointed as a coach for the American League. Martin would be meeting Mickey Mantle—listed as "honorary captain" of the AL—so the reunion of the Moonshine Boys would fortify the till in half the bars in Wisconsin.

The All-Star game demanded the focus of the baseball writers. Fans in Cincinnati were furious at Dodgers manager Walter Alston. The man who managed the National League team, upon announcing the pitchers he had selected, listed the names of three of his own (Don Sutton, Andy Messersmith, and Mike Marshall) and none of the Reds'. Cincinnati's Jack Billingham entered the All-Star break with a 10-3 record, and the Reds' followers were certain that he had gotten screwed. Billingham told reporters that it was not for him to say whether he deserved All-Star recognition, but he did question the presence of Marshall.

"The reason that Alston picked him was that if he didn't, then Marshall would start to cry and not pitch again all year," Billingham said.

The All-Star break was a three-day respite not only for the Rangers, but for me as well. I relaxed at home in Fort Worth, and in my paper, the *Star-Telegram,* read that the All-Star Game had been called off because of a bomb threat.

There was a local Little League all-star game, for eight- and nine-year-old boys, scheduled at Fort Worth's Cobb Park. Like the Cincinnati fans and the major league All-Star Game, somebody was upset by the Little League rosters, called the commissioner of the league, and said he was going to blow up the baseball field.

The story about that incident listed the name of the manager who'd stacked the Little League roster with his own kids. So the would-be bomber probably had a just cause.

July 15

Lou Brock of St. Louis was the only position player among National League starters who did not wear the uniform of the twin powerhouses that ruled the NL in 1975. The remainder of the lineup consisted of four Reds—Johnny Bench, Joe Morgan, Dave Concepcion, and Pete Rose—and three Dodgers—Ron Cey, Jimmy Wynn, and Steve Garvey.

Perhaps the most notable facet of the Milwaukee extravaganza took place in the pregame ceremonies. The man honored to throw out the opening pitch was United States Secretary of State Henry Kissinger. Ironic, isn't it, that a man who would later be described as "the real life model for Dr. Strangelove" had been selected as the ceremonial icon for the Great American Game?

The National League won the game, just as it always did. Three runs in the top of the ninth provided the margin in the NL's 6–3 ho-hum victory. All of the last-inning runs were scored at the expense of a couple of guys like Catfish and Goose. Perhaps American League manager Alvin Dark should have known to select a couple of pitchers from the baseball page instead of two refugees from the outdoor section.

Milwaukee's midyear baseball convention did have some histrionics. Those took place away from the field. The centerpiece item on the agenda of the annual owners meeting had been whether to extend the contract of Bowie Kuhn as commissioner of the game. Kuhn was in trouble. Major league baseball revenues were stagnant even at the top-echelon franchises. The owners needed an idea man. The free agent New World was bearing down on the sport like an eighteen-wheel semi with a pilled-up driver and burned-out brakes. Cable TV was in the delivery room, about to hatch. Baseball needed a person at the top who could institute reform and create new revenue sources. But Bowie Kuhn had been a corporate lawyer, meaning that he had all the creative intuition of a sack of hammers, and the personality of a morose eel.

But something strange happened at Milwaukee. At the last minute, Brad Corbett of the Rangers and George Steinbrenner of the Yankees changed their minds, and voted to support Kuhn. So the sport would be stuck with Bowie for an additional half-decade.

Charles Finley was furious, and felt deeply betrayed. He attended Kuhn's post-reelection press conference. He attempted to interrupt the commissioner with some media-directed comments of his own. Finley rose from his feet, and Bowie shot him down.

"Say what you want, Charlie, but right now, you're in *my* room," said Kuhn.

"That's just great, Mr. Commissioner. A real show of class," Finley fired back.

Afterward, Charlie found a forum of writers in the hotel lobby and vented. "Did you hear all the crap?" Finley demanded. "After Kuhn thanked all of the owners who voted for him, he said, 'I was not surprised by those owners who voted against me, considering the quality of the opposition.' And that was when I said to myself, 'What a joke!'"

Of the twenty-four owners at the meeting, the only one who did not cater to the media was the Angels' Gene Autry. The old cowboy, unlike the rest of the owners, had long been content with his own identity. The rest were the products of the private sector, and had invested in baseball because of the burning urge to become a celebrity.

What the game needed was a rule that allowed only already established celebrities to own baseball teams. Men like Mick Jagger, Jerry Lee Lewis, Chuck Berry maybe, people who long ago had gotten over the novelty of seeing their names in the paper. That way, sans the ego freaks, the game could have moved forward at a healthier level of sanity.

Chapter 10

July 19

As my Oldsmobile, the color of a cherry Popsicle, sped east toward the baseball stadium, KC and the Sunshine Band presented an appealing triple option via the car radio.

Do a little dance... make a little love... get down tonight!

Easy for you to say, KC.

Amid the strangulation of the rigidly controlled demands that faced the laboring baseball writer, there was no room whatsoever for leisure excess. No happy frivolities were permitted on Planet Deadline, where the trains always ran on time. That furlough known as the All-Star break, the fastest seventy-two hours in the whole universe, had shot by at the speed of light. Arlington Stadium had reopened for business. The New York Yankees were back in town.

First task of the day involved the latest readings on the Billy Martin Mood-o-Meter. Which manager would be at work that evening, Bello Billy or Acrimonious Alfred? Not surprisingly, the latter character awaited me in his office beneath the ballpark. Martin was back from his coaching duties at the Milwaukee All-Star Game and spitting hot oil. He expressed his utmost displeasure at

Alvin Dark, who had assigned Martin to coach first base instead of third.

"Who in the hell does he think he is?" Martin snapped. "If Alvin Dark is a great manager, then I'm a Chinese aviator [one of Billy's favorite bon mots, he said that a lot]. You talk about a push-button manager. Shit. Gretchen [Martin's wife] could win a World Series with that lineup of his, which Dark had nothing to do with putting together. It was all set when he got the job. He's up to his eyeballs in pitching. I guess he thinks he's some kind of mechanical genius because he knows how to flush a toilet."

"Can I put that in the paper?" I asked him.

"Sure, go ahead, if you want me to punch your goddamn lights out," Billy responded in that smoothly soft death row voice of his.

The season was at its halfway point, and no one could argue that Billy was not in midseason form. With his team approximately one light-year behind the Oakland A's in the standings, Billy the Battler found himself in the role of the cavalry officer who'd had his horse shot out from under him. So he'd ordered his bugler, general manager Danny O'Brien, to summon reinforcements, and what arrived wasn't much. Hell, not even the Salvation Army could rescue this team.

Dave Moates, an outfielder with the body of a teapot, and first-and-third baseman Tom Robson, otherwise known as Young Frankenstein, had come in from Texas's AAA Pacific Coast League outpost in Spokane. That meant a couple of players would receive exit visas, and one of them turned out to be the infamous lefty Mike Kekich, whom Martin decided had outlived his novelty value. The other player who left town with Kekich was a rookie pitcher, a Dallas boy, Mike Bacsik, whose then unborn son, Mike Junior, would someday serve up the pitch that enabled Bobby Bonds's little kid to break Hank Aaron's all-time home run record.

"There is more help on the way . . . I hope," Martin said. "I'm trying to get Tom Egan in here. We need a guy like that." Egan, a catcher for the California Angels, had attained the unofficial rank of master sergeant at baseball's NCO club. His ten years of active duty had seemingly come to an end three weeks earlier, when the Angels handed Egan his unconditional release. Egan's biggest asset had become his availability. The Rangers needed a catcher to back up Jim Sundberg. The guy who had been doing that, Bill Fahey, was hurt, and the player who had replaced Fahey on the roster, Ron Pruitt, was demanding to be traded away from the Rangers because he said certain aspects of the Texas cultural scene were too barbaric for his native Great Lakes sensitivities.

"Egan is exactly what this team needs," Martin insisted. "Great clubhouse personality. Funny as hell, when he wants to be, and he is nobody to fuck with when the fists start to fly." Unless Martin knew otherwise, Egan's clubhouse presence was about all that he appeared to offer, since he had compiled a career .200 batting average.

While Martin did not realize it, Egan would be the man who would get Billy's ass fired in Texas.

That night, Fergie Jenkins pitched a strong game, reminiscent of his dominant 1974 season-long presentation, when the Rangers' bats hammered the crap out of Pat Dobson. Texas won, 7–2, and the next night, Gaylord Perry shut out the Yankees, who wasted yet another glistening effort by Catfish Hunter in a 1–0 game. The two-game sweep served to permanently cripple whatever division championship hopes that George Steinbrenner might have been harboring.

The act of springing an ambush like that against the hated Bronx foe should have been the catalyst for happier trails in Rangerland, a good morale boost to launch the forced march that awaited the team following the All-Star break. Instead, as a weekend series against the Red Sox approached, Billy Martin's demeanor had generated enough raw fury to set off Civil Defense sirens.

Rangers general manager Danny O'Brien had informed Martin that Tom Egan would not be joining the Rangers. That had not been O'Brien's decision, ultimately. O'Brien's function as GM was mostly administrative. Owner Brad Corbett was the man who said yes or no to all personnel decisions. That was how Brad got his jollies. Everybody knew that. But in Martin's eyes, it was O'Brien who had become the source of all villainy. Wherever Martin had managed, more than good starting pitching, Billy had to have a scapegoat. In Texas, Danny O'Brien had become the logical and undeserving candidate to serve in that pain-in-the-ass capacity.

Martin had gotten on the phone with Brad Corbett. "You tell that son of a bitch [O'Brien] to stay the hell out of my office! You got it? I mean it, by God. I'm never going to speak to that god-damn bean-counting prick again!" Martin informed his owner. Since Brad Corbett felt that good communication served as the vital element for success in any operation, whether it involved baseball or selling plastic drilling pipe, Martin's mandate did not mesh with his owner's idealistic notion of a well-oiled machine. Corbett was concerned. A weekend earlier, a quartet of Corbett's players had informed the owner that other than the fact that Martin seemed poised to go on a nine-state killing spree, and that the entire roster should be vaccinated for rabies, everything was okay in the clubhouse.

With the Tom Egan issue, Martin had manufactured a crisis, and he intended to sustain it with all of his might.

Why?

Despite certain literary and theatrical efforts that suggest the contrary, it remains my steadfast view that Martin was forcing a showdown that he knew he could not win, and in the process, enable Brad Corbett—to mix sports metaphors—to dropkick Billy through the goalpost that Ruth built.

Martin knew that the one thing George Steinbrenner lacked most in life was patience, and after the Yankees had lost that pair of games in Arlington, Bill Virdon was cooked as the Yankees' manager. When Steinbrenner summoned the guillotine, and that would happen soon, Martin wanted to make damn sure his name appeared at the top of personalities free of conflicting contractual obligations, hastening his potential opportunity to manage in New York. Sure, when the time came, Martin played the ultimate hard-to-get role, and in the process, also played Steinbrenner like a snare drum. George had practically been compelled to crawl on his belly and spit-polish the self-styled Little Dago's lizard skin cowboy boots with his tongue before Billy coyly said yes. Martin's strategy was strange and daring, yet very calculated. He had a madness to his method.

I didn't care. That morning I had learned of the death in Nashville of one of my heroes, Lefty Frizzell. What a crappy year 1975 had been to the music scene. In April, Peter Ham, who formed the group Badfinger, had died. In late June, one of the genuine pioneers of the experimental psychedelic funk genre, Tim Buckley, had also departed. But Ham and Buckley had died of natural causes. Ham had hanged himself in his London apartment, and Buckley, woozy from a heroin-alcohol-barbiturate combo, had turned blue and died while watching TV. Frizzell, though, had died of a massive stroke. Men of Frizzell's stature were supposed to die in a private plane crash en route to a concert, or be found dead in a Cadillac in his driveway. This stroke business did not seem fair. I'd actually been fostering notions of a prolonged dry-out, but with the passing of Lefty Frizzell, those plans had been back-burnered quickly.

July 21

In an effort to boost anemic attendance figures, major league baseball teams had been resorting to more inventive promotional gimmicks to attract ticket buyers. The Dodgers gave away a new car. The Angels had scheduled special nights in which a ticket to the ballgame also bought the fan a ticket to Disneyland. In Cleveland, after fireworks displays and tightrope walkers failed to generate much excitement, the Indians introduced the Cash Scramble. Before the game, a few lucky fans would be selected to run onto the field where $2,000 in cash had been scattered, and given ninety seconds to scoop up as much as they could. And people had thought ten-cent Beer Night had been low-rent.

But it worked. Both the Angels and Indians had improved by over 100,000 at the midseason gate from the year before. Saturday, before a game against the Red Sox, the Rangers resorted to something more conventional—the Old-Timers Game. This would feature St. Louis Cardinals ex-greats against American League ex-notables.

Those Cardinals would be well received for sure. Before the big leagues had at last come to North Texas, many of the Dallas–Fort Worth baseball fans had adopted St. Louis as its team. It was closest to the area, after all, and the Cardinals games on clear-channel KMOX, with Harry Caray behind the microphone, had a strong audience.

The ex-Cardinals who appeared in Arlington included Enos Slaughter, Vinegar Bend Mizell, Solly Hemus, Harry "the Cat" Brecheen, Harry "the Hat" Walker, Bob Uecker, Paul "Daffy" Dean, Ken Boyer, and the living God himself, Stan "the Man" Musial, who had once said that the secret to a long career was to go to bed hungry and eat a good breakfast.

The American League roster was threadbare, but it included Joe DiMaggio, Bob Feller, and Mickey Mantle—a triumvirate of standing ovations if there ever had been one. Billy Martin played as well, attired, ironically and prophetically, in pinstripes, before donning his Rangers uniform before the scheduled game against Boston.

The postgame party in the Rangers' rec room saloon behind the press box was a beaut. Brad Corbett, if nothing else, knew how to lay out thick layers of hospitality. Now I was drinking tequila with one hand and champagne with the other, putting the liquid refreshment down just long enough to eat a fresh shrimp the size of my fist, all the while wandering amid living exhibits from the Cooperstown Hall of Fame.

These men had some stories to tell. Enos Slaughter talked about the occasion when he scored all the way from first base on a single to register the winning run in the fifth game at the 1946 World Series, one of perhaps three keystone events in baseball's decade of the 1940s.

"I've got a film of the play," Slaughter said. "I can't tell whether Mike Gonzalez [third base coach] tried to hold me up or send me. The film isn't very clear, but it looks kind of like he was just frozen. I knew one thing. I was going all the way, no matter what he was doing. I made up my mind rounding second that I should score on the play."

Bob Feller, the rocket-armed Cleveland Indian, was astonishingly candid when I asked him to compare his prime years to those of the fastest gun in baseball in 1975, Nolan Ryan.

"I read that they timed Ryan with radar and that he is supposed to throw harder than me," Feller said. "But what they timed Ryan with was the speed of his ball at the release point. What good does it do to time a pitch if it isn't a strike? When they timed me, nothing registered unless it went straight over the heart of the plate. Nolan is a good kid, but he is just a thrower and right now, he's struggling. People talk about his no-hitters, but no-hitters are just luck. I pitched 12 one-hitters, and nobody has come close to that."

Rapid Robert never held back. As the hour grew later and my head grew lighter, I found myself standing by the buffet table, and to my immediate left stood Joltin' Joe himself.

I wanted to speak to the man, ask him something, but what?

"Joe, everybody says that your hitting streak is the one record in baseball that nobody will ever break. But what about .400? Do you think anybody will ever hit .400 again?"

That was the best that I could do. DiMaggio was prompt, firm, sincere, and decisive with his reply. "Do you know what you're talking about?" he demanded. "You're talking about Ted Williams, and with a guy like Ted Williams, anything could have happened. There aren't any Ted Williamses around anymore. Right now, it would be more realistic to ask if anybody will hit .350."

Good answer. Two more glasses of Cuervo. Two more glasses of Moët. I found myself in the bathroom, staring at myself in the mirror and talking to myself. "You're getting some wrinkles around the eyes, big guy," I said. "Better get yourself some of that aloe vera moisturizer and let it work its magic, like they promise on TV."

Then another face appeared in the mirror, next to mine. It

was Mickey Mantle. He washed his hands, then asked an unusual question.

"What do you think of Hank Williams?" Mantle wanted to know.

"When I was four, I saw him perform in person on the Grand Ol' Opry," I told Mantle, which was true.

Mantle stared at me. "No shit?"

"No shit," I said, and to prove it, I sang the first two or three lines of "Lovesick Blues."

The Mick held up his hand and stopped me mid-song. "Listen, I was at some club where Hank Jr. was performing one night, and some guy beat him to a fucking pulp for trying to sing like his Daddy. And Hank Jr. sang a hell of a lot better than you do."

I took that simply as good advice, thanked Mickey, left the restroom, had a couple more drinks, summoned my designated driver, who was me, and headed for home.

July 21

After hearing of a behind-closed-doors meeting between Brad Corbett and Billy Martin, I realized that in the next few days my journalistic function would go beyond the pastoral realm of runs, hits, and errors. The topic had been Corbett's concerns about the "communication" issue between his field manager and his general manager after the Tom Egan fiasco. Afterward, the usually buoyant baseball owner looked seasick. "So how would you characterize your session with Billy?" somebody asked Brad. "Was it stormy?"

"Stormy? No, not stormy," said Corbett, the thick smoke from his cigar failing to conceal furrows the size of dry creek beds that had suddenly appeared in his great big brow. "I'd characterize the conversation as sticky."

Over the past six weeks, Martin had been enacting the role of the walking time bomb with Academy Award precision, the most convincing performance anyone associated with the sport of baseball had ever seen. Martin had forced a High Noon shootout with his boss, and no pocket watches were required to realize it was 11:59. Corbett had summoned his board of directors. That was an eclectic assembly that included, among others, the former owner of the *Star-Telegram,* Amon Carter Jr., a man who used to bet up to $25,000 and up on college football games, and Dallas shopping center magnate Raymond Nasher, overseer of what was probably the best private art and sculpture collection in Texas.

The topic of the emergency session: What the hell are we going to do about Billy? He's out of control. The board's consensus: If Billy thinks he is bigger than we are, then get rid of the motherfucker. I asked one of the board people about the meeting. "Are you going to let him go or not?"

"Not tonight, but stick around," he said. "Brad just can't believe that Billy is the source of all of the problems the team is having, but the more he talks to people, the more he is learning otherwise."

Corbett was the last holdout. He was savvy enough to realize that while his manager had embarked on a self-created suicide mission, the general public and ever-expanding Rangers fan base could not view the backstage hostilities. The act of canning the freshly minted American League Manager of the Year would certainly create a PR stink bomb. Corbett knew that he would become a casting director's dream to play the heavy when the sordid dramatics reached their climax. In the eyes of Joe Twelve-Pack, it was Billy, the ally of the lunch bucket brigade, versus Brad, the bloated capitalist.

Brad would close his eyes and dream that Billy would soon be overcome with a temporary burst of sanity, and offer some kind of let's-just-agree-to-disagree-and-still-be-chums-until-all-this-shit-blows-over compromise. Good luck with that, Brad. What Billy was doing was sitting in his office, and calling into his daily radio show, telling the listeners that fat Brad was going to fire him.

"I have been accused of being disloyal to the organization," Billy said, knowing that he was talking to a live audience. "You can kill me first, before you can accuse me of disloyalty. My reputation carried down here with me. I told them I wasn't a yes-man when they hired me here. But really, I am getting fired for one reason. Ego. The owner's ego. Everybody has got one, and his is as big as they come. Brad Corbett has owned his team for one year, and he thinks he is a baseball genius. Corbett knows as much about baseball as I know about plastic pipe."

Was public oratory like that the design of a man who was trying to hold on to his job?

After learning of that tirade, I sadly realized that for the next two or three days, I would be preoccupied with writing the front page obit for Billy Ball in Texas.

July 22

Shakespearean actors had been knighted for performing with less unrestrained histrionics than Billy Martin brought onto the tragic stage that his office became after the dismissal was formalized... *If you have tears, prepare to shed them now.*

Martin sat behind his desk, partially dressed, the Italian ram's horn that was fashionable in some circles at the time conspicuously dangling around his neck. Billy's eyes were red and moist, like a crocodile's eyes moments before suppertime in the swamp.

"Where did I go wrong?" he pleaded. He wiped the snot from

his nose with the back of his hand. "This has been an ordeal, trying to make this team the best that it could be," he went on, making gasping sounds. "I've got to gain my weight back." Martin also issued an apology to Brad Corbett for having popped off about his owner so harshly on the radio. Billy realized that George Steinbrenner read the papers.

Some writer asked Martin when and if he might manage again. "I am a proud man, and it would be hard to come back again," he declared with a very straight face. "My reputation precedes me everywhere I go."

His reputation preceded him at his house in Arlington, Texas, as well. I had driven to Billy's house to further the discussion of the events of the day, accompanied by a freelance writer named Tom Stephenson. He was an ex-linebacker at Missouri and had the face to prove it. Stephenson had been a reporter with the *Dallas Morning News* until he'd decided to travel through the block-long city room at the paper one night while leaping from desktop to desktop, and singing "I Did It My Way." On his first assignment as a freelancer, while pursuing a murder story, Stephenson had been arrested in the Dallas suburb of Blue Mound, initially suspected, he said of impersonating a law enforcement officer, attempted murder, and enticing a child. "Goddamndest misunderstanding I ever saw," he admitted. The allegations were dismissed.

So Stephenson landed a gig writing a baseball feature for a Dallas-area magazine. Martin liked having him around, because Stephenson had once joined him in a saloon rumble, and Billy, for some reason, thought Tom worked for *Sports Illustrated*.

We beat Billy home, by about a minute. As Martin wheeled his black Continental with its "Number 1" vanity plate into the driveway, the sound of shattering glass could be heard from inside the house.

"I don't know if you want to go in there or not," Stephenson told Billy. Martin smiled, and let us inside. Gretchen was busy in the kitchen. The charming and controlled Mrs. Billy Martin who occasionally appeared at the stadium clubroom was not the Mrs. Billy Martin we were witnessing then.

Gretchen stayed in the kitchen. She didn't know that Billy had media guests in her living room, and set about expressing her immense displeasure about his latest dismissal. Her remarks were sufficiently direct and unsparing to reduce the average man into ashes.

Billy seemed unconcerned, strangely content, and poured everybody a drink. "I just got an offer to manage again," he announced, grinning. "Bob Short [the previous Rangers owner, who had hired Billy to manage in Texas] called me, and asked me if I might want to manage that fleabag hotel of his in Minneapolis. He said he'd let me live on the whole top floor for free! Hey, Gretchen! Wanna move back to Minnesota?"

Then the phone rang. Billy picked it up. His third base coach, Frank Lucchesi, was on the line. Frank was telling Billy that Corbett had offered him the job to finish out the season as the Texas manager, and Lucchesi expressed reservations about accepting the post, lest Billy feel somehow betrayed.

"Listen, you dumb dago," Martin told Lucchesi. "When else and where else are you going to be offered a manager's job in the big leagues? This is your last chance. Take the damn job."

Martin hung up, and one hour later, I wrote a story that informed my readers that the new manager's name was pronounced "loo-kasee."

July 23

The thousands of fans who had adopted the early, awful Rangers like an abandoned stray puppy expressed widespread and also universal dismay that this loo-kasee guy was suddenly the manager of their team, instead of the fireball they had come to love as much as the handguns they kept beneath the front seats of their white pickup trucks.

I drove to the ballpark, listened to the talk shows, and cringed. "This is awful," some woman shrieked. "But I guess if you can get rid of the president of the United States, you can get rid of Billy Martin, too."

Brad Corbett was actively at work doing whatever damage control he could muster. He told a UPI reporter, "Ultimately, it depends on which general you want—George Patton or Omar Bradley. (Corbett didn't know shit about military history, but he did go to the movies.) With the kids we have, we need an Omar Bradley. Some of our kids were so frightened of Billy, they couldn't even play."

Inside the Rangers' offices at the ballpark, I talked to a woman who was GM Danny O'Brien's administrative assistant and who sometimes worked the phone lines.

"How's the pulse out there?" I asked her.

"Oh, I'd say I've answered about 250 calls—all pro-Billy," she said.

"Anything obscene?"

"Oh, sure," she said. "But being single, I get those at home, too."

July 24

Outside the Rangers' troubled universe, life, as usual, continued on.

According to baseball folklore, offensively challenged players are the stock from which great managers emerge. At Shea Stadium, Joe Torre, with a set of sideburns so thick that he looked more like an Allman Brother than a New York Met, polished his management credentials by grounding into four double plays in a game against the Houston Astros, tying a major league record.

In Baltimore, even though the Orioles had fallen seven games behind Boston in the American League East race, the Birds, who had won five of the last seven division titles, seemed coolly confident that they would still prevail. Just one season earlier, the Crab Cake Clan had overcome a seven-and-a-half-game post–All Star break deficit to overtake the Red Sox. Earl Weaver was confident that Boston would somehow choke again.

Along those lines, after a series finale against Oakland, somebody at Memorial Stadium punched out this scoreboard message to the departing A's: "Good-bye Oakland. See You in October."

In Cincinnati, Reds manager Sparky Anderson had been using Pete Rose more and more in left field. Pete said that he was not all that happy about being stationed in the cheap seat region because, "You deal with a better class of fan around third base."

In Atlanta, the Braves had been paying close attention to the Cash Scramble promotion in Cleveland. Rather than scatter a cheesy $2,000 across the outfield lawn, the Atlanta people pitched twenty-five grand onto the field and invited a handful of spectators to dig in. A wire photo of the event showed a sweet young Dixie dumpling stuffing greenbacks down her blouse with both hands, and the professionally satisfied expression she wore clearly suggested she'd done this sort of thing before.

Ah—American life in the 1970s. The CIA, which had been conducting mind-control experiments with LSD, was expanding its horizons with something new. They called it BZ, the superdrug. While LSD might mess you up for eight hours or so, BZ would keep you in orbit for three days, and according to the pharmacological experts, "Some people are not the same for weeks afterward." At some Army base, soldiers were sought to give this BZ a whirl, and 2,490 brave men volunteered.

July 25

After running four bold furlongs to begin the 1975 season, the Kansas City Royals could only watch the taillights of the Oakland A's as they thundered down the backstretch and into the far turn. Not only could the Royals not match the A's pace, they had lost six straight games and were about to run a white flag up the left and right field foul poles.

Jack McKeon, the Kansas City manager who had authored so many optimistic expressions back in the spring, sat near his telephone, awaiting the call from the warden inquiring of his menu selections for the last meal.

Joe Burke, the Kansas City general manager, went on the record. "We have no plans to replace Jack McKeon," he told Ken Leiker, who covered the Royals for the Topeka paper. "Yeah, right," Leiker told me a day or so later. "While Joe Burke was talking, in the next room I could hear this high-pitched, whining sound, like maybe somebody was sharpening an axe."

And so, while McKeon might have been on the line setting a golf date with Billy Martin, the Royals conducted a press conference. In Texas, the hiring of Frank Lucchesi to replace Bantam Billy would have little bearing upon the future of the Rangers, although Frank would achieve a certain immortality when he'd gotten his brains boxed around by his second baseman one day.

But when Royals owner Ewing Kauffman brought Whitey Herzog in to meet the Midwest media, the repercussions would last for more than a decade, both in Kansas City and, later, St. Louis. Herzog, who had been fired at Texas to make room for

Martin in 1973, had the most sharply tuned mind in baseball, and he was foaming at the mouth to prove it. He'd been coaching for Dick Williams with the Angels when he'd received the good news that K.C. desired Herzog's services.

More than any personality I ever met in public life, nobody was more compelled to speak the truth than Herzog, who also answered to the name White Rat.

When Whitey was asked to comment on the fate of his predecessor, he didn't trot out any "Gee whiz, what a surprise!" horseshit. "He [McKeon] knew he was on the brink even before the season started. I kinda knew that, too, and as the Royals began to struggle, I hoped I was the guy being considered."

Just as had happened in Texas a few days earlier when Martin was canned, the switchboard at the Royals' office quivered from the response of fans expressing their feelings about the departure of Jack McKeon. Unlike Texas, though, all the calls had been positive. But, the switchboard woman amplified, "not so much about the guy who is coming in, but against the guy who was going out."

When the Rat put on his white Kansas City uniform for the first time, he would dispatch his new ball club onto the Royals Stadium's steaming Astro Turf for a doubleheader against—of course—the Texas Rangers. It is said that cannibals refuse to eat divorced women because they are too bitter. There were few embattled ex-spouses who bore the animosity that Whitey Herzog carried in his heart when it came to the Texas Rangers.

As he sat in his new office in Kansas City, the Rat vividly recited the details of his last days in Texas. "As soon as Billy Martin became available, I knew that Bob Short was going to bring him in, and then Short had to wait until my son's birthday to fire my ass," he said. "I guess I can laugh about that now," Whitey added, and then he did.

Herzog was laughing after the doubleheader, too. Kansas City won both games. In the opener, John Mayberry, as was his custom, lit up Ferguson Jenkins. By the end of the game, his lifetime batting average against the future Hall of Fame right-hander had risen to .429. Did Big John have any explanation for his unprecedented success against a pitcher of Jenkins's pedigree?

"Hell, yes, I can explain it," Mayberry declared. "Fergie lays it there, and I just lay it back out."

In the nightcap, the veteran second baseman Cookie Rojas led the Kansas City hit parade against Texas with a single, a double, and a triple. So afterward, Herzog summoned Rojas's backup, a young infielder named Frank White. "Here's the deal," he told White in typical Herzog fashion. "I know you can play. I know that you can move to your left, move to your right, charge the ball, and also chase it into the outfield. You're perfectly suited to play on a Turf team. So from now on, you're playing second base, and Cookie gets to sit down. Just one note of caution," he said, finishing with Frank White. "Cookie Rojas is a big fan favorite around here, and they won't like his being benched. So just get ready, because no matter how well you field the ball, they're going to boo your ass for the next year and a half."

Chapter 11

July 27

Teams in both major leagues passed through the 100-game milestone in the season of 1975, most of them facing the remainder of the uphill grind with rosters full of players wearing the faces of men etched with forced-march agony. The outcome of three of the four divisions was already largely determined. Of the twenty-four teams, nineteen had no real hopes of a happy postseason afterlife. Once competitive psyches became overrun by the day-to-day, sadistic tedium of frustration. Two more months remained on the schedule, and the act of "playing them one at a time" seemed like trying to look graceful on an ice rink while wearing roller skates. The players of the time were working on one-year contracts, so the only incentive left was to embark on what they called their late season "salary drive." That called for padding the vital statistics, namely batting and earned run averages, which would determine the amount of next year's paycheck.

In the two clubhouses at Royals Stadium, before and after a Saturday afternoon game, the players on both teams seemed abnormally upbeat. Two teams, two new managers. Everybody seemed refreshed. On one of his classic baseball telecasts in the

1950s, Dizzy Dean talked about his old manager, Frankie Frisch, who sometimes acted the role of the tyrant, or, in Diz's own words, "One of them there Com-'nist dick-taters, like Joseph Stallion."

Certainly, there was fresh air in the Texas dungeon after the departure of Billy the Terrible. "Don't get me wrong. I respected Billy," admitted infielder Dave Nelson. "But every now and then, change is good. It's like putting on a clean pair of socks."

Kansas City Royals players seemed entirely revitalized with the appearance of Whitey Herzog in their manager's office, and were further delighted that Herzog's first move was to employ Charley Lau, the Dalai Lama of hitting coaches. After Herzog hit K.C., the baseball world for the Royals seemed to have arrived at a point like in *The Wizard of Oz*, where everything suddenly changes from sepia to color. The Royals unloaded on the Rangers, and Al Fitzmorris threw a 7–0 shutout, and Herzog was quickly 3-and-0 in his new job.

Herzog's postgame dissertations to the media, even when he was attempting to manage in Texas after having been dealt a hand that contained maybe a pair of fours, could be compelling. Whitey the Professor issued profound lectures on the basics of Baseball 101. Afterward, in places like the Banyan Room in Pompano Beach, or the bar in the Executive House in Chicago, or a three-hour dinner at Howard Wong's restaurant in Minneapolis, Herzog provided even more advanced lessons. Now the course would be Baseball 10W-40, because Whitey would be lubricated, and he would talk of how to create a slippery slope for the opposition. After beating the Rangers, Herzog issued two of what he regarded as baseball's simple truths:

- "We got the right bounces early. In baseball, more than any other sport, there is a very thin line that separates the heroes and the screwups."

- "A manager cannot win 20 games in a season, but he can lose 20 games by making the wrong moves."

Over in the Rangers' dressing quarters, the new man at the helm, Frank Lucchesi, talked about the perils of coaching third base for a team on which the signs might be too intricate. "One time, I was swatting a gnat, and the next thing I knew, my base runner was trying to steal home and got thrown out by thirty feet!"

Back at the Sheraton Royal, one of the Rangers players invited me upstairs to his room. He was in there with a Royals player who had brought some hashish. Technically, this gathering might have violated baseball's rule that forbade "fraternization" among players of opposing teams. However, if narcotics were involved, apparently the rule was waived.

That twelve-headed serpent that answered to the name of cocaine had not yet made its lethal presence too deeply in baseball by 1975. Players were not quite hip to the stuff, and according to the financial dictates of the time, not that many could afford it, anyway.

Who cared? That sweet-smelling, gummy material that the Royals player provided was amazing. Screw the white stuff. The hash emancipated my soul from my physical being, which was great, because I'd been traveling around the country with a couple of herniated discs in my lower spine, and life inside my body was a serious drag. I floated back down to my room, where the phone was ringing in a tone that I guessed was B-sharp. It was Burt Hawkins, the traveling secretary, mandating that I come to his room at once. He wanted me to meet somebody, and would not say who. It was a surprise.

I knocked, went inside, still dazed from the hash. Next thing I knew, Hawkins was introducing me to David Eisenhower, Ike's grandson. At first, I thought this might have been a drug-induced hallucination, but in the deepest recesses of my brain, I'd remembered Hawkins having talked of young Eisenhower working for him as a statistician with the Washington Senators. Not only was this Eisenhower in Hawkins's room, so was David's wife, Julie Nixon. The one-year anniversary of her father's resignation at the White House would arrive in about a week.

The couple could not have been more genuine. Julie looked so damn radiant, I was tempted to ask her if she wanted to sneak off for a couple of beers. Hell, about six years earlier, I'd hit on one of the Lennon Sisters, so why not Nixon's daughter? Inborn protocol prevented me from being that uncouth. (This Southern gentleman's upbringing can be a pain in the ass sometimes.)

After a chat that lasted about ten minutes, I adjourned. "I don't think they could tell how fucked up I am," I assured myself, and then walked into a janitor's closet in the hallway, thinking it was the elevator.

July 28

The Royals completed their four-game sweep of Texas. Rather than endure the rigors of the customary getaway day evacuation, a barbecue had been planned for the team at a ranch outside Kansas City that belonged to one of the team's minority owners. I had never been that fascinated with how the Other Half lived, since there was no chance of gaining admittance into the Other Half Club. But I was curious about how the Other Half ate and drank, and after the visit to the ranch, it is my testimony that they do okay. The guy served prime steaks, four inches thick, the best that I or anybody else had ever eaten. The players were thoroughly entertained, getting drunk before the serious drinking began on a late flight to the coast.

This journey offered an unusual hazard. On the trip to Oakland, the team would have to change planes in Los Angeles, where the new manager, Frank Lucchesi, feared that he might lose half his team. Frank did not wish to take on the task of a man trying to herd cats. On the bus ride from the barbecue to the Kansas City airport, Lucchesi, a man who was born to wear leisure suits, stood up and made a speech.

"I know most of you have already done some pretty good partying, but we've got a long night of traveling still to go," Lucchesi said. "You'll be seen by the public, and the people know who you are. So I expect all of you to remember that you represent the Texas Rangers, and you also represent major league baseball, so behave yourselves accordingly."

While Lucchesi spoke, one of his pitchers was standing in the back of the bus, urinating through an open window onto the traffic on the freeway outside.

After a four-and-a-half-hour blur, I found myself suffering through a bitter in-body experience. I sat at the counter of an all-night café across the street from the team hotel in Oakland, eating an omelet. Gaylord Perry sat to my right.

The café was filled with some guys I thought at first might be the Cleveland Indians, or the Houston Astros, wearing those garish uniforms of theirs. Instead, these were players on a team competing in a national fast-pitch softball tournament that was happening somewhere in the area.

One of them recognized Perry, and the softball players were pointing at him. A softballer finally approached him and asked for an autograph.

"He didn't want the autograph," I told Gaylord. "He wanted

to know if you could offer some tips on how to grease up under-handed, but he didn't have the cojones. You should have told him anyway."

"Finish your eggs," said Perry.

July 29–30

In a game that seemed of little consequence, just another passing event during the marathon season, the Yankees beat the Tigers, 4–2. The loss dropped Detroit to 10 games under .500, and Ralph Houk's team was just another outfit going through the motions of summertime survival. So nobody on the team, nobody in baseball, realized that the Tigers had just embarked on one of the most deflating losing streaks of its era.

The next day another name synonymous with Motown, a person, and not a team, began a losing streak of his own. Jimmy Hoffa, who, like Billy Martin presented himself as the blue-collar blood brother of the working class, had been scheduled for a lunch date with two acquaintances, Anthony Giacalone and Anthony Provenzano, at Machus Red Fox restaurant at Bloomfield Hills. Apparently, they were meeting to discuss the color scheme for some of the Teamsters floats in the Labor Day parade. Nobody had seen Hoffa since. An associate of Hoffa's said that he was not worried, and that Jimmy had merely been shot, put in the trunk of a car that was then run through a car compactor, and that he'd be just fine. But it would be quite some time before the Tigers or Jimmy Hoffa would experience the daylight of the win column.

Out in Oakland, where I was with the Rangers, the win column and the A's were hardly strangers. Alvin Dark, after his team had once again decked the Rangers, played the role of the cautiously optimistic politician. Any notions of planning yet another division championship party were still premature, Dark warned. Kansas City, on a winning streak with Whitey Herzog steering the boat, had crept to within single digits of the A's in the games-behind column. "Of course, Kansas City still has a chance," Dark insisted. "Until somebody has been mathematically eliminated, then they have a chance. Kansas City has a chance. Minnesota has a chance. California has a chance."

Dark didn't mention the Rangers. They weren't mathematically done, but Dark figured they didn't have a chance. His post-game gathering with reporters was unusual in that Charles Finley himself chose to attend, and contradicted everything his manager said. "Kansas City has a great club," said Finley. "Unfortunately for Kansas City, that team is not as great as the Oakland A's. Nobody is going to beat the A's in the American League West." Finley gave Dark a wicked smile that said, "If you don't win the division, Alvin, then next year, you'll be the guy walking my mule." Finley was supposed to have been the cover boy on *Time* magazine that week, but that story had been scrubbed, Finley said, after the furor he had created in Milwaukee when he'd staged his abortive coup to unseat Bowie Kuhn. The thing that impressed me most about Charlie O. was his eyebrows. There was something faintly satanic about them.

On the flight back to Texas after the Oakland series, three players sat in the back of the charter plane, guzzling the contents of those cute little bottles and playing cards. Between hands, one of them boasted of a nocturnal tryst that had occurred in the Disneyland Hotel. "This girl, she had a little tattoo, right at the top of her ass," the player exclaimed. Tattooed women were a real novelty in 1975, as were pierced nostrils, navels, and nipples. "It was a butterfly," the player added.

"The hell it was," said another of the card players, puncturing his teammate's balloon. "I hooked up with her on the last trip, and the tattoo was no goddamn butterfly. It was an eagle."

"You're both full of shit," commented the third party in the card game, pitcher Steve Hargan. "It was a buzzard."

While the Rangers were in the air, their departed friend, Billy Martin, fished for trout in Glade Park, Colorado. In the evening, he received a phone call. It was Gabe Paul, general manager of the New York Yankees, calling on behalf of his boss, George Steinbrenner. Paul apologized first for interrupting Martin's visit to the stream, but said that he wanted to discuss an interesting and important proposition.

August 1

Steam swirled atop the asphalt pavement of a residential Dallas street after a brief rain shower. I watched from the front porch of someone who worked as a radio man for a Dallas-based station. Since my bosses had commented on my lacking the natural investigative instincts of a good reporter, I was there to receive some pointers, and get high, before continuing on to the ballpark.

I inhaled deeply off one of his Panama Pall-Malls, and watched the little ringlets of smoke as they danced through the still, humid air. "You know what happens to good reporters?" he warned me. "They get awards named after them. Like Joe Holstead, who got too close to the fire at the gasoline storage tank. Blew his ass all the way to Oklahoma. No, you don't want to get an award named after you."

I felt better. Then the phone rang. The newsman went inside to answer the call, then reappeared, looking glum. "Goddamn," he said. "That was the day camp calling. My daughter just got run over, and her right leg is broken. She's on her way to the hospital in an ambulance, they can't reach my wife at work, and"—he issued a melancholy pause—"I'm supposed to meet this sweet thing at the Ramada Inn in half an hour."

"Doesn't sound like you have much choice," I said.

"Yeah, you're right," the newsman said. "It's a fine hospital. They'll take good care of her till my wife can get over there."

At the ballpark that night, before the Rangers played the Angels, Brad Corbett had some interesting news. "Here's a good story for you," he remarked. "Don't quote me. Just identify me as a source. I just talked to Gabe Paul, and tomorrow, the Yankees will announce that they are going to fire Bill Virdon and bring in Billy Martin."

So Brad, what is your reaction to this development? "I'm glad for Billy," the Rangers' owner declared. More than Billy, he was glad for Brad. According to Martin's contract, Corbett still owed Billy a year and a half's pay. With Martin employed elsewhere, Brad's obligations to his ex-antagonist were over.

August 2

The New York sporting print media, an assembly of humanity that smelled of stale tobacco and was habitually inclined to grossly overrate the people they wrote about, as well as chronically overrating themselves, crowded in the reporters' lunchroom at Shea Stadium. The Yankees had scheduled a press conference.

Back in June, many of these same faces had led the stampede to another press conference that Joe Namath had organized. This was it. Joe Big-Nose, the toast of Manhattan, would announce his retirement. Bring your hankies, everybody. Instead, Namath pulled a delightful con. Instead of issuing his official farewell to football, Namath informed the press that he had agreed to endorse the product of some perfume manufacturer.

The troops gathered at Shea, which served as the Yankees' temporary shelter for two seasons while their Great American Baseball Cathedral in the Bronx was getting a face lift and boob job. You had to get up awfully early in the morning to put one over on the New York media.

This time, they got what they came for. Gabe Paul stood up and made a simple two-sentence announcement. "There has been a change in management," Paul said. "Billy Martin is in."

From stage left, Billy Martin appeared. He had conveniently arrived in town to participate in the Old Timers Game. (One wondered if he had agreed to attend that event while he was still managing in Texas.) Martin took a long, deep breath, and savored the intoxicating aroma of retribution. Shipped off to the sticks by New York GM George Weiss for alleged conduct unbecoming a human being, Martin had returned to the center of the baseball universe after eighteen years in exile.

"Weiss, from wherever they have you stationed in hell, I hope that you are watching." Martin did not say that, but he was thinking it. "This is one of the biggest thrills of my entire life. It's great to be back where it all started," was what he did say. Martin could not resist the urge to issue some body punches to the small-peckered, off-Broadway nobodies who had been unable to comprehend his strategic brilliance. "Everybody fired me, then tried to explain why. But my track record speaks for itself." He stopped just short of saying, "What this team needs is Tom Egan, and if Gabe doesn't bring him in, I'll stomp his ass."

After Martin finished, Gabe Paul huddled with a group of

reporters and admitted, "If Billy Martin had not been available, then Bill Virdon would still be managing the Yankees." Nobody connected any of the obvious dots that presented the conclusion that Martin had made damn sure he was available when the opportunity arrived. Billy's gift of timing went unappreciated.

The man Brad Corbett had compared to General George Patton now managed the Yankees. (Coincidentally, on the same day, General George Patton III assumed command at Fort Hood, a huge U.S. Army installation in Central Texas. Asked to comment on his father, General Patton III hesitated and finally said, "He was colorful, yeah." Anybody who ever dealt with Commander Billy would offer the same epitaph.)

The banner headline jubilee that Steinbrenner's new hire generated was greeted with muted response in the Yankees' clubhouse. Several players thought that Bill Virdon had simply gotten screwed. "We didn't play up to our potential, some of us, and that wasn't Bill's fault," Bobby Bonds said.

Sparky Lyle, the relief pitcher who would later write a book that described life with the Yankees as a visit to the animal house, was more direct. "I spent two months this season watching guys come in, look at the lineup card, and walk away, sulking and hanging their heads. What should Bill have done, gone up to those guys and said, 'I'm sorry'? Ultimately, you've got to have a little pride in yourself. We should have taken it upon ourselves to go and play better ball."

One of Bill Virdon's starting pitchers, Pat Dobson, expressed a different view. It had been rumored that Dobson had approached Steinbrenner and Paul and bitched about Virdon behind his back. Dobson did not deny that but disagreed that he was the reason his manager was dismissed. "If I have the ability to get the manager fired, then what manager would want to hire me in the first place?" he reasoned.

As the ex-greats from New York's pinstriped past mingled about before the Old Timers exhibition, Martin posed for news photographs with Mickey Mantle and Whitey Ford, who ironically had been present at the Copacabana rumble that caused Weiss to chase Billy out of town back in 1957. It would not have been out of the question to suggest that Billy had phoned the club for postgame reservations.

After the aging legends had performed their exhibition, Martin took charge for the actual contest, the Yankees vs. the Cleveland Indians. New York won, 5–3, on key hits by Thurman Munson, Graig Nettles, and Chris Chambliss. The Martin Regime was officially in place and underway. Despite the reputation that shadowed Billy throughout his managerial career, there were two reasons to think that, finally, he might be there to stay.

Martin was confronted with a clubhouse that included a lengthy cast of calloused veteran players. Those had been the character types that gained Martin's approval, and in return, they maintained a skin thick enough to endure whatever abuse Billy might inflict. Also, and more importantly, Martin now worked for an owner and general manager who would not be inclined to take much crap off the scrappy skipper. Gabe Paul had endured an immediate past in Cleveland, and having lived through that, he was numb, uncaring, and unafraid. George Steinbrenner, people had been inclined to forget, had worked as an assistant football coach at two Big Ten schools in the 1950s, shouting orders to a bunch of Eastern European steel puddlers with tree trunk necks and wedge-shaped heads. After dealing with those types of thugs, Steinbrenner would not be fearful of any outbursts from some skinny-ass Roman candle.

Mindful of this, would Martin be more inclined to modify his off-the-field binges, and harness his natural resentment of authority? The adventures that lurked on the road ahead offered high potential for entertainment value.

August 4

The Texas team that was supposed to win the American League West, and march from there into the World Series, was on the field at Arlington Stadium. Too bad these all-conquering legions showed up about four months too late. Ferguson Jenkins never looked sharper as the Rangers defeated the regal Oakland A's, 12–0.

Jenkins left the game after seven innings, complaining of nausea. "It wasn't anything that I ate," Fergie insisted. "My wife fed me her good old beef stew four hours before the game. I just think the heat got to me a little bit."

Alvin Dark, huddled in the visiting manager's office, appeared kind of queasy himself. "I'm a man of faith, and proud of it," he insisted. "A game like this will make me pray even harder." I felt almost sorry for Dark, and was tempted to offer him one of the big pain pills that Rangers trainer Bill Zeigler had kindly provided me before the game, to soothe my tortured back.

Back upstairs, Brad Corbett was hosting a cocktail party for the commissioner of baseball, Bowie Kuhn. The American League president, Lee MacPhail, was there, too. The purpose of the gathering, according to Corbett, had been a clear-the-air festivity after all the unpleasantness that happened at the All-Star Game, where the Rangers' owner participated in the insurrection to oust Kuhn. In reality, Corbett didn't give a shit about clean air, and neither did Bowie Kuhn. The actual purpose of Kuhn's and MacPhail's trip to steamy Texas had been to devise a strategy to put the squeeze

on the city of Arlington to build an upper deck on the joke of a
ballpark where the Rangers played home games.

The party lasted late. As usual, media representatives con-
versed with baseball people on topics that involved not only the
dynamics of the sport, but also such matters as politics and the
world economy, religion, and pussy. On the drive back to Fort
Worth, I made it two blocks from the stadium, and then the pain
pills kicked in in a bad way. Earlier, Fergie Jenkins just thought he
was sick at his job. What I had was the real thing, and this was an
emergency. I pulled the Olds off the road and into the parking
lot of the Dos Gringos restaurant, opened the door, leaned out,
and hurled. Three full flushes. That done, I started the car and
saw flashing colored lights swooping at me from behind. An Arlington cop had been parked beside the restaurant, watching the
whole sorry bit. One of the great things about living in Texas was
that if you were a white guy and said "yessir, nossir " to the cops,
you were always free to go. I wasn't worried now. I should have
been. Mostly due to run-ins with Billy Martin, the Arlington cops
despised anyone remotely connected with the Rangers, and had
declared open season on those leaving the ballpark after hours.

"Get out of the car," said the cop.

"Sure, officer. Gee. Sorry about the mess I made here. But
have you ever eaten in that restaurant? I'm not the first guy who
ever had to blow his beets in this parking lot. Ha-ha."

Ha-ha, my ass. The cop pinned my arms behind me and applied the cuffs. Shortly after that, I sat in the police station, where I
was about to be booked. Everybody was surly as hell, and I no longer had anything to gain by offering undue measures of respect to
pricks wearing badges.

"Don't I get a phone call?" I said, getting ready to play the
long shot of my journalistic career. "I need a phone book, too."

The cop, who had already happily informed me that I needed to hire a lawyer, gave me the directory with some reluctance. I looked under the Vs, thinking that Tommy Vandergriff, the mayor of Arlington and the man solely responsible for bringing the franchise to his city from Washington, D.C., might actually be listed. Jackpot! He was. I dialed the number from a phone attached to a wall next to a door that led to the beckoning cells. The time was about 2:30 A.M. The phone at Vandergriff's house rang about seven times, and I was about to surrender when Vandergriff's wife answered. I asked for the mayor, and Mrs. Vandergriff seemed truly underjoyed.

I had never met Vandergriff in person, but he listened while I explained my predicament. "You don't sound drunk to me," he said. "Could I speak to an officer?" I handed the telephone to the cop and watched while his eyes bugged out. "Uh...sir, let me switch to another phone," he said and disappeared into another room. I felt better. Two minutes later, the cop was back, all smiles. "W-e-l-l-l!" he said. "You certainly are fortunate to have a friend like Mayor Vandergriff."

"That's right," I said. "Now kindly return my car keys, and without further ado, I'll get the fuck out of here."

"Well, that's going to be a problem, I'm afraid," said my newest best friend. "Your car was impounded, and now the city lot is closed and locked up for the night. So Mayor Vandergriff is on his way over here, to drive you home."

"Why can't *you* drive me home?"

"Well...um...that wouldn't look...um...appropriate."

Vandergriff arrived shortly. About four cops, including a captain, gathered around the mayor, falling all over themselves to be first in line to kiss his ass. I watched that scene, and decided to have some fun. "Listen, Tommy. I still have to write my P.M. story about the game, and my typewriter, and my notes, are in the trunk of my car that these gentlemen have locked up." That was bullshit. I'd already written the P.M. story. I just wanted to repay them for the grief that they had already brought upon me. So one of the policemen was sent to the car pound, where he had to scale a chain link fence, retrieve the typewriter, and climb back over.

On the drive back to Fort Worth, Vandergriff wanted to talk baseball. He was curious. Why in the world had the Rangers fired Billy Martin? I told the Arlington mayor that the reasons were complex. I should have told him the truth—that Billy got the chop for pulling the kinds of stunts that I had just pulled back at the police station. (If anybody wished to verify this story, they'd have to get it from Vandergriff himself, since the paperwork involved with the incident disappeared without a trace. That, by the way, had nothing to do with Tommy.)

August 6

Cincinnati manager Sparky Anderson was complaining bitterly about people in baseball who whined about injuries to key personnel as an excuse for losing. Sparky was not directing his criticism toward anybody in the Reds' organization. He was fed up with some sad songs he'd been hearing from the God-almighty Los Angeles Dodgers. In fact, Anderson had grown to resent the patrician attitude that the lordly Dodgers inflicted upon the rest of the baseball world. Maybe he remembered that Jim Murray of the *Los Angeles Times* had come to Cincinnati and insulted the place, writing that it had taken the city over a decade to finish construction of an expressway project because, "It was Kentucky's turn to use the steam shovel."

"Guess what? We have some guys out, too," Sparky fumed.

"We haven't had Pat Darcy available for a good part of the season, and in the spring, he was our best pitcher." By then, Sparky could say whatever he wanted to. His Reds were putting on a great impersonation of Secretariat at the Belmont Stakes two years earlier.

August 7

Oakland reverted to form and blitzed the Rangers, 10–1, with Vida Blue on the mound, in a game that finished Texas's home stand. Reggie Jackson stood alone at his locker, toweling off after a postgame shower. In the past, Jackson managed to deflect questions to Sal Bando. But Sal was in the trainer's room, so I thought this would be a rare opportunity to allow Reggie to express himself.

"Were you surprised that the Rangers didn't make a run at the A's this year? Quite a few people actually picked them to beat you guys in the division," I said.

A rather professorial frown crossed Jackson's face as he pondered the query. "A lot of people failed to factor in the reality that the Rangers' showing last year was a fluke," Jackson said. "Ferguson Jenkins is a pitcher who will always be on schedule to win 20 games, but not 25, like the Rangers had been counting on again this year. Last year, they got away with a one-man bullpen. You don't get away with that year after year. Last year, they put Cesar Tovar in center field, and he played like Willie Mays. This year, Tovar has played like the player he his, which is a nice utility man who is pushing age forty. Last year, Jeff Burroughs was the Most Valuable Player in the American League. This year, he played back down to his actual level, which is that of a man who'll finish around eighth among the outfielders in the All-Star voting. Even if some of last year's pieces had fallen into place again, Texas had no chance against us. Look at the players in this room," he said, with his right arm gesturing expansively across the men-in-mustaches dressing quickly in the Oakland clubhouse. "We are head and shoulders above the rest of the league."

In yet another postgame presentation, Vida Blue defined the A's' success ethic in a poem that he had composed. He recited his work. *"Sometimes you can, sometimes you can't. Sometimes you is, sometimes you ain't. Sometimes you will, sometime you won't."* Short but meaningful, Vida's verse was vastly superior to that horseshit of William Butler Yeats and his ilk that so many of us had been forced to read in school.

His words were comforting. Also comforting was the reality that anybody experiencing inclinations of self-pity needed only to watch the downpour of misery that had inundated the Detroit Tigers. They'd lost a 7–6 heartbreaker to Baltimore, making their losing streak climb to a calamitous 13 straight. One more, and the Tigers would break a franchise record for futility. They'd get that one more, too, and several more after that. Gary Sutherland, a Detroit infielder, detailed the state of the floundering team. "Our attitude," Sutherland said, "is great. It's the play on the field that's killing us."

Chapter 12

August 8

According to the lyrics of a long-ago literary ballad, two women gazed upon F. Scott Fitzgerald as he lay in his casket.

"He looks so peaceful," said one of the women.

"Well, he ought to," responded the other woman, whose name was Dorothy Parker. "He hasn't had a drink in three days."

I had matched Fitzgerald's record. But there was no joy in that accomplishment. The act of typing newspaper stories "on the 'natch," as the musicians called the condition of going on stage unstoned, proved bitterly nonfulfilling. Seen through sober eyes, the players on the field seemed more lethargic than graceful. Only once did something occur that was really worth watching. That happened when Joe Rudi stroked a screaming line drive into the stands behind first base at Arlington Stadium that struck an old man right square in his dentures, and three beer-bellied fans sitting nearby nearly killed each other fighting for the bloodied baseball. Meanwhile, the action on the field limped along at the pace of a five-act opera. Yet, the minutes on the electric clock out on the scoreboard clicked by at an alarming rate. Deadlines seemed more threatening.

Three days without the solace of bottled amnesia had been at least two too many. I was going to quit at three anyway, since the Rangers' never-relenting schedule mandated a weekend visit to Milwaukee. How terribly rude would it have been to arrive as a guest in the premier drinking city in all of North America and not participate—along with the locals—in a liver-withering bender? According to the ad slogan, this was a city made famous by a beer. Schlitz. Or was it Pabst Blue Ribbon? Being the native of a city (Fort Worth) that was made famous by a whorehouse (the Jackson Hotel), I could appreciate that. So what kind of chickenshit would dare to dishonor the heritage of the greatest German metropolis in the New World, where everybody's surname included the "oeh" letter combination, by ordering a diet cola?

Any flimsy notion of continuing the futility of my self-imposed dry siege vanished when I read of a confession by Don Newcombe, who had become the lead crusader of an abstinence cause for baseball players. Newcombe, the ex-Dodger, contended that drinking was a hazard to the health and career of a grassroots majority population of big leaguers. One of the latter-day heroes of Ebbets Field, Newcombe had resorted to the sedation of fermented fortitude because he was terrified of air travel, and the demon in the jug had led the pitcher to the altar of self-destruction. The heart of the game was darkened by an 86 proof secret. After years of trembling tribulation, Newcombe had successfully abandoned the bottle, and encouraged others to follow his example. Then, out of nowhere, he announced with pride that six years had passed since he had experienced the taste of *ice cream*. Ah. Now the truth had emerged. Once the person bade bye-bye to the liquid substances that buzz-bombed the brain, the sugar syndrome made its attack. After a while, dried-out Newk was unhappy to watch his waistline expand.

While the Rangers began the first of a four-city (Milwaukee, Detroit, Baltimore, Cleveland) summertime tour of the skeletal remains of America's industrial age, I beefed up the free lager refreshment available in the County Stadium press box with a quart of Christian Brothers brandy. I drank straight from the bottle, and drew an admonishing stare from some Milwaukee sportswriter. "What do you think this is, a Packers game?" he said. What did he know? Bingo! Mission accomplished! The magic of baseball was back! On the mound, Ferguson Jenkins was an artist, a maestro, as he left the Brewers spellbound in a 4–2 win.

Then Jenkins offered the most candid assessment of the business reality among the big leaguers' job force, circa 1975, that I would hear all season. "I got the win and that is the only statistic that is really going to matter when I go to talk contract with Mr. Corbett this winter," Jenkins said. (Note the word "agent" did not appear in that sentence. Note also that even though Jenkins's contract was up, the concept of selling his services to another team also went unmentioned.)

"A pitcher can't make any money in this game if he doesn't win 20 games. At least, a finesse pitcher like me can't."

The Rangers, obviously more relaxed after Billy Martin's departure, had been playing a better brand of baseball. They beat Milwaukee in two of the games in the series, and were rewarded for their efforts by being herded onto a two-engine DC-3 for the short flight across Lake Michigan to Detroit. That plane hadn't been in the sky since the Berlin Airlift. A flight attendant wisely handed out barf bags full of miniature liquor bottles to the players as they boarded this relic from aviation's yesteryear. Even though the luggage and equipment were not on board, the aircraft barely made it off the runway at Milwaukee's General [Billy] Mitchell Airport. "This is just the fun part," said Jeff Burroughs, who puffed nervously on a menthol cigarette even though he didn't smoke. "Wait until they parachute us out over enemy territory."

August 11

The origin of the word "fan," as related to sports, has been assigned to three sources. Fan might come from "fanatic," which describes the nature of the truly addicted beast, or might have come from "fantasy," which is the world in which most true fans live their lives of loud desperation. But in Detroit in 1975, the fan was what the shit hit when the Tigers fell apart like a poorly assembled Nash Rambler. Amid the crumbling-factory landscape of the Michigan subtopia, some people referred to the Tigers' midsummer disaster as Jimmy's Jinx, while to others the calamity had become Hoffa's Hex. By any name, since the labor boss had vanished, so had the home team's chances of winning any ballgames. In a city with a proud-as-hell baseball history, a 15-game losing streak ventured beyond embarrassment. Henry Ford, in his grave, found solace in the fact that the alarming decline of the ball club had led many Detroit natives to forget the Edsel debacle, but in Motown, Marvin was not Gaye.

One of baseball's top stories of the time had been Tigers outfielder Ron LeFlore, who had been discovered in the recreation yard of the Michigan state pen in Jackson, and had advanced from prison walls into the major leagues. Then, as the Tigers' August miseries grew more glaringly intense, LeFlore was denying rumors that he wanted to be returned to the joint. Joe Falls, the bare-knuckled columnist for the *Detroit Free Press*, wondered and thundered in print, "What in the name of Ty Cobb is going on here?" Falls threatened to start writing about soccer if the calamity was not corrected soon.

Several American League teams, the Red Sox in particular, had been padding their win column résumés at the Tigers' expense, and the Rangers were eager to fatten theirs as well.

On Monday night, Texas extended Detroit's chain of despair to 16 games. Gaylord Perry pitched a shutout, the Rangers won, 7–0, and I typed a lead paragraph that read: *"The Rangers made it look easy because it WAS easy."*

Not only were the Tigers on a collision course with the all-time big league losing streak—23 games—they also were closing in on another possible measure of ignominy, the record for consecutive innings without scoring a run. The record was 48, and after Perry's performance, the Tigers' run drought reached 29 innings. Until the losing streak had set in, the 1975 Tigers had been grinding along at a marginally sub-.500 pace most of the season, just like the other American League teams had been doing... jogging in circles while the Red Sox and A's disappeared beyond the horizon. Why, all of a sudden, had this Detroit team suddenly become so nontransparent in its on-the-field futility? The answer, ultimately, was simple enough. A few too many individuals on the Detroit roster were imposters who had fooled the scouts into the clubhouse with forged IDs. Baseball tradition dictated that the least gifted—the "how in the hell did that guy get in here?"—players became the best managers. Two of the game's best future managers, Gene Michael and Jerry Manuel, seldom appeared on the field, but they were wearing Tigers uniforms while the team performed its Dead Man Walking routine.

I joined a handful of other reporters who entered the Tigers' clubhouse, and was stricken with the awkward feeling that came with a funeral home visitation. I hadn't been sure whether I was supposed to take notes or send flowers, and could only hope that the lid on the casket was closed. The reporters asked questions in whispers. Ralph Houk, the Tigers' manager, offered the quintessential portrait of dignity amid disaster. This was the man who had managed the team that was acknowledged as the greatest since the onset of the Depression: the 1961 Yankees.

But prior to that, Houk had been a hero fighting Nazis in World War II. He'd earned a battlefield promotion from private to major. Houk had been awarded a Bronze Star, a Silver Star, a Purple Heart. So if anybody could withstand this siege of despair on the baseball diamond, it was Ralph Houk. He reminded me of Ben Schwartzwalder, the football coach at Syracuse, who had said of a particular referee, "When I was a paratrooper in the war, I stuck eight-inch knives into guys I hated less than I hate him."

The Tigers' manager was calm now, his priorities in place. Houk sat, with no show of emotion, sipping on a bottle of Coca-Cola though a straw, and eating Planter's Peanuts that were piled on a plate next to the can. "There is no dissension. There is no morale problem. Nobody is bawling anybody else out. A manager can't ask anything more. Believe it or not, unlike this game against Gaylord Perry, we've played pretty well. We're not playing ball to make people laugh; at least I'd better not catch anybody laughing."

After having witnessed Ralph Houk's exhibition of bravery, I needed a drink. The obvious location to secure that was within walking distance of Tiger Stadium, a haven for the thirsty known as the Lindell AC on Cass Street. That particular stroll was sometimes a high-adrenaline event, where I found myself moving with hurried strides amidst the silhouettes of people harder even than the sidewalks of downtown Detroit. The Lindell might have been America's original sports bar. It was a dive owned by the same guy who helped spring Ron LeFlore from the Michigan state penitentiary in Jackson. The walls were coated with glossy black-and-white autographed photos of the warriors from Detroit's proud professional athletic past—the likenesses of men whose names and faces resounded throughout the after-shave generation. That lasted about fifteen good years, starting with Old Spice and running all the way to English Leather. Alex Delvecchio, Night Train Lane, Dave DuBusschere, Frank Lary—by the dozens—storied names from a glorious past. The Lindell was a museum, and at the same time, the stars of the present (that being 1975) mingled with the ghosts of the past. An eternal procession of visiting players from baseball, hockey, and hoops drifted through the doors of the Lindell on a nightly basis.

Naturally, an array of personalities like those attracted a collateral assembly of persons of the groupie persuasion. If a ballplayer couldn't get lucky at the Lindell, then he either had some kind of disease or just didn't care. On Monday, I sat at an empty booth, accompanied by a scotch and soda. Then I heard a woman say, "Oh, look. It's Timmy Ecclestone! Hi, Timmy!" She slid into my booth. I knew two things: that Tim Ecclestone was a hockey player, and a former Detroit Red Wing, and I knew that I was not Tim Ecclestone, but was going to try to be him, anyway.

The key to pulling that off would be an ability to speak Canadian. I'd covered minor league hockey back in Texas, and thought I knew how. Simply begin every sentence with "Jeez" and conclude it with "eh?" Hell, it was easier than pig latin. Another key to speaking fluently in Canadian: Always state the obvious.

"Jeez, that's a white blouse you've got on there, eh?"

She nodded, looking giddy.

"Jeez, so it's all right if I buy you a drink, eh?"

That worked for about half an hour. But with every passing cocktail, I started sounding less Canadian and more Texan, and was starting to feel as out of place as a sombrero in a synagogue.

The woman was growing suspicious. Finally, I made the mistake of making a quick run to the bathroom. As I sauntered back, it was evident that I was no goddamn hockey player. In the colored reflective light from the jukebox, my front teeth looked real.

"You're not Timmy!" the woman shrieked.

"Jeez, I never said I was, so I guess I'm not, eh?" I said. I thought she was going to slap me. A guy at the next table enjoyed the show. That was the Rangers' irrepressible backup catcher, Ron Pruitt, who had remained on the Texas roster because the team had refused to succumb to Billy Martin's demand to hire Tom Egan. Then Pruitt informed me that he was finally leaving. "Just got my traveling orders," he said. "Shipped to Spokane, so I'm in here for a farewell drink or three. Tell the folks back in Texas not to take it too hard."

August 13

Detroit's losing streak had added still another chapter, and stood at 17. A crowd of 10,200 came to Tiger Stadium to watch. They wore the curious expressions of passers-by at a bus wreck. When the PA announcer informed the throng that after that night's game, the Tigers would leave on an extended two-week road trip, the people cheered.

Those cheers of derision changed to cheers of hope, then cheers of actual jubilation as Bill Freehan, one of the leftover figures from the Tigers' championship team of 1968, belted a home run. After seven innings, the Tigers had mounted a 5–1 lead. The Detroit fans applauded almost every pitch. The witch was dead. Then came the top of the eighth inning, and the Tigers' dark destiny lurked in the night sky. Mike Hargrove lined a hard opposite field double to left. Joe Coleman, who had been mowing down

Rangers with the zeal of a man on a mission of vengeance, struck out Jeff Burroughs.

The next batter, Jim Spencer, looped a lazy blooper into short right field. Leon Roberts charged the ball, got there late, then turned and chased the ball as it rolled to the wall. Hargrove scored, Spencer stopped at second. Detroit's lead was cut to 5–2. The next batter, Toby Harrah, cracked a sharp single to left. Spencer stopped at third.

Ralph Houk emerged from the Tigers' dugout. Joe Coleman, he realized, had run out of petrol. Houk signaled for a right-handed reliever, Bob Reynolds, to work against Tom Grieve. Grieve was a home run threat, and, as a slow runner, an even better double-play threat. That was what Ralph Houk counted on. Instead, Grieve swung a little late on a fastball and delivered the ball to deep right field, just far enough and high enough to clear the screen atop the wall.

The game was tied now, 5–5, and the crowd issued the most thunderous sigh...a muffled lamentation of Old Testament proportions...ever heard in the history of the ballpark.

In the top of the 11th inning, the power of negative thinking put its fingers around the throats of the Detroit Tigers and squeezed hard. With Rangers on first and second with one out, and Gene Pentz pitching for Detroit, Lenny Randle cracked a hard grounder up the middle. Detroit shortstop Tom Veryzer fielded the ball cleanly, stepped on second for the first out, then fired to first. The ball landed in the dirt, skipped past first baseman Dan Meyer, and Cesar Tovar scored the go-ahead run, unearned. Detroit lost, 6–5. Eighteen straight.

In the press box, I shook my head and typed. "*It is now official. Jimmy Hoffa will sit in the right field upper deck with Amelia Earhart as his date before the Detroit Tigers will ever win another baseball game.*"

As the Rangers got dressed for a flight to Baltimore, the players collectively reacted like some person who had received a check in the mail that was intended for the guy next door. If Tom Grieve had been the hero with his clutch, game-tying, three-run homer in the eighth inning, he concealed it. "I cannot imagine," he said, "what it must be like over in their clubhouse right now." Toby Harrah, who had been gathering a reputation among managers as the most underrated player in the American League, was less compassionate. "Shit, I don't feel sorry for them at all. I originally signed with the Washington Senators, remember. When I came into the big leagues, I played for teams that had losing streaks that lasted for three years."

August 16

Like most vacations, the days of the Rangers' respite from genuine big league competition had zoomed by and ended abruptly. Despite an appeal to the league that would have allowed the team to follow Detroit around for the remainder of the season, the pilot landed the team charter flight at Friendship Airport in Baltimore, which meant that the Texans would once again be going to bat against the Big Boys. Earl Weaver's Orioles had launched into their customary late season victory binge, and were marching in steadfast pursuit of the front-running Red Sox.

Weaver, a man who could have kept the tobacco industry afloat through his efforts alone, was a craftsman when it came to dugout mind games. He convinced his players to relax, let the fatigued opponent make the key mistakes, don't press for vital wins—let the other team hand those to you on a room service platter—and merely look complacently confident while Boston stared at what was looming from behind in the rearview mirror. The Orioles had gotten the Sox' attention. Back in early June, right around D-Day, at a time in the season when most teams had played enough games to establish their true identities, the Orioles had been nine games under the break-even mark.

At the time, Weaver had seemed supremely unconcerned, and I had wondered if that had been an act. It hadn't been. With two stellar starters—Jim Palmer and Mike Torrez—and two more solid ones—Ross Grimsley and Mike Cuellar—plus a well-fortified bullpen—Grant Jackson, Wayne Garland, and Doyle Alexander—Weaver knew that the most natural laws of the game would bring another satisfactory outcome. All Earl needed to do was open another pack, light up, inhale, and watch. With the Rangers arriving in town, packaged as easy meat, Baltimore had risen from the dregs of June and had climbed up to 12 games above the blue sky side of .500. Since the All-Star break, the Birds had posted a 23-8 record.

Before a Friday night doubleheader against Texas, Weaver expressed some concern that the Rangers might offer trouble. "The guy they have who worries me is that Mike Hargrove. You know what he is? He's a goddamn white version of Tony Oliva, that's what he is," Weaver allowed. "Get two strikes on him, and then watch what happens. He'll step out of the batter's box, and fiddle with his cap, and adjust his jockstrap, and then he'll step back in, and foul one off. Then, he'll step back out of the box, fidget some more, and then foul off another one. You know what that does to a pitcher? Drives him nuts, that's what it does. Finally, Hargrove gets the pitch he wants, and hits a line drive, and where does the ball land? Right into the most open space available in the outfield, that's where." Earl smoked about a pack and a half during that soliloquy.

Since Hargrove's destiny was to become a successful manager, he could not have been all that good. Still, he bedeviled poor old Earl with a couple of two-strike line drive base hits that each brought home a run, and the Rangers won the opener of the double-dip, 10–6. Steve Foucault, the relief pitcher who looked like Archie Bunker, except for having less hair, came into the game while it was still close and proceeded to shut down the Orioles. Foucault had been the Rangers' 1974 one-man bullpen that Reggie Jackson had talked about. In '75, Foucault had faltered, and as a result, the Rangers had entered American League combat with a no-man bullpen, and garish numbers in the games-behind column had been the result. But with the arrival of August, something changed, and in four relief appearances, Foucault had recorded two wins and two saves.

What happened? Why the turnabout? Foucault credited Billy Martin, or more specifically, Martin's late-July departure.

"Billy, when he was managing us, called all of the pitches from the dugout," Foucault noted. "And when I was pitching, everything Billy called was a breaking ball. When Frank Lucchesi took over for Billy, he had the catcher call the pitches. Since then, in my last four appearances, I've probably thrown four breaking balls, total, and now I'm getting guys out."

So much for the man who'd appeared on the cover of that June issue of *Sports Illustrated*...Baseball's Fiery Genius.

In the second game, Earl Weaver got into a screaming match with umpire Ron Luciano, and got thrown out. Actually, Weaver was leaving town to attend his daughter's wedding in St. Louis, and needed to catch a plane. The Orioles did not need Weaver in the nightcap. Baltimore won, 13–1. With the game out of hand and the Rangers running out of pitchers, Lucchesi was forced to leave a pitcher without his stuff in the game as a sacrificial offering to the realities of baseball.

Tommy Moore, a left-hander who arrived in the gift basket of spare parts that Texas had received from St. Louis while unloading Willie Davis, toiled for three innings, and was pounded for seven runs. The next morning, I saw Moore in the coffee shop of the rather half-ass Holiday Inn in downtown Baltimore where the team was billeted, and he offered the best quote I'd get all year.

"I've got bruises all over me," Moore said. "I fell out of bed three or four times last night—dodging line drives."

August 17

What was with the Rangers, all of a sudden? The Baltimore Orioles had been baseball's version of a runaway train for a month and a half, and now the Texas team had dynamited the tracks. I knew the answer. I was drinking again, so God, in His merciful wisdom, had thrown me a bone, and given this world-weary straggler in the press box infantry something worth describing to the calloused readership.

Gaylord Perry, himself prospering during the Rangers' life-after-Billy renaissance, bolted down all of the escape exits and beat Baltimore, 5–1. Over a stretch of 67 innings, Perry had registered an earned run average of 0.40. So I wrote, *"Matched against the hottest team in baseball, Perry, the grizzled gentleman farmer, seemed about as in awe of the Orioles as he would be of a bale of hay."*

Bobby Grich marveled at what Perry had been throwing. "Those weren't spitballs," Grich confirmed. "Those were some of the nastiest fastballs I have seen all year. All I could do was walk away from the plate and shake my head."

Texas had jumped ahead early when Jim Fregosi hit a three-run homer off Ross Grimsley. Of the batting star of the game, I wrote, *"Fregosi is old enough to be somebody's grandfather, although, to the best of his knowledge, he's not."*

In major league baseball, the top story of the day had come from Anaheim. Detroit beat California to end its losing streak at 19 games. Some pitcher named Ray Bare had thrown a two-hitter. But when it came to the big picture, the more meaningful event was what had been occurring in Baltimore. The Texas Rangers, in their own small way, had provided the key that would unlock the gates of Fenway Park at World Series time in October 1975. They had blunted Baltimore's late season momentum, and the Orioles never were able to sustain the push that they would need to catch the Red Sox. And that was too bad, in my estimation. I liked Earl Weaver. I liked his players and the way they played the game, I liked the food in the Baltimore press box, and I liked the stadium PA announcer, the ever congenial Rex Barney, the ex–Brooklyn Dodgers bullpen star. What I did not like about the Orioles was that they played, and played loudly, "Thank God I'm a Country Boy" during the seventh inning stretch. I'd known the man who sang the song, John Denver, in high school. I liked John Denver, too, but I didn't like that goddamn song, and if Denver was a country boy, then I was J. Edgar Hoover.

So it was with some reluctance that I packed my suitcase and headed off to Cleveland on getaway-day Sunday, and said so in the paper. *"Next stop on the Rangers' tour of the Mysterious American League East: That noted resort city of Cleveland, otherwise known as the Big C."*

August 18

In Oakland, the A's Gene Tenace violated one of baseball's most carefully tended protocols. He owned up to the fear factor that silently lurked among every hitter who stepped into a batter's box.

"I hate to bat against anybody that wild," said Tenace. He was talking about Milwaukee pitcher Pete Broberg, who had yielded three runs in the second inning without surrendering a base hit. After walking a trio of hitters, Broberg hit Sal Bando and Tenace on consecutive pitches.

Broberg, who'd gone to Dartmouth, had been a top draft choice with the Senators, just prior to moving to Texas. He had a 99-mile-per-hour heater. Finally, Texas gave up on its "live young" arm and shipped him to Milwaukee. Given Tenace's confession, it was clear that the Rangers had screwed up when they tried to teach Broberg some control.

August 19

While the Rangers and Indians entered the final stanzas of a season largely etched in futile frustration, and played before crowds of a magnitude usually seen at the grand opening of a Conoco station, an intriguing baseball dispatch arrived from Atlanta.

Since Willie Davis had been acquired by St. Louis, he'd been batting .308 in a Cardinals uniform and demonstrating flashes of the Willie Davis of his prime, the Willie Davis who had scored from second base in an exhibition game against the Chicago Cubs in 1968.

Then, with his team on the road in Georgia, Davis showed the Cardinals a different kind of speed, as he had hauled ass out of the clubhouse, out of town, and out of baseball. In sports sections around the United States, under the agate-type heading of "Transactions," the Cardinals had officially placed Davis on the Disqualified List. Some enterprising St. Louis reporter tracked Davis down, via the miracle of the telephone, and Willie explained his situation.

"My ex-wife is trying to collect all of my wages, which would, in effect, leave me playing for nothing," Davis announced. Willie was, in the end, a narcissist and somehow pictured himself as the only man in the world who experienced that predicament. "The way the laws are set up, she can garnish my entire salary, and that's what she's doing. So—if she's going to get my money, then let *her* play centerfield."

Danny O'Brien, the Rangers' general manager, was on the road with his team in Cleveland. I showed him the story about Willie Davis.

"Willie's available again, Danny," I said. "Any plans to bring him back to Texas?"

"None that I know of," Danny said.

"Then how about Tom Egan?" O'Brien laughed out loud at that one. Since Billy Martin had left Texas and found a nest in Gotham City, O'Brien had been seen laughing a lot.

Downstairs in the Texas dugout, the manager, Lucchesi, was not only matching O'Brien, grin for grin, but he looked like a man auditioning for a role in a toothpaste commercial. His boss, Brad Corbett, had removed the term "interim" from Lucchesi's job description, and presented him a contract that guaranteed his paycheck for the remainder of the 1975 season and the following two as well.

That came as a relief to Lucchesi, since underground whispers had hinted that Bill Virdon, the manager displaced when Martin went to New York, was headed to Texas. Lucchesi lit a cigar and talked of the future. "My intention is to cooperate every way I can with the owners and everybody in the front office," declared Frank, "but if I ever hear any talk about trading Toby Harrah, unless it's for Tom Seaver, they'd better be ready for a fistfight."

Lucchesi was kidding. But when those words appeared in black ink on white newsprint, he sounded just like his hyper-combative predecessor. Poor Brad Corbett. He was learning that baseball team owners, like boat owners, list their happiest moments as the day they buy and the day they sell it.

August 20

A couple of poignant news dispatches appeared from baseball's outer precincts. Tony Conigliaro had abandoned his brave attempt to work his way back into the major leagues, finally admitting that he no longer had what it took to succeed even in the minors. He had a good excuse for quitting. "My body is falling apart," he said.

Meanwhile, another former big leaguer was laboring in the sticks. Jim Bouton, author of the 1970 best-seller *Ball Four,* was pitching again, in the minors. He threw a six-hitter against Walla Walla, and in the process perhaps confirmed that people who write books need to sustain a day job.

August 24

Baltimore had come to Texas in dire need of a four-game series sweep. Their annual scorched-earth march through the AL East had lost its steam. The Boston Red Sox had been standing firm, and the Orioles were running out of time. Earl Weaver's team won the first two games—but then encountered Ferguson Jenkins at his best, and lost, 1–0. Weaver felt that a win in the fourth-game finale was essential.

The teams played Ping-Pong with the lead, back and forth. The Rangers scored twice in the eighth to go ahead, 7–6. Over the span of almost a decade, nobody in the big leagues performed better in clutch situations than Baltimore. In the top of the ninth, Ken Singleton homered to tie the game. Texas loaded the bases in their half of the inning, and with one out, it was pressure cooker time. Mike Hargrove tapped a slow bouncer to short, and Tim Nordbrook, subbing for Mark Belanger, fired the ball to the plate, looking for the force. Len Randle, running from third, slid, and home plate umpire Jerry Neudecker extended both arms, palms down. Safe! Game over!

Earl Weaver blew his top, and what came shooting out was a long season's worth of hopes, fears, and frustrations. People filing out of the stadium thirty rows up could hear Earl screaming at Neudecker.

"FOUR FEET! HE WAS OUT BY FOUR FUCKING FEET! JESUS CHRIST, JERRY! I'VE GOT TO MAKE A FUCKING LIVING, TOO!"

Neudecker seemed supremely unconcerned. En route to the umpires' dressing room, he actually sat down in the Orioles' dugout and took a drink from the water cooler. He was still relaxing in the dugout, and enjoying the solitude, when I walked down there to speak with Earl. "Two things wrong with Earl's argument," the ump said. "The runner beat the throw, and then Elrod [Hendricks, the catcher] took his foot off the plate."

On the Rangers' side, Frank Lucchesi assessed the win. Frank was a classic specimen of the Mafioso prototype, but the only thing he'd ever mangled was the English language. "It was a bleep-bleep play," he said.

August 26

Baseball's eternal season registered its usual pre-September body count. Loss of key personnel translated into losses in the standings. Somehow the managers who could least afford the attrition of injuries always seemed to be the hardest hit.

Frank Quilici, vainly struggling to save his job in Minnesota, got bad news. His third baseman, Eric Soderholm, had been declared finished for the remainder of the season. So what happened to Soderholm? Hurt his leg in a hard slide? Screwed up his shoulder, diving for a fly ball?

No. Soderholm had been exploring some rural property he had purchased, fallen into an open sewer well, and broken two ribs. Frank Quilici knew that it was time to clean out his desk.

Chapter 13

September 1

Concealed amid the monastic solitude of his underground bunker, he hid his work with a zeal that was untethered, unrestrained. This agent of Satan had been assigned a mission: to extinguish any and all elements of hope from the human condition. They called him the Major League Baseball Schedule Maker. He wore a black hood, and beneath that was a diabolically contoured face, white as bone, and stainless steel, dagger-shaped teeth, coated with dry possum blood left from his morning breakfast ritual. On his days off, he moonlighted as an interrogation expert for the KGB.

From Cap Anson to Hank Aaron—it didn't matter. Nobody escaped the ravages of the Schedule Maker. What the fiendish son of a social worker liked to do best was schedule night games. People who resided in free countries were not intended to labor after dark, unless they were some kind of pervert. Because of the Schedule Maker's handiwork, I calculated that I had devoted forty-four of my last fifty nights to either typing in a press box or going somewhere on an airplane. As the 1975 season tiptoed quietly in the general direction of a conclusion, I went to my boss at the newspaper and begged for a one-night reprieve. I needed a Saturday night off, for reasons of health.

"All right," said the boss. "You can have Saturday off, but first, take my car and get it washed."

That was all that I needed. One night off. I wanted to experience the decade of the 1970s. From people with more standard occupations, I'd been hearing good things about the 1970s. The quality of the nightlife was generating especially promising reviews, and I'd been isolated from all of that, trapped inside the constrictions of the tightly wrapped cocoon of baseball. The 1970s would not be around forever, and they were passing me by.

So—with my certified furlough that entitled me to thirty-six hours of shore leave—I accompanied two old friends, both freshly minted divorcés, to an outdoor concert in Oklahoma with a talent ensemble appropriate to the time and the region, entertainment geared for the dope-smoking goat roper.

My friends included me in this adventure because, with my newspaper connections, I had been able to obtain three backstage media passes for the event that was promoted as 48 Hours in Atoka. One of the friends had become a lawyer, and he represented the *Dallas Morning News*. He'd obtained an assignment from the entertainment editor to cover the concert, without a byline. His motive, I think, was to demonstrate to the newspaper people that he'd produce a better story than they could. A lot of lawyers shared that delusion. Still do.

There was a point during my night off in the open fields of southern Oklahoma when I abandoned the protective womb of the backstage area and ventured out among the people...the fans of the music of their era. What I encountered out there was a five-course feast for the various senses, but the main course didn't involve sight or sound—it was the stench. The tableau presented one feature that was vaguely similar to a baseball game. A concessionaire meandered through the crowd, hawking his products, but instead of "Popcorn...peanuts!" the concert vendor yelled, "Psi-locybin! White crosses! Psilocybin! White crosses!"

Next morning, after an all-night cultural experience and three showers, I lay on a sofa at my lawyer friend's house, watching him attempt to write his concert review on a legal pad. He was on deadline, and choking, just like the lawyers always did. In that gigantic area where the printing presses were housed, there was no such thing as a motion for continuance. The lawyer, Steve, solicited my assistance.

Don't get me wrong. He did all of the writing. I simply told him what to say. I kept the resulting clip, still have it, as a trea-sured snapshot of the 1970s. These were some of the printed highlights:

- Despite heat, dust, and drastic scheduling failures, Saturday's crowd, estimated between 85,000 and 115,000 by the Okla-homa Highway Patrol, consumed staggering quantities of beer and wine and appeared in good spirits.
- A highly publicized pre-concert schedule listed a star-studded assembly of names from the country genre. But most of the evening, the stage was occupied by Willie Nelson's drastically overworked backup band, and by midnight, only Larry Gatlin had performed. It was near midnight when Jessi Colter arrived from a Holiday Inn in McAlister, without her vocalist husband, Waylon Jennings. Colter had been scheduled to entertain at 10 P.M. But instead of performing, the songstress disappeared into a backstage trailer. An aide advised the press that the singer was not feeling well.
- Some crowd discontent was voiced, complaining of the ab-sence of advertised shade and an adjacent lake. Security per-sonnel piqued resentment for high-handed treatment of the

ticket buyers, and for frequent statements that they had been officially deputized by the sheriff of Atoka County. Upon arriving, the music fans, many carrying heavy coolers, had been forced to walk four miles, through thick, choking Oklahoma red dirt, to the concert site. Even so, the crowd displayed more upbeat spirit than the performers.

- A crowd of performers and aides gathered backstage to watch a girl being transferred into an ambulance. Although there were rumors that the girl had been stabbed, medical personnel confirmed that she was in good condition after a drug overdose. Rumors also circulated that the Hell's Angels had arrived from Oakland, California. But investigation proved the thirty-member motorcycle club to be the Rancid Riders from the east side of Fort Worth. (Okay. I made up the name Rancid Riders, but this was the lawyer's story, not mine.)

After a sixth visit to the shower, my entire body remained coated with a veneer of concert dust. Now that I had seen the 1970s, I was eager to return to the sanitized sanity of the baseball press box, and supplicate myself again to the Schedule Maker and his heinous proclivities.

September 2

A pregame exploration of the Rangers' clubhouse revealed a glaring absence. Cesar Tovar, the man whose contagiously cheerful presentation could fill the big room by itself, was missing. Tovar's locker was empty. The man called Pepe was gone, gone to Oakland, exchanged for the most immortal name in baseball history, the Player to Be Named Later. (In all of the seasons I covered baseball, I somehow never met a player named Later.)

Charles Finley was stocking up with the veteran personalities that he liked to see on his roster as the postseason approached, the party time that most American League teams seldom enjoyed, when the stakes and the rewards loomed large. Reggie Jackson said he always enjoyed the late-season influx of experienced labor as it arrived in the Oakland dugout. "The great thing about playing for this team is that sooner or later, I get to meet all my boyhood idols."

A couple of weeks earlier, Texas manager Frank Lucchesi had been ejected from a game at Baltimore after losing an argument to Armando Rodriguez, an umpire. Lucchesi could be funny as hell when he wanted to be, and afterward he said, "I think Armando and I have a language barrier problem, because apparently, 'he missed the tag' is Spanish for 'motherfucker.' So next time I dispute a call with Armando, I'll take Tovar with me as an interpreter."

Tovar's Latin heritage might have been a reason for his transfer to Oakland, but his command of the language had nothing to do with it. The A's shortstop, Bert Campaneris, had been out of the lineup for a month with a lingering leg injury, and according to speculation, it would be Tovar's job to goad Campaneris to get off his ass.

Tovar, for sure, had gone on to a better place. School had started; the crowds at Arlington Stadium were drastically outnumbered by empty seats; football season was breaking out all over in Texas; and my Rangers stories were spotted at the bottom of the sports page, nestled obscurely next to an ad for the Handy Dandy store offering furnace filters for 44 cents.

A crowd of about 5,000 came to the stadium on Sunday night to watch the Rangers complete a series against the Minnesota Twins, the team that was identified as Texas's blood enemy for the third-place prize in the American League West standings.

The Twins led, 5–4, but the Rangers had the bases loaded and one out, with Jeff Burroughs at the plate. Burroughs had been fulfilling his home run allotment for the Rangers, but his batting average was way down, and it was becoming apparent that the league's incumbent MVP might not be the elite hitter that so many had thought he was. With a full count, reliever Tom Campbell threw a curveball, down and away, an out-of-the-strike-zone pitch to tie the game. But Burroughs swung and missed. Had Jeff declined to swing, the fly ball that the next batter, Toby Harrah, hit to left field would have served as the game-winning sacrifice fly. Instead, it was the game-ending third out.

Frank Quilici, the Twins' lame-duck manager, was asked to assess the key pitch of the game, the one on which Burroughs had whiffed. "I think it was a ball," said Quilici, rather curtly. Frank knew that he was gone at the end of the season, and there was no longer any reason to sling around any superfluous bullshit.

September 3

Dick Williams didn't say so, but through the serenity of his demeanor, he must have sensed that managing the last-place Angels for Gene Autry was the happier alternative to managing Charles Finley's World Series champion A's. Williams was a very watered-down reproduction of Willie Mays when he labored in the Dodgers' minor league chain. He knocked himself into a deep stupor after running into the center field fence at LaGrave Field in a game I attended in Fort Worth in the year 1950. A quarter of a century later, Williams sat in the pregame dugout and discussed his theory of pitching.

"I've offered $200 to any of my starters who can get 18 or more ground ball outs in a game," Williams declared. (Hey, Big

Spender, that's more than $12 an out! But this was baseball, '75 style.)

Williams says his incentive plan stemmed from his postwar tenure with the Dodgers, when their farm system was more extensive and far more efficient than anything that the Soviet Union had to offer. "Branch Rickey himself used to come and watch the AA pitching prospects warm up, and then he'd tape a dollar bill into the catcher's mitt and tell some guy, 'Hit the mitt and win the buck.' Nobody ever lost, and then Mr. Rickey would say, 'See, there? Control is concentration. Nothing more, nothing less.'"

September 5

I was in Oakland, and I was cold. I was also feeling a little repentant for thinking that California, on the whole, was constituted of the last remnants of the Pod People from *Invasion of the Body Snatchers*. They never looked you directly in the eye. They looked right through you, focused and fixated on the something beyond. Well, the fault was mine, and not the Californians. Then the telecast of *The Newlywed Game* was interrupted by a major news bulletin. Just over in the next town, practically—Sacramento to be exact—somebody had tried to shoot Gerald Ford, interim manager of the United States of America.

He was shaking hands after an appearance in the state capital, and said he knew something was going on when, "I saw a row of hands extended toward me, and then I saw a hand coming up between several others and obviously, that hand had a gun in it."

Squeaky Fromme, ex-follower of Charles Manson, pointed a .44 automatic at the president and pulled the trigger. The gun was loaded but the chamber was empty when Squeaky tried to shoot it. "Don't worry, fellas," Squeaky yelled at the Secret Service people.

"It didn't go off." Later, Fromme said that she belonged to an unofficial order of red-clad nuns, who were intent upon cleaning things up in anticipation of the Messiah's encore. "America is a mess," Squeaky announced. And in every major league city except Oakland, Boston, Pittsburgh, and Cincinnati, Squeaky was absolutely right. Among the remaining twenty teams, the lights that remained burning were vague beacons of promise that flickered in the faraway dreamland of Next Year.

September 6

Fergie Jenkins watched his hopes for another season of 20 or more wins vanish with one swing of Reggie Jackson's bat. Jenkins sat in front of his locker, a man at peace. A young reporter from the *San Mateo Times* ruptured the tranquillity. "Reggie Jackson said he hit a good pitch." Then he stared at Jenkins, awaiting a response.

"Yes, it was good, about 400 feet worth of good," Jenkins finally said, measuring his words tactfully.

"What kind of pitch was it?" The kid from San Mateo was clearly into that pitch.

"It was..." responded Jenkins, now adopting a Delphic pose, "a change-up."

The reporter left in a hurry, satisfied. Jenkins watched him go, and said, ever so quietly, "I lied to the dickhead. It was my Jamaican voodoo ball. Hops six ways at once."

September 8

Oakland inserted the golden spike into whatever distant ambitions Whitey Herzog and his Kansas City Royals might have fostered about overtaking Oakland in the season's final month. In a game fraught with more symbolic gestures than a Navaho mating dance, before a big home crowd of 38,000, the A's pounded K.C., 8–2. Herzog, ever the pragmatist, reviewed the show and said, "Looks like they got some bats. You play Oakland, you ain't playing no kids."

Sal Bando, who'd been hitting .205, had the keynote at-bat of the game when he hit a three-run homer. "That proves once again that we play a little better when the game means a lot, and a lot of people turn out to watch us." At a certain level, Bando's comments, brimming with the confidence of the well-weathered champion, might have served as the harbinger of storm clouds soon to form out past the Bay. Bando all but conceded that the A's had been flying over the American League landscape all season on automatic pilot.

With a World Series ring on their right ring finger and two others locked in a safe, Bando and the rest of the A's had a right to feel cocky. They should have known, of course, that many were the teams that had reached for the extra gear at the grand prize moment, only to learn that it was no longer there. Charlie Finley remained oblivious to the impending peril. His focus drifted away from the standings and his attention directed toward business issues. Japanese investors were probing the notion of buying Finley's rival for the Bay Area sports entertainment dollar, the Giants. Horace Stoneham, who'd moved the team from the Polo Grounds to Candlestick Park, was eager to sell. After one of the games against Texas in Oakland, Charlie, wearing some eye-catching gold cuff links, made a rare appearance in the modest media lounge and produced a quiet sermon. "This is a one-team market, and we're not going away," said Charlie. "The only 'if' in my equation is who our competition will be. If it's the Japanese, there will be no competition. The Japanese will find out what competition really is."

The pressroom man who supplied the generous spread of deviled ham and Nabisco saltine crackers chimed in. "Hey, Mr. Finley," he said. "Did you hear about the guy who was half-black and half-Japanese? Every December 7, he attacked Pearl Bailey."

Everybody stood there trying not to laugh, and then Finley said, "That's a good one." It was the only instance during the nearly three-decade span of Finley's ownership tenure that he was ever known to compliment an employee.

September 9

The Cincinnati Reds, operating in their own, separate galaxy, had already clinched the NL West division, and had left lordly Los Angeles so far behind that a *Rand McNally* road atlas was necessary to find them. Twenty games. So the Reds entertained themselves during the final thirty days of the regular season by decorating their bandwagon with stats and cheap frills.

Tony Perez had tied Frank Robinson's franchise record for career RBIs—an even 1,000. Then he broke it. "My children wanted to be at the stadium to see me break the record, even though I didn't want them there, because they had school the next day," Perez acknowledged. "So when I broke the record in the sixth inning, I sent word into the stands to tell the kids to go on home." Still, Perez could not help but express pride in the accomplishment. "Everyone in Cuba will hear about it," he said. "The Voice of America reports all of the baseball news."

September 10

Throughout my concentrated cross-country meanderings, I'd learned one enduring truth. With the advent of cool weather, persons living anywhere north of around Kansas City, up in the Corn Belt and Rust Belt, started to become edgy, staging an inward struggle to ward off dark moods.

The sky was sullen and gray and a mean-spirited breeze, the morning-after breath from Siberia, blew a mist along the streets of downtown Minneapolis. For all of the *Prairie Home Companion* types of portrayals of the rock-willed Minnesotan as the somehow colorfully stoic but ultimately harmless creature of the snows, I always sensed a population on the verge of blowing its stack.

Those suspicions got confirmed at the ballpark. It was a Wednesday, last night of the next-to-last trip of the season. The weather was so disagreeable that the big sliding press box windows had been pulled shut. In the Metropolitan Stadium stands, the beer vendors provided the only discernible signs of human life. The press box was practically deserted. One man stood out. About fifty. Full-figured farm build. He wasn't working for any media, and didn't work for the Twins. He was just some pragmatic, plainclothes Lutheran who'd wandered into the press box to stay dry, and with the season entering its final cheerless chapter, nobody cared.

And nobody cared when he violated the ultimate press box rule of expressing any type of enthusiasm, vocal or otherwise, about what was happening on the field.

Frank Quilici was ending his tenure as Twins manager by inserting a few of the minor league people summoned for the September roster into his lineup. One was a tall third baseman, Dave McKay.

In a 1–1 game, McKay stepped into the batter's box against Gaylord Perry with the bases full. The press box intruder went into action. He stood up. He clapped. "Okay, big guy. Let's go! Knock one outta here, kid! You can do it!" Nobody beyond the press box could hear him, since the windows were closed. Perry put Dave McKay away on three pitches, and the batter and his press box patron sat down simultaneously.

Two innings later, the same scenario occurred. McKay, with a couple of runners on base, watched three strikes go by, just standing there like a wooden Native American in front of a cigar store. In the bottom of the seventh, the score stood at 2–2, the bases were full, and McKay once again entered the batter's box.

"This guy's got nothin'! Come on, big guy! You're the one...you're the one!" Perry required four pitches this time, but again McKay went without a whimper, and as he carried his bat to the dugout, the mystery man upstairs soundlessly watched and rubbed the knuckles of his left hand into the palm of his right hand, like he was trying to crush walnuts.

In the top of the ninth, the Rangers broke the 2–2 tie and scored seven runs.

In the bottom of the ninth, Dave McKay, with two outs and his team trailing, 9–2, hit a 430-foot home run into the left field stands. The man in the press box stood again, but quaking and jerking, as if he were being electrocuted. He stumbled toward one of the big windows, and it slid open. While McKay circled the bases in the field of a totally vacant stadium, the man began to shout:

"YOU GUTLESS COCKSUCKER! YOU MISERABLE, BALL-SUCKING SON OF A BITCH! NOW YOU DO IT, YOU SORRY MOTHERFUCKER!"

His Scandinavian aria echoed across the empty arena, and players in both dugouts stood and peered up at the press box, craning their necks and wearing looks of concerned curiosity as they sought the source of the madness.

September 16

Oakland came to Texas for a one-day, two-game series. They were the makeup games for the happy "snow day" postponements of April, coming back to haunt the players in the trying form of the late-season doubleheader. The A's hit town, literally bubbling with aerated spirits and inflated with hubris.

For my readers, I offered a portrait of what a baseball dynasty, circa 1975, looked like:

> Outfitted in traditional postseason playoff costumes, this year all of the A's will be conspicuous in their Charles O. Finley cowboy hats. They're gold and green with a white A's insignia sewn onto the front, the kind of thing that's designed to make women faint, children scream and cause fist fights in the bars on the Jacksboro Highway.
>
> "Everybody who travels on the team plane—the players, the coaches, the manager, the broadcasters, Mr. Finley—is supposed to wear our hats and smile at all times," remarked one of the A's dubiously.

The A's player who was quoted was Paul Lindblad, a relief pitcher. Later, he'd also said, "What is this? The fucking 4-H Club?"

But the old buckaroos went out and mopped up on the Rangers, winning both games. Afterward, the players displayed measures of modesty not seen since the prime of Julius Caesar.

Vida Blue said, "Everybody talks about the '27 Yankees. This year, this Oakland team has to be remembered as one of the best of all time."

Billy Williams, who had toiled heroically with no postseason reward during his long career as a Chicago Cub, anticipated the sweetness of the completed mission of the division championship, and the richness of what lay beyond. "Champagne in the clubhouse. I can't wait," Williams admitted. "I've drunk a lot of things in the clubhouse, but never champagne."

Reggie Jackson was born for the mantle of the victor, and he bore it well after the Rangers had been kicked aside. "We had to prove ourselves more this year, because we lost Catfish Hunter. There was a lot of pressure on us. If we'd lost, then everyone would have said, 'See . . . see? They couldn't do it without the Cat.' "

Then the Oakland A's, lords of the baseball universe, packed up their gear and headed for the airport in search of new conquests.

I never saw them again. The machine, the dynasty, had only a few days to live. Postseason calamity sat in ambush, just around the next bend, and Charlie Finley would disassemble the guts of the apparatus. The grandeur of the Swingin' A's would vanish—poof—just like the muttonchop sideburns and leisure suits and open love trappings of the decade of their reign. Boston ended Oakland's season with the suddenness of a guillotine in the playoffs. First round bye-bye. If ever a championship-caliber team committed a self-inflicted early departure, it was those A's. Bloated with the assumption of invincibility, the A's overlooked the Red Sox in anticipation of the later confrontation with the Reds.

In the stunning aftermath, Charles Finley was prepared to show the baseball owners that in the New Day of the free agent marketplace, a man could wreck a franchise quicker than he could ever build one up. By the end of the next season, Finley would have jettisoned Reggie Jackson, Joe Rudi, Sal Bando, Gene Tenace, Bert Campaneris, and Rollie Fingers. Seldom had any dynasty been so hastily relegated to the scrapbooks than Finley's A's.

September 20

According to the crumpled cynics, it matters not who you were, or what you've become, it's the lives you have touched. But the truth is, the turnout at your funeral is totally dependent upon the weather.

The wind—the voice of ice—was coming in hard off the lake, bringing a soggy overcast with it, which might have partially explained the emptiness of White Sox Park in what was being billed as perhaps the last game in major league baseball's oldest stadium.

The '75 White Sox had registered a big-league-bottom season draw of 770,000. The Chicago owner, John Allyn, was having discussions with some envoys reporting that a Seattle group desired to transport the White Sox to their new Pacific home. Because Chicago was ending the season on the road, the place was already about to be locked up for the winter.

Dismal weather or not, the Sunday crowd of 4,000 provided a cruel send-off to a facility with such an active past. The spectators, with plenty of room, sat scattered among the deserted grandstand, bundled in quilts and blankets. I tried to capture the feeling of the ballpark as much as possible when the opportunity came along in my newspaper stories. This time I wrote: "*From the outside, White Sox Park looks like a long-abandoned munitions factory that was built during the Civil War. It looks like that on the inside, too.*"

So Nancy Faust, best ballpark organist of her time, played "Take Me Out to the Ball Game" in the middle of the seventh inning, and from elsewhere in the press box, the voice of Harry Caray resounded and echoed as he declared, "Why in the hell aren't they playing 'Auld Lang Syne'?"

Texas won. I asked Jim Spencer if he'd felt any sense of history in playing in the final game in the ancient pavilion, Home of the Black Sox, if nothing else. "I don't know if shit like this was history or not. I'd hate to think so." he said. "I do know that my balls are frozen harder than a brass monkey's."

As it turned out, the White Sox were not going anywhere, and as for the stadium, well, there was plenty of life still left in that old corpse.

The Rangers boarded a bus that was to transport them to O'Hare Airport for a flight to Kansas City and the final road series of the season. The driver managed to get lost, and the bus was zigzagging through the back streets of South Side Chicago. Bus drivers had to take a bunch of crap from ballplayers under the best of circumstances, and this poor man, already flustered, absorbed the flogging.

"This guy is so fucked up he ought to be an umpire," shouted Dave Nelson. A car sped past the bus, on the left, going seventy at least, and then: BOOM! The bastard drove straight into a telephone pole. The bus stopped, and that was the moment when I found out a lot about the 1975 Texas Rangers.

Half of them liked to look at dead people; half of them didn't. And the ones who did liked it a lot. I'd never—and haven't since— seen a collective gleam of anticipation in people's eyes that could compare with that of the players running to the wreck scene. I got off the bus with them. I didn't like to look at dead people but thought it was interesting to look at people who were looking at somebody who was. The group was disappointed. The driver was alive, so I checked him out, a man wearing an overcoat of blood and broken glass, the perfect metaphor for end-of-summer base-ball. He was finished for the season, but dead set on being good as new come the spring.

Joe Lovitto stared at the man whose car was impaled on the wooden pole. "Hey, man," Lovitto said to the driver. "You look like you could use a drink. Here…" Lovitto held an airline mini-bottle—vodka—through what was left of the passenger-side door. Joe was a man determined to squeeze the last drop out of the life that the baseball of his generation had to offer.

September 27

The Baltimore Orioles, under Earl Weaver, had been as smirk-ingly impervious and immune to the notion of death as fire ants. In mid-September, they won 10 out of 11 games. Baltimore had been almost supernatural in its tenacity. Billy Martin's Yankees finished the Orioles' desperate, clawing quest. New York beat Bal-timore in a doubleheader, the Magic Number was then zero, and the championship belonged to Boston.

September 29

One out remained in my season of '75. Jim Wohlford of the Roy-als stood at the plate. Two-and-1 count. Wohlford took the pitch, and the umpire gestured with a pulling motion of his right arm. One strike now. Two-and-2 pitch. Wohlford fouled it into the dirt, and as he did that, most of the 6,000 people at Arlington Sta-dium jumped up and cheered. Wohlford looked around, confused by the reaction of the foul tip. He didn't know that most of the people in the stands sat with a beer cup in one hand, small radio in the other, listening to the Dallas Cowboys game against St. Louis.

Dallas made the winning touchdown just as Wohlford had swung his bat. He swung again and lofted a lovely arc across the bluest of wide-open-spaces skies, high into left field, where the ball began its peaceful descent into the glove of Lenny Randle to complete a seven-month saga that I knew would never be replicated.

The Arlington Stadium organ man—no match for the woman in Chicago or the man in Anaheim—played "Thanks for the Memories."

So those memories, of whom and of what was I supposed to be thanking? Thank you, spring training. Thank you, Willie. Thank you, Jose Cuervo. Thank you, Lindell AC.

Mike Hargrove remained among the few in the Rangers' clubhouse, where Joe Macko, the equipment manager, directed a mass exodus of golf bags.

"What do you think about the season, now that it's over?" I asked him.

"Disappointing." But not for him. Hargrove had followed his Rookie of the Year act with a plus-.300 sophomore season. He'd been selected for the All-Star team. An unlikely product of the Texas Panhandle, land of tumbleweeds and faraway train whistles, winter wheat and serial killers, Hargrove was in the big leagues to stay.

He pondered his situation. "I haven't been around long enough to even think about money," he said. "But I can't help but wonder how many seasons like this it'll take before they offer me forty grand." Then Hargrove smiled and walked out of the clubhouse, while a certain time of sweet simplicity left with him and, once through the door, disappeared completely and forever in the early autumn dusk.

Epilogue

October 10, 1975

Since the conclusion of the 1974 spectacle-bereft Oakland vs. Los Angeles confrontation, I'd accompanied the planet earth through another tortured odyssey around our vengeful sun, and once again it was time to become culturally immersed in the World Series. The alterations in the setting were drastic.

Cincinnati, the team that was supposed to be in the Series since opening day, had done its part. But the Reds were going to play Game 1 in Boston instead of Oakland, and that ranked high on the improbability scale during the sporting decade of the 1970s. Should it have been? In major league baseball, it was well known that two things cometh before the fall: summertime and pride. As the American League playoffs began, Oakland was unfocused, unready.

Who could have predicted that their Bay Bridge postseason monopoly would vanish in three swift strokes? Nobody in the sports pages had predicted it, although the outcome was foretold in the scriptures. "...*the blind shall see and the lame walk; the lepers are cleansed and the deaf hear; the dead are raised up...*"

And the Boston Red Sox would saw off the likes of Reggie and

Rollie; Bando and Blue. The entire A's roster was genuinely stunned. And since the World Series money had been taken for granted as part of the Charles Finley–designed compensation package, it was rumored that winter ball in the Latin nations would be graced with some gringos wearing handlebar mustaches. Relief pitcher Paul Lindblad, speaking for the players of his time, said, "Missing out on the twenty-five grand was a tough hit. Now I guess I'll be spending the holidays working on a Christmas tree lot."

I arrived in Boston on Friday, and got a copy of the *Globe* at Logan Airport. Peter Gammons wrote a story on the front page. It said, in part, that *"the Old Towne Team stands ready to hoist the World Series banner for the first time since our grandfathers were in the Argonne Wood."*

Since Gammons seldom sought to reach such grandiose octaves in his day-to-day coverage of the Sox, it was easy to conclude that the city was seething with postseason baseball passions. After I checked in at the Sheraton, I walked over to the Ritz-Carlton, the press headquarters, to obtain my media credentials. Autumn had arrived in Boston and the sidewalks were strewn with wet leaves from the shedding chestnuts. Dusk approached, and I tried to read the faces of the New Englanders on the eve of the huge event, faces that mostly seemed gripped with the intent of making it to the bank before it closed. Of course, this was a city where the colleges outnumbered the saloons, and with all these inscrutable eggheads, their true emotions were hard to gauge. But beneath the oft-described stoicism and pragmatism of the Northeast natives lay a bedrock stratum of fatalism, and that seemed to be at work there. As deeply as their Red Sox devotion extended, the essential burning question remained: How long would it take Cincinnati to wrap this up? Four games or five?

The Reds were one of perhaps three or four teams in the entire panorama of the sport that didn't have to rely on good pitching to win a World Series. Their demeanor was apprehensive—everybody kept glancing back over their shoulders, as if the Strangler were still on the loose.

The World Series pressroom at the Ritz was crammed with the familiar faces that had congregated at the Biltmore in L.A. just a year earlier. Given the turbulently eventful ride of '75, "just a year earlier" seemed a lifetime ago. It was good to overhear the wounded madrigal of baseball's traveling newsmen:

"...So finally, I got her up to my room and, the next thing I knew, I woke up the next morning and looked around and...*she stole my goddamn typewriter!*"

The hotel was starting to hop when I walked out. A half-circle that consisted of about eight men stood around a man seated at the lobby bar. It was Pete Rose, sipping beer out of one of those narrow-at-the-bottom glasses used in a lot of commercials. Pete talked. They listened. I cannot recall ever, in my life, seeing a person more content with who, what, and where he was than Pete Rose as the World Series of 1975 was about to begin.

By virtue of my elevated status with the Baseball Writer's Association, I got assigned one of the best seats in the cramped press box at Fenway Park—rustic and open air, like a duck blind.

Below, in the ancient stands, people stood shoulder to shoulder, and the aisles disappeared into an ocean of humanity. The top of the billboard advertising Canadian whiskey, visible beyond the Green Monster, was lined with spectators, silhouetted like crows on a telephone wire. When the pageant began, they all joined as a vast chorus, and the reaction to each pitch, every gasp, or moan or basso shout of approval, came in unison, as if Arthur Fielder were directing the program from a podium out beyond the center field seats. It continued like that for the duration of the competition.

One of baseball's signature moments happened in the 12th inning of Game 6—Carlton Fisk waving at the ball—sending it sailing to the fair side of the flagpole by sheer force of his will. Hardly anybody who was actually there at the ballpark saw that. Every one fixated on the baseball, and its spellbinding trajectory, not on Fisk himself.

From the inventory of everlasting recollections from the 1975 World Series, mine happened in the press box. It was Game 2, and a fine, slow rain fell throughout the entire game. I sat behind and slightly above Sherm Feller, the lyrical Fenway Park public address voice. Bob Fowler, who covered the Twins for a big time Twin Cities metropolitan daily and who stood out among the reporters as one of the sane ones, had the seat to my right.

Feller sat behind a plexiglass screen that protected his PA lineup card from the rain that gusted occasionally inside the box. With every third pitch or so, Feller would stand up and wipe the beaded drops from his screen with a rag. In the sixth inning, Bob Fowler snapped.

"God awmighty, Sherm! If you don't sit down, I'm gonna bust your skull open."

Sherm turned, looked at Fowler, spoke distinctly and directly into his microphone, and said, "If you don't like it, then why don't you get your ass upstairs and sit on the fucking roof?"

I didn't know, for a second, that Feller had clicked the mike off before making his comments to Fowler. Too bad. For a moment, I thought I had just witnessed one of the game's historic episodes. That hardly mattered, because more than any single episode, I'd been a passenger on the sort of season-long joy ride that started to become obsolete the moment the Reds—the last of the great homegrown baseball locomotives—recorded the last out to win Game 7 of the Series.

December 3, 1975

Baseball was still coping with the meaning of the free agency menace at the winter meetings in Miami.

I was sick. Brad Corbett and the Rangers traded Fergie Jenkins to the Red Sox for Juan Beniquez, the hot dog man, and Roger Moret, a left-handed pitcher with a vicious curveball and profound emotional problems.

In the lobby, I bumped into Billy Martin, managing the Yankees and enjoying his capacity as the Prom Queen in the eyes of the media. We sat on a sofa and had a quick drink. It was 11 A.M., and Martin was buzzed. He said that after the finish of the last season, he'd gone to George Steinbrenner seeking $30,000 to handle a personal emergency. "George pretty much said, 'Uh-uh. Don't even think about it.'

"Then," Martin said, "he brought up this business about my history for getting involved in all these off-the-field distractions, and I said, 'Screw it, George. You know what history is? History is bullshit!'"

Martin laughed, took another swallow, and said, "And that's right. The past *is* bullshit. *But...* it's a hell of a lot more certain than the future."

Acknowledgments

With alarming frequency, the characters in this book, names that then appeared beneath bylines and in box scores, are the same names that show up listed among the obits. That happened three or four times during the summer of 2007, when most of the narrative was produced. After more than thirty years, I guess that shouldn't be so surprising. Leading cause of death has been liver-cide.

Other than those macabre distractions, writing this was as close as you get to encountering a project that could be described as fun. It was easy, too, because what amounted to a personal diary for the baseball season of 1975 was available in the nicely preserved pages from the *Fort Worth Star-Telegram*. Some other information was taken from the *Dallas Times Herald*. That's the beautiful feature about newspaper archives. They have long memories and never change their stories, which is exactly the opposite of what comes from the mouths of living eye-witnesses.

I spent quite some time at the public libraries in downtown Dallas and Fort Worth. So I'll begin my acknowledgments by offering thanks to the staff at both places. Apart from the research resources available at these library facilities, they offer some jaw-dropping people-watching opportunities.

Some other individuals who offered aid and comfort to this work:

- Jim Donovan, my book rep who provides me with small details like topic and title;
- Whit Canning, for the stuff that he did;
- Pickslay Cheek, my cousin, for info on our grandfather and the Nashville Vols;
- Bobby Bragan, for elevating the message of the game;
- the publishing team at Grand Central, including my editor Rick Wolff, Tracy Martin, David Palmer, Fred Chase, and Karen Andrews, Esq.
- and my wife, Karen, for turning me on to glucosamine, without which I would not have been able to complete this.

Also, thanks to Johnny Langdon, David Hatchett, Dick Gordon, Brad Stribling, and Steve Connatser, Toby Harrah, Ken Suarez, and Tom Grieve, for the kind remarks that he has made on his Rangers telecasts.

—Mike Shropshire, 2007

Index

About the Author

Author/journalist Mike Shropshire is a New York–born native Texan. His actual baseball playing career "was tragically cut short by an absence of ability."